Making a Difference:

Meeting diverse learning needs with differentiated instruction

Acknowledgements

Alberta Education would like to acknowledge the generous and committed individuals and groups who contributed to the development of this resource, including the following.

Teachers, administrators and consultants from the following school authorities and associations who provided valuable feedback and suggestions during the field review:

Alberta Teachers' Association
Aspen View Regional Division
Battle River Regional Division
Boyle Street Education Centre
Calgary Learning Centre
Calgary School District
Chinook's Edge School Division
Christ the Redeemer Catholic Separate Regional Division
Edmonton Catholic Separate School District
Edmonton School District
Evergreen Catholic Separate Regional Division
Fort McMurray Roman Catholic Separate School District
Fort McMurray Public School District
Greater St. Albert Catholic Regional Division
High Prairie School Division
Holy Family Catholic Regional Division
Lloydminster Roman Catholic Separate School Division
Medicine Hat Catholic Separate Regional Division
Northern Gateway Regional Division
Northern Lights School Division
Palliser Regional Division
Peace River School Division
Red Deer Catholic Regional Division
Red Deer Public School District
St. Paul Education Regional Division
Wild Rose School Division
Wolf Creek School Division.

Participants in the Spring 2009 Curriculum Coordinators Meetings held across the province, including representatives from the Alberta Regional Professional Development Consortium and Alberta Teachers' Association.

$\pi \approx 3.141\,59\,20$

i

Expert reviews who provided valuable feedback and suggestions related to the professional learning needs of pre-service and new teachers
- Dr. Maureen Stratton, Assistant Professor, Concordia University College of Alberta
- Barb Milne, Consultant
- Lenora LeMay, Director of Educational Services, Hope Foundation of Alberta

Alberta Education staff who reviewed and validated subject-specific content:

Becky Pretli	Ken Ealey
Bernie Galbraith	Lisa Caouette
Bryan Ellefson	Lise Belzile
Christine Henzel	Marliss Meyer
Corinne Sperling	Martine Moore
Debbie Duvall	Natalie Prytuluk
Heather Dechant	Pam Halverson
Héléne Gendron	Patricia Rijavec
Jennifer Bushrod	Paolina Seitz
Jim Rubuliak	Ron Sperling
Karen Sliwkanich	Shelley Wells
Katherine Deren	Wai-Ling Lennon
Kathy Salmon	
Keith Millions	

Contributing writers

Patricia Shields-Ramsay and Doug Ramsay, InPraxis Consulting
Dana Antaya-Moore, Resource Development Services, Edmonton School District
David Harvey, Principal Consultant, Elk Island Public Schools Regional Division
Graham Foster, Consultant
Joanne Neal, Associate Professor, Concordia University College of Alberta
Kathy Howery, PhD candidate, University of Alberta
Sandra Gluth, Consultant, Edmonton School District
Greg McInulty, Consultant, Edmonton School District

Production team

Desktop publishing	Dianne Moyer and Lee Harper
Copyright	Sandra Mukai and Genevieve Bowman
Editor	Rebecca Pound
Cover and design	Lime Design
Indexer	Judy Dunlop
Project manager	Catherine Walker

Table of Contents

iii

Differentiated Instruction: An Introduction

Contents of this chapter

1

1

"Differentiated instruction has the potential to create learning environments that maximize learning and the potential for success for ALL students—regardless of skill level or background."
– McQuarrie, McRae and Stack-Cutler, in *Differentiated Instruction: Provincial Research Review (2005)*

Differentiated instruction is a philosophy and an approach to teaching in which teachers and school communities actively work to support the learning of *all* students through strategic assessment, thoughtful planning and targeted, flexible instruction. According to Carol Ann Tomlinson, one of the early advocates of this approach, differentiating instruction means 'shaking up' what goes on in the classroom so students have multiple opportunities for taking in information, making sense of ideas and expressing what they learn.

Most teachers naturally incorporate elements of differentiated instruction to some degree in their classrooms every day. Every time you use a pre-test to help you plan a learning activity, present information in multiple ways or offer choice in the format for a final project, you are reflecting the key belief of differentiated instruction—that all students can learn, in their own ways and in their own time. In other words, making a commitment to a more differentiated classroom does not mean starting over, but rather building on current best instructional practices in an explicit, intentional, focused and systematic manner.

Purpose and contents of this resource

This resource is a synthesis of current research and an introduction to the theory and practice of differentiated instruction within an Alberta context. The resource is organized into three parts.

Part 1 offers general information and strategies for differentiating instruction, including why and how to:

- use a thoughtful planning process
- develop learner profiles
- assess student needs and student progress
- create differentiated learning experiences
- leverage technology to support differentiation
- develop schoolwide support.

Part 2 provides ideas for differentiating learning and teaching for specific student groups, including English as a second language learners, students with disabilities and students who are gifted. Although these groups of students will benefit from the same process and strategies used to differentiate instruction for other students in the classroom, planning effective instruction to meet their specific needs requires additional considerations.

Part 3 offers practical, curriculum-specific ideas and strategies for differentiating learning and teaching within four core subject areas:

- English language arts
- mathematics
- social studies
- science.

Benefits of differentiated instruction

Today's classrooms are increasingly diverse. Students come from a variety of backgrounds and have a wide range of interests, preferences, learning strengths and needs. Differentiated instruction makes it possible for teachers to reach *all* learners and can particularly enhance the success of:

- students with disabilities (as part of or in addition to an individualized program plan)
- English language learners
- students who are gifted
- students considered at risk for leaving school before completion.

At the same time, the recent Alberta Initiative for School Improvement research indicates that many of the strategies used to differentiate instruction for students with disabilities were also effective within the general student population across grade levels and curriculum areas. Several projects also noted a spill-over effect where gains in one subject area had positive impacts across the curriculum, or where all students (not just the target group) benefited from differentiation strategies.

An important part of differentiated instruction is a way of recognizing that education needs are not as straightforward as just regular or special. On any given day, in any given subject area, or for any given type of activity, *different* students may have difficulty engaging in classroom activities, or learning new skills and concepts. Differentiated instruction offers multiple pathways to learning, so that all students are engaged and successful learners each and every school day.

Effective differentiated instruction also helps students understand what they are expected to learn, evaluate their own progress, and articulate their learning strengths, challenges and interests. Starting where students are at, providing meaningful choice, and creating opportunities for students to demonstrate their interests and skills increases students' motivation, self-confidence and willingness to assume responsibility for their learning.

3

Key elements of differentiated instruction

When done effectively, differentiated instruction is a seamless part of everyday instructional planning and practice. It is woven throughout the school day for all students and is integrated into how the physical space is organized, what learning resources are used, how instruction is planned and delivered, and how student learning is assessed.

The very nature of differentiated instruction means that it will look different in different learning contexts and environments, depending on the students, teacher, and/or curriculum. In all contexts, however, effective differentiated instruction involves:

- knowing your students
- understanding the curriculum
- providing multiple pathways to learning
- sharing responsibility with students
- taking a flexible and reflective approach.

Knowing your students

Differentiated instruction begins with truly knowing your students, both as individual learners and as a community of learners. It is important to intentionally create opportunities to learn about students' strengths, needs, interests, preferences and ways of learning.

It also is important to know about students' cultural and linguistic backgrounds. These have an important impact on how students view and interact with each other, how they tend to process and use information and what their expectations of school and learning might be.

Learner profiles, interest inventories, and ongoing formal and informal assessment can all provide essential information for planning instruction that goes beyond general student needs to address the specific, identified needs of your students. Throughout the instructional cycle, continue to systematically study learner traits to understand what each student brings to tasks and what he or she needs to succeed. For strategies and tools you can use to get to know your students, see *Chapter 3: Developing Learner Profiles* and *Chapter 4: Differentiated Assessment*.

Understanding the provincial curriculum

Differentiated instruction is built on a recognition that students learn at different rates and in different ways. For activities and assessment to be useful and fair, they must sometimes be different for different students. At the same time, within an Alberta context, all students are expected to achieve outcomes from the provincial, standardized program of studies. Effective differentiated instruction supports and strengthens this quality curriculum; it does not replace it. The first step is to thoroughly understand the provincial curriculum you are working with. Then you can begin to identify ways to help all students achieve learning outcomes by asking yourself questions such as the following.

- What are the big ideas in this curriculum?
- What are the implications of these learning outcomes for student learning and growth?
- What skills and processes are essential to meeting these learning outcomes?
- What are logical sequences of instruction for these outcomes? At what different points will students need support?
- How will these outcomes relate to different experiences and backgrounds that students have?
- What will motivate and engage students?
- How can I help each student build his or her own map of understanding and skill related to these outcomes?

For more information on purposeful planning in an Alberta context, see *Chapter 2: Purposeful Planning*, as well as relevant subject-area chapters in *Part 3: Diverse Learning Contexts*, of this resource.

Providing multiple pathways to learning

Differentiation depends on knowing and using a variety of teaching methods so that students have opportunities to learn and demonstrate their learning in multiple ways. For example, this may involve teaching to different intelligences or to different learning styles, or appealing to a variety of interests during a unit, term or course. You can address differing levels of readiness and ability by building open-endedness, choice and the potential for simple or complex responses into activities. In this way, you not only create opportunities for students to show their learning in different ways, but also make it possible for students with differing degrees of readiness or skills to respond. Offering a greater variety of challenging, engaging and curriculum-linked activities means a better chance of reaching more students.

Students also need opportunities to work in a variety of contexts including independently, with partners or small groups, with larger groups, and as a whole class. The contexts and ways in which these groups are organized is an essential component of differentiated instruction. Learning groups should change over the course of the day and over the course of the year, and should be based on a variety of differing factors including student interests, learning preferences, background experience, social preferences, readiness level or learning needs.

For more information on differentiating learning experiences by providing variety, choice and flexible grouping, see *Chapter 5: Differentiated Learning Experiences*.

Sharing responsibility with students

One of the ultimate goals of education is to gradually transfer responsibility for learning to students so that they become capable and motivated lifelong learners. In differentiated instruction, teachers actively work toward this goal by:

- scaffolding instruction so that all students can experience success
- building on student interests and skills to increase motivation
- providing opportunities for appropriate student choice and independent learning
- helping students to build a personalized repertoire of strategies to organize information, make sense of ideas, communicate clearly, and retain and retrieve information, concepts and ideas
- providing frequent opportunities for students to set goals, reflect on their own learning and develop self-monitoring and self-assessment skills.

The nature of students' involvement in their own learning and the degree of independence will vary depending on students' ages and development levels, and the demands of the curriculum.

Taking a flexible and reflective approach

Putting this philosophy into practice requires proactive planning, in which teachers identify, from the beginning, multiple routes for students to succeed, rather than retrofitting one-size-fits-all approaches after the fact. At the same time, it is important to plan with flexibility in mind. This flexibility, in terms of both scheduling and attitude, allows you to respond as much as possible when new student needs or interests emerge in relation to a topic or concept of study.

In differentiated instruction, ongoing assessment of students drives and extends instruction and helps you to continually refine your efforts. Along with ongoing assessment, differentiated instruction also demands that teachers systematically reflect on their instructional practices and use this information to improve their practice. Consider the following self-assessment.

Does my instructional approach:

1. use assessment strategies at the beginning of the instructional cycle, to determine what students already know and understand?
   ☐ Yes   ☐ Not yet

2. use varied instructional approaches including discussion, demonstration, guided reading and discovery activities?
   ☐ Yes   ☐ Not yet

3. emphasize critical and creative thinking and the application of learning?
   ☐ Yes   ☐ Not yet

4. use varied instructional groupings, including whole class, small groups, partners and individuals?

    ☐ Yes   ☐ Not yet

5. provide opportunities for students to choose activities based on their interests and preferences?

    ☐ Yes   ☐ Not yet

6. provide opportunities for guided and independent practice of new skills and concepts?

    ☐ Yes   ☐ Not yet

7. incorporate ongoing assessment strategies to check student learning and understanding throughout instructional sequences?

    ☐ Yes   ☐ Not yet

8. accommodate for learner differences by providing a variety of ways to show learning?

    ☐ Yes   ☐ Not yet

9. use strategies for reteaching, which are different from those strategies used to teach the skills and concepts the first time?

    ☐ Yes   ☐ Not yet

10. ensure those reteaching activities demand higher-level thinking skills while reinforcing basic skills and content?

    ☐ Yes   ☐ Not yet

11. provide enrichment activities that demand critical and/or creative thinking and the production of new ideas, thoughts and perspectives?

    ☐ Yes   ☐ Not yet

12. provide learning activities and ways of organizing that will scaffold student learning?

    ☐ Yes   ☐ Not yet

Links to other instructional theories and practices

Differentiation is a compilation of many theories and practices. It is grounded in an understanding of effective pedagogy and learning theories, including current research and best practice in the areas of brain-compatible learning, multiple intelligences, Bloom's taxonomy of thinking, and universal design for learning.

Brain research

Over the past 30 years, new technology has created new understanding about the brain and how we learn. Researchers and educators are using this information to support and inform classroom practice. Politano and Paquin (2000) outline nine factors to create brain-compatible teaching and learning environments in a differentiated classroom.

- *Uniqueness*—To be truly engaged, students need opportunities to identify their unique strengths and needs as learners and community members. They also need choices on how to process their thinking and represent their learning. This choice and variety allows students to work in ways that most suit their unique learning styles, developmental stages and personality.

- *Assessment*—A differentiated approach uses classroom assessment to find out what students know and what they need to learn, which in turn helps inform instruction. Assessment is most authentic when learning is demonstrated through tasks and assignments that closely reflect previous work in the classroom.

- *Emotions*—Emotion strongly affects learning, attention, memory and overall health and well-being. Learning activities such as storytelling, singing, humour and drama help to emotionally engage students. Students also benefit from approaches that enhance their understanding of their own emotional states, and create opportunities to develop strategies for managing and expressing their emotions.

- *Meaning*—The brain is always trying to create meaning. Teachers can help students create meaning by providing opportunities to explore the big picture perspective of concepts and issues, and by making links between what students are learning and how they are living in the world.

- *Multi-path*—The brain is constantly making new connections between ideas and experiences, which allows us to understand and remember material. Presenting information to students through a variety of rich, multidimensional, sensory experiences encourages students to make those brain connections.

- *Brain–body*—Using physical activity as part of instruction helps motivate and energize students. Role-plays, cooperative games and service learning projects, all tools of differentiated instruction, have instructional potential for helping the brain learn more effectively and efficiently. Activities such as dance and dramatic movement also can help learners process and represent abstract concepts.

- *Memory*—Memory plays an important role in learning. There are many strategies teachers can use within a differentiated instruction approach that will help students build strong personal memories, including role-plays, reflective journals and storytelling.

- *Cycles and rhythms*—Brain functioning is affected by the varying body rhythms and energy cycles of the individual. By providing choice and variety, wherever possible, teachers create the most productive learning climate for the most number of students.

- *Elimination of threat*—The flight or fight response is a well-documented phenomenon in brain research. A safe and supportive classroom climate is critical to engaging students in the learning process. Teachers need to observe students, identify common stressors that inhibit learning and then work proactively with students to minimize and manage the effects of these stressors.

Multiple intelligences

A differentiated instruction approach uses a variety of curriculum and instructional strategies to respond to student diversity and differences in learning needs. Multiple intelligences, a concept developed by Howard Gardner in the early 1900s, offers one flexible framework for planning for differentiation. Gardner identified eight basic types of intelligence that could provide potential pathways to learning. These are:

- verbal-linguistic intelligence (or word smarts)
- logical-mathematical intelligence (or number smarts)
- interpersonal intelligence (or people smarts)
- intrapersonal intelligence (or self smarts)
- spatial intelligence (or picture smarts)
- musical-rhythmic intelligence (or music smarts)
- bodily-kinesthetic intelligence (or body smarts)
- naturalist intelligence (or nature smarts).

Purposefully planning to engage as many of these intelligences as possible throughout the school day will ensure more students have additional opportunities to learn.

Bloom's taxonomy of thinking

Bloom's taxonomy provides another useful framework for planning for differentiated instruction.

Bloom's taxonomy is a hierarchy of thinking skills including:

- knowing (ability to remember something previously learned)
- comprehending (demonstrating basic understanding; e.g., paraphrasing)
- application (ability to transfer learning from one situation to another; e.g., build a model)

9

- analysis (understand how parts relate to whole; e.g., develop solution to problem)
- evaluation (judge value of something; e.g., decision-making process)
- synthesis (rearrange parts to make a new whole; e.g., invention)

Differentiation involves making decisions about what level of thinking skills are required for a particular task for different students.

The amount of time students spend at each level may vary depending on their academic readiness and the particular task. For example, some students will require more time to learn new skills and practice in a variety of contexts. However, these students still need plenty of opportunities to use their creativity and higher-reasoning skills. Ultimately, all students need opportunities to explore and apply a range of thinking skills at all levels of the taxonomy.

Universal design for learning

Universal design for learning (UDL) is an educational approach that aims to increase access to learning for all students by reducing physical, cognitive, intellectual, organizational and other barriers. UDL describes three main principles to guide the selection and development of learning environments, resources and activities that support individual learning differences:

- *multiple means of representation*, to give learners various ways of acquiring information and knowledge
- *multiple means of expression*, to provide learners alternatives for demonstrating what they know
- *multiple means of engagement*, to tap into learners' interests, challenge them appropriately and motivate them to learn.

UDL is based on the concept of universal design in architecture, which proposes that designing for the divergent needs of special populations increases usability for everyone. A classic example is the sidewalk curb cut. Although it was originally created to allow wheelchairs to move more freely between roads and sidewalks, an unintended consequence was that other people, including parents with strollers, cyclists and people with shopping carts, also found it easier to move from the sidewalk to the street.

Likewise, educators began to realize that many teaching strategies and materials that were originally designed for students with specific learning needs often can be useful for all students. For example, the use of visuals to support English language learners or students who are hard-of-hearing also will enhance learning for all students who learn visually.

10

The principles of UDL overlap with and complement the approach of differentiated education. Much of the application of UDL principles relies on the use of technology to make learning resources and environments more flexible. Within this combined approach, the classroom is *inclusive by design*. All students have access to the learning because teachers:

- assume that there will be diverse learning needs in their classroom and plan in advance to meet all student needs
- ensure learning materials and activities are available in flexible formats and options
- intentionally and proactively work to eliminate barriers in the physical environment, materials and learning activities
- maintain high, appropriate expectations for all learners.

For more information about the UDL visit the CAST Web site at www.cast.org.

11

12

Purposeful Planning

Contents of this chapter

2

13

"Good plans shape good decisions."
– Lester R. Bittel, in *The Nine Master Keys of Management*

Differentiated instruction focuses on diversity and flexibility, two characteristics that can easily overwhelm a teacher. However, with active and strategic planning processes differentiated instruction can be both effective *and* manageable.

Differentiated instruction involves considering not only the commonly identified elements of content, process and product, but also how these elements intersect with programs of study and with students' personal contexts and experiences, skills and abilities.

In Alberta, the starting point for all differentiation must be a sound understanding of the provincial program of studies, followed by the deliberate question, "What do I need to do to make these learning outcomes accessible for every student?"

Through this process of planning, you will have the opportunity to reflect on and apply your fundamental beliefs about learning, and about your role in creating effective, meaningful learning environments. Planning for differentiated instruction can start with an exploration of the following questions.

- What do you believe about the individual needs of students?
- What do you learn from your students?
- What range of abilities, interests and aptitudes do you see in the students you have taught?
- What languages do they speak and what cultural backgrounds do they represent?
- What range of skills, concepts, values and attitudes are reflected in the program of studies?
- What are your abilities, interests and aptitudes as a teacher? How do these connect with your students and the curriculum?

Consider planning models

There are an increasing number of educational models and instructional approaches that emphasize purposeful planning and differentiated instruction. As you make planning decisions on how you will structure your instruction, consider what the impact will be on the overall effectiveness of teaching and learning, as well as how these decisions will address individual learning needs.

14

A purposeful learning experience connects curriculum outcomes and expectations to relevant, meaningful contexts. These contexts are created when students have opportunities to:

- build deep and meaningful understandings of content
- transfer those understandings to different contexts
- develop skills and understandings of critical processes
- ask questions relevant to them and conduct inquiries
- explore and act upon values, beliefs and attitudes
- make connections to build their own evolving sense of purpose and identity.

These elements of meaningful context-building are not new; they are repeatedly reflected in educational provincial research, theories and approaches. They also are commonly reflected in provincial programs of study and other curriculum documents.

Planning to create such contexts and to meet the individual needs of students involves processes of reflection and purposeful design. A purposeful design is a meaningful sequence of learning opportunities that starts with learning outcomes, clustered and aligned with essential learnings, assessment approaches and strategies, resources, and teaching and learning strategies (see diagram below). This alignment is critical to purposeful planning.

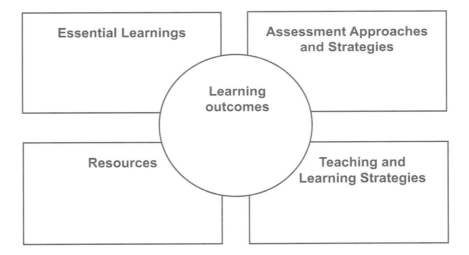

Your planning approach also should consider:

- the levels of difficulty at which curriculum outcomes can be interpreted
- the materials, resources and tasks needed to support varied interests, aptitudes and abilities
- the scaffolding or supports required to facilitate student learning
- how to include varied approaches to assessment and evaluation
- time requirements.

It is essential to have a thorough knowledge and understanding of the provincial curriculum before making decisions about what and how to teach. You may begin simply by critically and thoughtfully exploring curriculum outcomes with students in mind. Then consider the question, "If this is where I have to take my students, how do I most effectively get them there?" You also may consider questions such as the following.

- What are the overall expectations for students in this program of studies?
- What conceptual understandings and big ideas are emphasized within these overall expectations?
- What are the organizing constructs; e.g., strands, themes, topics?
- What are the specific expectations for learning in this program of studies? What concepts, skills, processes, values and attitudes are emphasized?
- If the learning outcomes in this program of studies are not already organized, what organizing constructs can be brought to the outcomes?[1]
- What prior knowledge, experiences and interests correlate or connect to these learning expectations?
- What have students learned in previous years of the program? What will they be expected to learn after they complete this year of this program?
- What differences in prior knowledge, understandings, experiences and interests might be found between individual students?

Be flexible when planning with differentiated instruction in mind. The planning process should be one of continual assessment, reflection and adjustment, as it is centred on the premise that instructional approaches should be varied and flexible for both teachers and students. Recognize also that successful implementation includes a range of learning situations, including individual, small group and large group experiences. This range should be explicitly planned in the learning sequence. The planning process, therefore, is cyclical and considers the key elements of instructional design as checkpoints that should be revisited and realigned as an instructional sequence unfolds.

Know every student in the classroom

Knowing and responding to each student as an individual is perhaps the most fundamental element of differentiation. Effective teachers naturally get to know their students over time; however, in a differentiated classroom, you will *plan* specific ways to learn about your students and to use the information you gather. This allows you to move from planning, based on how students *can* differ in general, to a more proactive approach of planning, based on how your students *do* differ in particular. Learner profiles, discussed in-depth in *Chapter 3: Developing Learner Profiles*, are a valuable tool for identifying and recording student strengths, needs, readiness, learning preferences and interests.

---

1. Text to this point adapted from Douglas Ramsay and Patricia Shields-Ramsay, *Purposeful Planning* (Edmonton, AB: InPraxis Learning Systems, 2006), pp. 1–7.

Identify essential learnings[2]

Essential learnings are the big ideas of the curriculum. These big ideas help students to connect facts and skills to conceptual frameworks and prior experiences. They encourage students to recognize and apply familiar ideas and help students build deep understandings through transferring what they learn to new and different contexts. A planning approach that is based on broad concepts and process skills, or essential learnings, is more effectively differentiated than one based on specific, narrow facts and topics. Both you and your students have more flexibility to make choices and to develop meaningful, personally relevant connections. Students have more opportunities to question existing conceptions, develop skills and establish their own learning goals.

Purposeful planning is centered on essential learnings, including knowledge and understandings, skills and processes, and values and attitudes, that are articulated explicitly from a program of studies. Develop essential learnings that are closely aligned with the curriculum by using clusters of recurring concepts, words, terms and processes to reflect broad topics, themes, concepts, ideas or questions. Well-aligned essential learnings should offer numerous opportunities to make connections both within and between subject areas.

Expand essential learnings into essential questions[3]

Essential questions are a critical planning element. These questions help students to focus on the important aspects of the essential learnings. Essential questions also help to emphasize that continual questioning is a critical component of a unit. Together, essential learnings and questions identify the understandings and processes that all students must attain and, in doing so, provide the anchor for a unit.

Each essential question should:
- be directly related to the programs of study
- contain critical concepts and important vocabulary or terms that recur in the curriculum
- be written at a level that students can understand and use
- be written in a way that avoids 'yes' or 'no' answers
- facilitate critical thinking by starting with "Why…"; "How…"; or "To what extent…"
- be written at different levels of difficulty to scaffold learning and support the learning of all students
- provide a logical sequence that can guide the construction of an instructional unit.

---

2. Section adapted from Douglas Ramsay and Patricia Shields-Ramsay, *Purposeful Planning* (Edmonton, AB: InPraxis Learning Systems, 2006), pp. 8–11.
3. Ibid.

Essential questions are developed from essential learning statements and emphasize key concepts and processes. For example, the essential learning statement, "Changing social and economic conditions can influence movement and migration patterns" can be developed into the essential question, "Why do changing social and economic conditions result in movement and migration?" Essential questions encourage exploration of authentic problems and queries that are open-ended, with the potential to include a variety of perspectives and approaches.

Other examples of essential questions include the following.
- Why do communities change over time?
- How does change result in the movement of peoples?
- Why is change inevitable?
- Why do living things adapt in response to their environments?
- How can individuals participate in decision-making processes?

These types of questions facilitate effective differentiation because they typically reflect recurring and authentic life issues, and create more possibilities for differentiating processes and products.

The open-ended nature of essential questions creates opportunites:
- for all learners to reflect and respond
- to make connections to students' cultures, backgrounds and life experiences
- to accommodate a range of student differences, including skill levels, interests and learning preferences.

The conceptual planning model developed by Erickson (2002) suggests that essential learning statements and questions should be scaffolded to represent different levels of complexity and sophistication. She suggests a process based on "how, why and to what extent" questions.

Scaffolding essential learnings[4]

Level 1:

All cultures have celebrations.

How do cultures celebrate special events?

Level 2:

Celebrations express the traditions of a culture.

Why are traditions important to cultures?

Level 3:

Traditions reflect the beliefs, values and heritage of a culture.

To what extent do celebrations and traditions reflect the beliefs and values of a culture?

You also can provide opportunities for students to develop their own "how, why and to what extent" questions at varying levels.

Break essential questions into unit questions[5]

Unit questions are a way of breaking down the essential questions of a unit into more focused pieces. They can focus on the specifics of the unit, such as:

- developing vocabulary
- exploring terms and concepts
- guiding research.

To make them most useful, unit questions should be:

- written to guide inquiry and uncover the essential questions and learnings of the unit
- sequenced to provide the flow of the unit.

For example, unit questions that support the essential question, "Why is change inevitable?" could include the following.

- When does change occur?
- How do people react to change?
- What are the visible results of change?
- When is change a good thing?
- When is change challenging?
- How does change help solve problems?

---

4. Adapted from H. Lynn Erickson, *Concept-based Curriculum and Instruction: Teaching Beyond the Facts* (Thousand Oaks, CA: Corwin Press, Inc., 2002), p. 87.

5. Section adapted from Douglas Ramsay and Patricia Shields-Ramsay, *Purposeful Planning* (Edmonton, AB: InPraxis Learning Systems, 2006).

19

To support differentiation, develop unit questions that provide options and flexibility for students with different interests, backgrounds and abilities. Tier or scaffold questions to accommodate different paths and allow students to investigate what is most interesting and relevant to their learning needs.

Identify assessment tasks

Initial and ongoing assessment is an essential teaching tool in differentiated classrooms. Considering assessment early in your planning process will help you to make more effective decisions about student learning needs.

Essential learnings and questions reflect expectations for student achievement across the curriculum. When outcomes are clustered around these "big ideas" they become the basis for articulating expectations, selecting strategies and developing activities. Well-aligned units and lesson plans incorporate a series of learning experiences that are designed around a process (see diagram below).

Clearly identifies a cluster of learning outcomes around a big idea or concept

Describes what students should understand, know and be able to do to meet the outcomes

Provides learning activities that lead students to attainment of the outcomes

Uses these indicators of student learning to select instructional approaches or strategies

Assessment can be thought of as the "arrows" in the process of planning. In a differentiated approach to planning, assessment considers questions such as the following that focus the planning process on students and help set the direction of the unit.

- What do students know and understand about the essential learnings?
- What do they need to learn?
- What will help them to learn?
- How well are students developing understandings during the unit?
- How are students responding to the processes used in the unit?
- What assessment tools will best gather this information?
- How will students be involved with the assessment process?
- How and when will students assess themselves?
- In what ways can assessment be used to motivate and engage students in the learning process?

Plan a series of performance tasks that will open the unit, guide students through learning experiences and wrap up the unit. The final performance task typically involves culminating projects that require students to synthesize and apply understandings. These projects should be closely aligned with the values and attitudes, knowledge and understandings, and skills and processes outcomes from the learning clusters. In differentiated planning, performance tasks also should provide for different modes of demonstrating learning as well as options for student choice.

Chapter 4: Differentiated Assessment provides an in-depth exploration of differentiated assessment and its role in instructional planning, student learning and effective evaluation.

Plan differentiated learning experiences

There are countless strategies and activities that you can use to create differentiated learning experiences. How can you choose the right ones for your classroom? Planning for purposeful instruction is intended to promote maximum student achievement. Strategies and activities are planned to move students toward the learning goals represented by essential learnings, questions, outcome clusters and assessment tasks. In a differentiated unit, strategies and activities also incorporate such elements as:

- flexible grouping options
- scaffolded instruction
- choice
- different learning modalities
- interests.

When selecting differentiated learning experiences, the activities, resources and materials should:

- focus on essential learnings and questions
- develop opportunities for students to explore unit questions and inquiries
- capture rich, compelling and engaging relationships between concepts
- enable students to apply what they have learned in multiple contexts
- involve, support and develop higher-order thinking skills
- form the basis for students to test and question generalizations and expand their learning to new and different contexts.

Consider the following questions to help you to select learning experiences.

- What strategies and instructional practices align with essential learnings and questions?
- How will the learning environment in the classroom support these strategies and instructional practices?
- What learning activities and tasks will engage and motivate students?
- How will these learning activities, tasks and materials build understandings, skills, values and attitudes?
- What are the roles of the teacher and students in different learning contexts throughout this unit?
- What learning supports will students need throughout this unit?

22

Developing Learner Profiles

Contents of this chapter

3

23

To effectively meet the learning needs of students, classroom teachers must begin with an understanding of the needs of the learners, both collectively as a classroom unit and as individual students.

A classroom is a community of learners, each with unique learning preferences, interests, strengths, needs and potential. Planning instruction that acknowledges and honours these differences means providing each student with opportunities to learn in different ways so that each can reach his or her maximium potential. It means thoughtfully selecting learning and teaching strategies, materials and supports that will maximize student achievement. Learner profiles and class profiles offer a starting point for this planning.

What is a learner profile?

A learner profile describes the ways in which a student learns best. A comprehensive learner profile includes information on student interests, learning preferences and styles, and differences related to gender, culture and personality. It also might include information on student learning strengths, needs and types of supports that have been successful in the past. A learner profile needs to be dynamic, as individual learners are constantly growing and changing.

Learning preferences and styles
Learning preferences typically refer to the general environment in which a student learns best. This may include preferences for:
- a quiet versus noisy room
- a busy room with lots to look at and interact with versus a bare room with few distractions
- a movement friendly room versus one in which sitting still is valued
- a flexible schedule versus a fixed schedule
- a warm versus a cool room to work in.

Learning styles typically refer to how a student tends to use senses to learn. Rita and Ken Dunn (1987) identify three types of sensory learning styles.

- **Auditory learners**—like to hear directions aloud, discuss what they are learning, use word games, puzzles, riddles and songs, work with partners, do choral reading, teach others for clarification.

- **Visual learners**—like to draw pictures to represent ideas, use games and puzzles, use visual clues to remember, go on field trips for a "being there" experience, use visualization to see pictures in their minds, use graphics and flowcharts, use videos for review, look at books, watch others to see what to do.

- **Kinesthetic learners**—like to have opportunities to move around, trace and outline, act out concepts and stories, make models or do experiments, write or draw while listening, walk while talking, imagine themselves in the situation, examine and manipulate material.

Closely related to learning styles are thinking styles. These typically describe how a student organizes information and solves problems. Based on the work of Gregorc (1982), Judith Dodge presents four general thinking styles.[1]

- **Concrete random thinkers**—are creative, make intuitive leaps, enjoy unstructured problem solving, like choices, are self-motivated, see the big picture and not the details.

- **Concrete sequential thinkers**—like order, respond to step-by-step instruction, enjoy learning with concrete materials, attend to details, work within a time line, appreciate structure.

- **Abstract random thinkers**—are guided by emotion and interest, seek environments that are active, busy and unstructured, like to discuss ideas and interact with others.

- **Abstract sequential thinkers**—enjoy theory and abstract thought, focus on knowledge and facts, thrive on independent investigation and research, usually prefer to work alone to prove things for themselves.

Learning preferences and learning styles develop and change over time in response to ongoing experiences. One style or preference is not better than another. What does matter is the fit between the individual learner and the learning task and/or material. The way in which we respond to different preferences and styles can vary across tasks and situations. For example, one learner may prefer to study on his or her own at home, but prefer to work with a small study group in the classroom.

Individuals also differ in the strengths of their preferences and styles. Some learners also can shift easily between different kinds of learning, while others cannot be as flexible.

The goal of a learner profile is to find out as much as possible about how an individual learns. The goal is *not* to label students as certain kinds of learners but rather to help them develop multiple pathways for learning. When working on unfamiliar and/or challenging tasks, students will be more confident and motivated if they are able to work in their areas of strength.

---

1. Adapted from Judith Dodge, *Differentiation in Action* (New York, NY: Scholastic, 2005), p. 11.

25

Students need frequent opportunities to work in their preferred sensory and thinking styles. At the same time, it also is critical to ensure that students have learning opportunities that stretch them beyond their preferences and allow them to develop a wider repertoire of learning skills. This will help them become more confident learners who can work through challenges.

Types of intelligence

Another framework for reflecting on how individuals learn is examining different types of intelligence. An intelligence can be defined as a brain-based predisposition to excel in a particular area. Howard Gardner (1994) identified eight intelligences that individuals possess in varying combinations. Thomas Armstrong (1994) came up with student-friendly terms for each intelligence:

- verbal-linguistic intelligence (or word smarts)
- logical-mathematical intelligence (or number smarts)
- interpersonal intelligence (or people smarts)
- intrapersonal intelligence (or self smarts)
- spatial intelligence (or picture smarts)
- musical-rhythmic intelligence (or music smarts)
- bodily-kinesthetic intelligence (or body smarts)
- naturalistic intelligence (or nature smarts).

Similarly, Robert Sternberg (1985) identified the following three intelligences that he suggests exist in varying combinations and strengths in each individual.

- **Analytic intelligence** (or schoolhouse intelligence) involves the linear type of learning found most often in schools.

- **Practical intelligence** (or contextual intelligence) involves seeing how and why things work as people actually use them.

- **Creative intelligence** (or problem-solving intelligence) involves making new connections and seeking innovation.

Sternberg argues that recognizing where each student's strengths lie and teaching to those strengths, particularly when introducing a new concept, can maximize student learning. At the same time, your goal should be to develop all intelligences as fully as possible in every student, so that he or she can succeed in a variety of contexts.

Influences based on gender, culture and personality

Learning patterns can be influenced by student gender and culture, as well as unique personality. Some of these influences include:

- being expressive *or* reserved in class interactions
- preferring competition *or* collaboration
- preferring to work individually *or* in a group
- approaching learning with a creative *or* practical way of thinking
- preferring part-to-whole *or* whole-to-part learning
- preferring contextual and personal learning *or* learning that is discrete and impersonal

- viewing time as fixed and rigid *or* fluid and flexible
- being more impulsive *or* more reflective in one's thinking and actions
- valuing creativity *or* conformity.

Interests

Students are most motivated and engaged when they are learning about something they are interested in. Having areas of interest identified as part of learner profiles helps you to regularly consider these interests in your instructional planning to vary projects, themes and examples used in your instruction.

Gathering information for learner profiles

Students often know which ways of learning are most effective for them and what things get in the way of their success. Listening to what students have to say about their own learning can be a great starting point for creating learner profiles. Inventories and other assessment tools also may provide you with valuable information.

Inventories

Consider the following types of inventories. Samples of these inventories are included at the end of this chapter. Additional strategies and tools for getting to know your student are available in the Alberta Education resource, *Building on Success: Helping Students make Transitions from Year to Year* (2006), available at http://education.alberta.ca/media/352661/build.pdf.

Learner preference inventories provide students with ongoing opportunities to reflect on and talk about their learning preferences. These opportunities help students to develop the self-knowledge, vocabulary and confidence to tell you what works best for them. See Tool 6: What Works for Me Inventory.

Each new unit of study provides a useful opportunity to explore individual learning preferences. For example, at the beginning of a unit on classroom chemistry, you may ask students to order the following choices based on their favourite way to learn.

> The best ways for me to learn about classroom chemistry would be to (number from 1 to 6):
> _____ read a book about chemistry
> _____ visit a chemist working in a lab
> _____ do a chemistry inquiry at school
> _____ research a famous chemist
> _____ create a display about chemistry to share with the class
> _____ look for examples of chemistry in my home.

Reading inventories are typically given at the beginning of the year. They provide an opportunity for students to share information about the kinds of reading they enjoy, as well as their understanding of themselves as readers. Used again at the end of the year, a reading inventory can reveal how student perceptions have changed and can generate new information to share with the next year's teachers. See *Tool 3: A Reading Interview*, *Tool 4: Reading Attitudes Interview*, *Tool 5: Reading Stategies Survey*.

Social inventories provide valuable information for assessing social competence. Understanding how a student gets along with others and functions in group situations can be helpful for both you and the student. See Tool 7: Getting Along with Others Inventory.

Interest inventories, including general interest and "All About Me" inventories, should be administered at the beginning of the year. They offer a variety of insights into student likes and dislikes, interests, affinities and lives. You can use these insights to plan learning activities that engage and motivate students. See *Tool 1: 20 Questions About Me* and *Tool 2: Interest Inventory*.

Assessment information

Assessment and diagnostic information is an important part of a learner profile. You can gather this information from a variety of sources, including:
- cumulative records
- report cards
- individualized program plans (IPP)
- standardized assessments
- parents
- previous teachers and other school staff involved with the student.

Assessment information helps you to identify each student's developmental level and particular challenges, so that you can plan accordingly.

Helping students identify and understand how they learn best and how they can use this information can help students learn-to-learn throughout their lives.

Recording learner profiles

Individual learner profile information can be recorded in a variety of formats. Many teachers find it most practical to use individual file cards that can be kept close at hand for reference. One way to organize the information on the cards is as follows.

Interests books sports–hockey, soccer music	Thinking style concrete random	Learner and sensory preferences kinesthetic hands-on movement
	Caleb	
Intelligences practical creative	Other individualized reading goals	Other preferences group work

What is a class profile?

The information gathered about each student can be compiled to create an overall picture of the class as a community of learners. A class profile identifies the strengths and challenges of all students as well as the stage each student is at in his or her learning. It is a resource for planning that conveys a great deal of critical information at a glance. It is a living document that can be added to and revised throughout the year based on your observations or other information that you receive.

The class profile is developed at the beginning of the school year or semester. It is a tool for recording and summarizing information gathered through diagnostic assessment that happens prior to instruction and through formative assessment that happens during instruction. For additional information on assessment, see *Chapter 4: Differentiated Assessment*. Class profiles can be organized in a few different ways. The class profile helps you:
- collect, sort, categorize and summarize classroom data
- identify patterns of similarities and differences among students
- plan assessment and differentiated instruction on a daily basis
- form flexible groupings
- monitor student progress by noting results of ongoing assessments
- share information among educators and parents.

Overall academic profile

An overall academic profile for a class can be compiled in a chart for quick reference. This type of profile indicates, at a glance, any current assessment information for each student, additional supports a student requires or is receiving, and other relevant information as determined by you or the school. An overall academic profile might look like this.

Class/Teacher: Mrs. Cromwell		Grade: 2	Year: 2008–2009
Student name	Joanne	Marc	Sunita
Reading level 1 – below 2 – grade 3 – above	1	2	3
Math level 1 – below 2 – grade 3 – above	2	2	2
IPP Y/N	Y	N	N
In-school support	buddy reading	none	none
Out-of-school support	none	none	Big Sister mentor
Technology	dedicated word processor	none	none
Learning preferences	enjoys partner work; responds well to feedback	enjoys partner work; needs to move around	prefers quiet
Social/ emotional	persistent; cheerful; cooperative	cooperative; hardworking; confident	persistent; independent
Interests	horses; soccer; swimming	soccer; hockey; nature programs	piano; drawing; singing

Subject or unit specific class profile

Using information from various inventories, assessments and observations, you can create class profiles specific to a subject (e.g., language arts, mathematics or science) or a unit of study (e.g., poetry, sky science or a novel study).

A class profile for a language arts class might start like this.

Grade: 9	Teacher: Mr. Benson	Subject: Language Arts
Strengths	**Challenges**	**Preferences**
Amanda – extensive repertoire of reading strategies **Mary** – understands relationships between ideas **Marcus** – understands the use of literary devices **Sisi** – extensive vocabulary **James** – communicates ideas clearly **Beth** – makes connections between self, text and the world around her **Marcel** – loves poetry **Kara** – enjoys challenge **Lorne** – loves talking about what he reads	**Suki** – beginning to learn English **Ben** – difficulty expressing understanding **Fiona** – difficulty identifying main ideas **Nora** – difficulty discerning key concepts when reading **Brianna** – impulsive when responding **Oscar** – needs constant encouragement **Petra** – often loses focus	**Rhiannon** – nonfiction **Stephen** – anything to do with computers **Tabitha** – listening to books on tape

Literacy or numeracy class profile

A class profile focused on literacy or numeracy can be developed using a checklist format. Use a system of "met/not yet met" to record information in the profile, or make a more descriptive note for each student. You can use the information in the profile to inform planning, determine groupings for various learning activities, and assist in tracking and reporting growth.

31

Using learner and class profiles

Knowing your students—intentionally reflecting on who they are and how they learn—is what makes differentiated instruction possible. Learner and class profiles help you to identify the individual and collective strengths, needs, challenges and interests of the students in your class. This information is vital to selecting effective instructional strategies, supports, resources and interest-based topics for individual students and the class as a whole. Most, if not all, of the assessment and instructional strategies described in the following chapters either depend on or can be enhanced by considering learner and class profile information. By using both individual learner and class profiles as living documents, you can do more thoughtful and supportive planning throughout the school year.

Developing your own learner profile

To maximize the value of student learner profiles, you may want to better understand your own learning preferences and how they influence your planning and teaching.

You can use the information and inventories in this resource to think about your own learning. Other adult-focused inventories related to learning and communicating are readily available on the Internet, and many are free.

Take time to do some self-reflection and ask yourself questions about your own learning strengths, how they have changed over time, and what the implications are for teaching and learning with your students. Consider questions such as the following.

- What are my learning strengths?
- How have I developed these particular strengths over the years?
- How do my strengths and preferences affect my teaching?
- What types of intelligences and preferences do I want to more consciously incorporate into my teaching?

Developing your own learner profile puts you in a better position to see when student learning is being hindered by your preferences. For example, a teacher who is a concrete random thinker likely enjoys unstructured problem-solving situations, opportunities for divergent thinking and big picture ideas. If all of his or her instruction and classroom organization reflects these preferences, those students in the class who are concrete sequential thinkers (e.g., who like order, step-by-step instruction and detail) will most likely find learning difficult.

32

Likewise, a teacher who is a strong visual learner may plan instruction that focuses primarily on using graphic organizers and visual representations. Those students who learn best through small group conversation (auditory) or movement (kinesthetic) may be challenged by not having opportunities to learn in their preferred ways.

Recognizing and respecting the differences that exist between you and your students is the first step to intentionally adjusting instruction and valuing different kinds of learning in the classroom.

As you find out more about your own learning strengths and preferences, it is useful to share this information with your students. Talk with them about how knowing this information will help you to learn and teach more effectively.

33

Tool 1: 20 Questions About Me[2]

Student Name _____ Date _____

1. What is my favourite activity to do at school? _____
    _____

2. What is my favourite subject? _____
    _____

3. What is my favourite activity outside of school? _____
    _____

4. What sport do I like to watch? _____
    _____

5. What sport do I like to play? _____
    _____

6. What would I like to learn more about? _____
    _____

7. What kind of books do I like to read? _____
    _____

8. What is the best book I ever read? _____
    _____

9. How much time do I spend reading for fun every week? _____
    _____

10. What is my favourite television show? _____
    _____

34

2. Reproduced from Alberta Education, *Building on Success: Helping Students make Transitions from Year to Year* (Edmonton, AB: Alberta Education, 2006), pp. 26–27.

11. What kind of music do I like? _____
    _____

12. What is my favourite activity to do on the computer? _____
    _____

13. What kind of technology do I like to use? _____
    _____

14. Who are my best friends? _____
    _____

15. What do I like to do with my friends? _____
    _____

16. What makes me smile? _____
    _____

17. What makes me laugh? _____
    _____

18. What part of the world interests me the most? _____
    _____

19. What do I plan to do after high school? _____
    _____

20. What kind of career do I want when I'm an adult? _____
    _____

35

Tool 2: Interest Inventory[3]

Student Name _____   Date _____

1. My most interesting subject is _____

2. My most challenging subject is _____

3. What I enjoy most about school is _____

4. What I find most challenging about school is _____
    _____

5. Books I read recently _____

6. Activities I do outside of school _____
    _____

7. Three words to describe me _____

8. Careers that interest me _____

9. An ideal job for one day would be _____

10. My favourite television programs are _____

11. My favourite Web sites are _____

12. My questions about next year are_____
    _____
    _____

13. School situations that are stressful for me are _____
    _____

14. I deal with stress or frustration by _____
    _____

15. Some interesting places I've been to are _____

16. If I could travel anywhere, I would like to go to _____

17. If I can't watch television, I like to _____

18. I would like to learn more about _____

---

3. Reproduced from Alberta Education, *Building on Success: Helping Students make Transitions from Year to Year* (Edmonton, AB: Alberta Education, 2006), p. 28.

36

Tool 3: A Reading Interview[4]

Name _____

1. Do you like to read? Why or Why not?

2. Do you think you are a good reader? Why?

3. What was the last book you read?

4. What kinds of books do you like to read?

5. Do you think it is important to be a good reader? Why?

6. What do you do when you come to a word you can't read?

7. Do you read at home?

8. What do you usually do after school when you get home?

4. Adapted with permission from Patricia Pavelka, *Create Independent Learners: Teacher-tested Strategies for all Ability Levels* (Peterborough, NH: Crystal Springs Books, 1999), Reading Inventory.

Tool 4: Reading Attitudes Interview[5]

Name _____   Date _____

1. How do you feel about reading?

2. What kinds of books do you like to read?

3. Who are your favourite authors?

4. How do you decide what book to read?

5. a. Who do you know that is a good reader?

    b. What makes _____ a good reader?

6. If you knew someone who was having trouble reading, how would you help him or her?

7. Do you think you are a good reader? Why or why not?

8. What would you like to do better as a reader?

_____

5. Reproduced with permission from a form by Christa Svenson, Lawton Junior High School, Edmonton Public Schools, Edmonton, AB.

38

Tool 5: Reading Strategies Survey[6]

Name _____ Date _____

	Usually	Sometimes	Never
1. I use the title and pictures to predict what the selection is about.	❑	❑	❑
2. I try to predict what is going to happen next in the selection.	❑	❑	❑
3. I break new words into familiar chunks.	❑	❑	❑
4. I think about movies, TV shows or books that might be similar in some way.	❑	❑	❑
5. I study the illustrations, photographs or diagrams for information.	❑	❑	❑
6. I reread when I don't understand.	❑	❑	❑
7. I imagine myself right in the story.	❑	❑	❑
8. I talk to others about confusing parts.	❑	❑	❑
9. I think about how the story is like something I have experienced.	❑	❑	❑
10. I try to figure out the main idea of the selection.	❑	❑	❑
11. I try retelling the story in my head.	❑	❑	❑
12. I look up new words in the dictionary.	❑	❑	❑
13. I correct myself when I mispronounce a word.	❑	❑	❑
14. I ask questions about what I read.	❑	❑	❑
15. I change my reading rate for different tasks or texts.	❑	❑	❑

6. Reproduced with permission from Edmonton Public Schools, "AISI Middle Literacy Project" (Edmonton, AB: Edmonton Public Schools, 2001).

Reading Strategies Survey (continued)

16. How has your reading changed this year?

_____

_____

_____

_____

_____

_____

17. What strategy helps you the most when reading?

_____

_____

_____

_____

_____

18. What skills or strategies do you need to continue to work on?

_____

_____

_____

_____

40

Tool 6: What Works for Me Inventory[7]

Name _____   Date _____

A. How I look after myself:
- How much sleep do I need? _____
- What kind of food makes me feel the most alert? _____
- What snacks are good energy sources? _____
- What times of the day do I need to eat? _____
- What time of the day do I have the most energy? _____
- What time of the day do I have the least energy? _____
- What type of exercise makes me feel energized? _____
- What kinds of activities help me relax? _____

B. Tools that help me learn:
- What writing tool works best for me; e.g., type of pen, pencil, colour of ink?
  _____
- What kind of paper helps me keep organized; e.g., wide-ruled, unlined, wide
  margins, prepunched? _____
- What colour of paper do I find the easiest to read? _____
- What binder system works for me? _____
- What other supplies help me keep organized; e.g., white-out, post-it notes, ruler?
  _____
- What calculator works best for me; e.g., size, features? _____
- What spellchecker works best for me? _____
- What is my favourite dictionary? _____
- What other reference books help me learn? _____
- What computer programs are helpful to my learning? _____

C. In the classroom:
- What seat in the classroom works best for me? _____
- What do I read best from?
  _____ chalkboard   _____ overhead   _____ projector   _____ chart paper
  _____ my own copy   _____ interactive white board
- Does the colour of ink (or chalk) make a difference? _____
- Does the type of print; e.g., printed, handwritten or typed, make a difference?
  _____
- Does the size and spacing of print make a difference? _____

41

_____

7. Reproduced from Alberta Education, *Make School Work for You: A Resource for Junior and Senior High Students who want to be More Successful Learners* (Edmonton, AB: Alberta Education, 2001), pp. 85–86.

What Works for Me Inventory (continued)

D. Rank in order from 1 (being the most useful) to 12 (being the least useful) which type of learning experiences work best for me:

_____ teacher explains aloud

_____ teacher writes directions on the board

_____ teacher does example on the board

_____ teacher asks another student to demonstrate

_____ teacher asks all students to try a sample at their desks

_____ I read the directions while the teacher reads them

_____ I read the directions on my own

_____ teacher shows me at my desk

_____ another student explains a second time and answers my questions

_____ I watch what another student does

_____ I try it on my own and then check with teacher

_____ I try it on my own and then compare with another student.

E. Tricks I use to keep myself organized:

_____

_____

_____

_____

_____

_____

F. Tricks I use to keep myself focused and on task in class:

_____

_____

_____

G. Special things that teachers can do to help me learn:

_____

_____

_____

_____

_____

_____

Tool 7: Getting Along with Others Inventory[8]

Name _____ Date _____

In class	always	usually	sometimes	not yet
• I arrive to class on time.	❑	❑	❑	❑
• I bring needed books and supplies.	❑	❑	❑	❑
• I say hello to other students as I enter the classroom.	❑	❑	❑	❑
• I answer questions with a few sentences.	❑	❑	❑	❑
• When I start a conversation, I check that the other people appear interested.	❑	❑	❑	❑
• I keep small talk to before and after class.	❑	❑	❑	❑
• I sit up straight.	❑	❑	❑	❑
• I remove distracting hoods and hats.	❑	❑	❑	❑
• I make eye contact with others.	❑	❑	❑	❑
• I show active listening by nodding my head and turning to the speaker.	❑	❑	❑	❑
• I volunteer at least two answers per class.	❑	❑	❑	❑
• If I've missed directions, I look to other students for clues.	❑	❑	❑	❑

With partners and in small groups				
• I am willing to work with a variety of partners.	❑	❑	❑	❑
• I try to make others feel comfortable by talking to them.	❑	❑	❑	❑
• I show that I'm willing to work with others by moving closer.	❑	❑	❑	❑
• I am polite to people even if I would rather not work with them.	❑	❑	❑	❑
• I listen carefully to directions.	❑	❑	❑	❑

43

_____

8. Reproduced from Alberta Education, *Make School Work for You: A Resource for Junior and Senior High Students who want to be more Successful Learners* (Edmonton, AB: Alberta Education, 2001), pp. 95–96.

Getting Along with Others Inventory (continued)

	always	usually	sometimes	not yet
I check directions with my partners.	❑	❑	❑	❑
I make a rough plan.	❑	❑	❑	❑
I check the time lines.	❑	❑	❑	❑
I use a quiet voice.	❑	❑	❑	❑
I stay with my group and focus on the task.	❑	❑	❑	❑
I try tasks even if I don't really feel like it.	❑	❑	❑	❑
I do my share of the work.	❑	❑	❑	❑
I volunteer ideas.	❑	❑	❑	❑
I show good listening.	❑	❑	❑	❑
I encourage others to contribute their ideas.	❑	❑	❑	❑
I don't put down other people's ideas.	❑	❑	❑	❑
I am willing to try new roles, even if I'm uncomfortable.	❑	❑	❑	❑
I support my partners in group presentations.	❑	❑	❑	❑

Solving problems

	always	usually	sometimes	not yet
I use all my skills to build a positive working relationship with partners.	❑	❑	❑	❑
I let partners know when I think we have a problem.	❑	❑	❑	❑
I am willing to make a new plan and start over.	❑	❑	❑	❑
If necessary, I'll share my concerns with the teacher.	❑	❑	❑	❑

Getting connected

	always	usually	sometimes	not yet
I participate in at least one extracurricular activity each term.	❑	❑	❑	❑

44

Differentiated
Assessment

Contents of this chapter

4

45

"Assessment informs practice, and we take action."
– Rick Wormelli in *Fair Isn't Always Equal: Assessing and Grading in the Differentiated Classroom.*[1]

In a differentiated classroom, assessment is a rich ongoing source of information to help plan meaningful learning activities, establish organizational and grouping structures and mold the classroom environment. Assessment supports the learning process by helping teachers identify and begin to address student strengths and needs. It is ongoing and responsive, changing over the course of a unit in response to student growth and development. It serves multiple purposes— assessment for instructional planning, assessment *for* learning and assessment *of* learning.

Differentiated classrooms, therefore, require what Wiggins and McTighe (2005) describe as a "photo album" approach to assessment, as opposed to a "snapshot" approach. An assessment photo album relates to instruction through the following two reciprocal processes.

- **Differentiated assessment informs differentiated instruction.**
  Differentiated assessment provides information about each student's readiness, strengths and needs in relation to particular outcomes or activities. This information shapes your planning.

- **Differentiated instruction leads to differentiated assessment.**
  In a differentiated classroom, students work toward learning outcomes at different paces and in different ways. As a result, you will need assessment tools and strategies that accomodate diversity while still usefully measuring learning outcomes.

Differentiated assessment means selecting tools and strategies to provide each student with the best opportunity to demonstrate his or her learning. As you get to know your students, and as student differences emerge, assessment naturally becomes more differentiated, because its purpose is to meet students where they are and to coach them to the next step. In this way, assessment and instruction continue to support and inform each other.

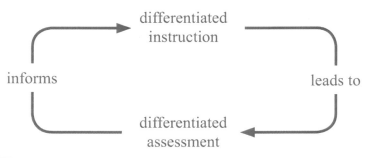

Moving toward differentiated assessment

Like differentiated instruction, differentiated assessment is based on the reality that the needs of students cannot all be met in the same way. Successfully meeting student needs involves using your understanding of each student to guide your selection of a reasonable range of assessment tools and strategies. The goal is not to have an individualized assessment plan for each student, but to have a manageable class assessment plan that is flexible enough to accommodate a range of student needs.

The following scenarios illustrate sample ways of moving toward differentiated assessment practices in different contexts.

Supporting students with learning difficulties

A student with learning disabilities has a goal in his individualized program plan (IPP) that points toward the use of particular assessment tools and strategies. The teacher sees the potential of these practices for some of the other students in the classroom, who do not have a diagnosed learning disability but appear to have some similar learning needs. The teacher uses similar assessment methods with these students.

Rethinking grading practices

A teacher is rethinking his grading and reporting practices. He sees that he has been using a one-size-fits-all approach that does not consider individual student readiness, interests or learning preferences. He redesigns his grading and reporting practices to include some student choice, different supports for different students as required, opportunities for students to better their performance on major assessment tasks, and some flexibility in the timing of major assessment tasks.

Assessment-for-learning practices

A teacher adopts a number of assessment-for-learning strategies and realizes two things. First, assessment-for-learning practices (such as the use of exit slips to determine students' level of understanding after an activity) help identify student strengths and needs and, therefore, support differentiated instruction and assessment. Second, some assessment-for-learning strategies (such as having students keep growth portfolios, learning logs and reflective journals) are, by their nature, already differentiated assessment since these strategies provide students with choice and a broader scope for how they can respond.

Facilitating metacognition

A teacher is pursuing one of Alberta's Teacher Quality Standards: "… [teachers] help students develop the ability to diagnose their own learning needs and to assess their progress toward learning goals." He has reviewed the programs of study for the subjects he teaches and identifies metacognition, including goal setting, choice, self-assessment and reflection, as an important underpinning of the curriculum. He realizes that using a more personalized assessment practice is an important way to encourage his students to reflect on their learning processes and needs.

47

You can use assessment-before-learning, (sometimes called pre-assessment or diagnostic assessment), to help plan effective instruction at the start of a new term or unit. Instructional decisions can be improved by having early information about student:

- readiness
- interests
- learning preferences
- background knowledge
- existing understandings.

Consider the two scenarios below.

- A teacher is preparing for a new term. Several of her students have portfolios created over the last year, several others have learner profiles, and one has an individualized program plan (IPP). The teacher reviews all of this information and develops a preliminary instruction plan for the first unit of study. She also creates a pre-assessment plan to gather information from the remaining students in the class. This plan might include an interest inventory and doing a short survey to identify preferred learning preferences.

- A teacher has his science class complete a pre-test for the next unit in order to fine-tune his planning for the opening learning activities.

Learner profiles and pre-testing are two types of assessment you can use for instructional planning.

Learner profiles

Learner profiles can help you to understand and track your students' unique learning journeys. As a student progresses through the grades, a wealth of information can be amassed about his or her achievements, interests, learning preferences and general strengths and needs. Much of this information does not need to be rediscovered each year.

You can use a variety of strategies to assemble student profiles, such as:

- reviewing profiles and files of student work
- conferencing with each student
- conferencing with parents
- administering interest, learning preferences and other inventories
- consulting with previous teachers.

You can use the contents of individual learner profiles to create various types of class profiles and to plan for differentiated instruction. For more information on creating and using learner and class profiles, see *Chapter 3: Developing Learner Profiles*.

Pre-testing

Pre-testing is a way to determine ahead of time what understandings and levels of readiness students have regarding a particular topic. Pre-tests are generally administered well before a topic is introduced, to help you answer the following types of questions.

- How much prior knowledge or experience do students have?
- What level of achievement and readiness do students have?
- Are any students missing the skills or understandings they need to learn this material?
- Will students need help to overcome any misconceptions about this topic?

The information gathered from pre-tests can help you make decisions and differentiate instruction in the following areas:

- pacing of instruction for the whole class or for small groups
- how much time to spend on review
- how to schedule assessment of achievement
- flexible grouping of students
- tiering assignments
- acceleration.

In addition to supporting differentiated instruction, pre-testing can itself be differentiated, since it can enable students of various abilities and with varied experience to best show some of what they know. For example, one student may not know the details or have the vocabulary but might understand some key concepts in the subject. Another may have a lot of general knowledge, but also have significant misconceptions. Use a range of question types, from knowledge and recall to evaluation and even speculation, to allow a range of students' understanding to emerge. Open-ended questions, such as "Write what you know about…" also can allow more students to respond.

Assessment *for* learning seeks to gather information to meet not only an assessment purpose, but also an instructional purpose. The instructional purposes of assessment *for* learning include:

- to help students connect different learning experiences (e.g., the "cubing" strategy can help students use their prior knowledge to look at a topic from different points-of-view; in this strategy an 8-sided cube has a different perspective or type of task printed on each face and a student chooses one or more of these prompts to complete a task)

- to engage students in learning or create a context for learning (e.g., the "jot-pair-share" strategy can help create conversations between students about a topic as they jot down the main idea of a presentation, share what they wrote with a partner and then with whole class)

49

- to remind students of essential skills or knowledge (e.g., asking "How does the design of the structure you have built affect its strength?" reminds students that, although they have enjoyed decorating their structures, the main expectation is that they will understand the principles of strength in structures)

- to provide immediate feedback and model strategies that help students to improve their own learning (e.g., using an "exit slip" strategy encourages students to habitually ask themselves questions like, "What have I learned?," "What am I learning?" or "What could I learn next?" and write their responses to these questions and give them to the teacher as they leave the classroom at the end of the class).

Assessment *for* learning

Assessment *for* learning (also called formative assessment) can include pre-assessments (which in addition to supporting planning also can motivate students and activate prior understandings and knowledge), ongoing assessment and other strategies. Ongoing assessment strategies quickly gather information from all students in the class. Other assessment *for* learning strategies are focused on articulating the learning of individual students, both for the teacher's and student's benefit. These strategies are differentiated by nature because they deal with the unique qualities of each student.

There are a number of assessment strategies that allow all students in the class to be assessed quickly and often simultaneously, providing you with assessment information you can use immediately to adjust the difficulty, pacing and other factors in a lesson. Ongoing assessment strategies typically have a narrow focus on a single skill or concept, and are not appropriate for assessing complex understandings or integrated skills.

Assessment *for* learning strategies typically have the following characteristics.

- **Informal**—The setting does not resemble that of a test and requires no standardizing. For example, in the simplest form of ongoing assessment, teachers use focused observation to listen to and watch their students at work in order to determine if and how they are learning. In the "K-W-L" strategy, students simply add things they know or want to know to the columns of an ongoing chart labelled "what I know", "what I want to know" and "what I learned."

- **Focused on learning**—Students can expect that when they do not meet a goal, they will soon have an opportunity to meet it. For example, students use a "traffic light" graphic to indicate "Green–I understand this. I'm good to go.", "Yellow–I need to go a little slower to better understand." and "Red–Stop, I need help!" By choosing Green, Yellow or Red to represent their learning, students self-report their current level of understanding so teachers can use this information to inform upcoming instruction.

- **High response**—All students are expected to respond within a short period of time. For example, with the "response cards" strategy, the teacher asks a question and all students write a response. Simply by walking around the room the teacher can quickly see who is responding correctly and can use the opportunity to do some on-the-spot prompting and teaching for students who need it.

- **Foster metacognition**—Students self-assess and reflect on what they have learned and on how they learn. For example, students may be asked to complete an "exit slip" at the end of class. This is an opportunity for them to reflect on their own learning, record their reflections and then pass this written record to the teacher as they exit from the classroom.

What assessment *for* learning strategies you use will depend on your existing knowledge about your students, as well as the specific purpose for the assessment and where in the activity the assessment will occur; e.g., at the beginning, in the middle or at the end.

	Position in the learning activity		
	Beginning	**Middle/During**	**End**
Example of assessment purpose	To find out whether students have retained a skill learned in a previous activity.	To find out if the remainder of the learning activity should be restructured to accommodate differing learning needs.	To find out the extent to which students have overcome a misconception common to the topic.
Example of instructional purpose	To help students recall what they learned in the previous activity and to remind them of an expectation.	To help students remain engaged in the learning, and to take ownership for their own learning	To help students bring closure to the activity and to focus on a big idea.
Sample strategy	"Response cards"	"Post a point"	"Exit slip"

Planning for assessment

Planning for assessments *for* learning is part of short-range planning, as the strategies are directly related to current learning activities and outcomes. The following steps suggest a process for using assessment *for* learning strategies. In some cases, you might run through all six of these steps in a few minutes, while in others, it might take a more extended time.

1. Determine the purpose

The purpose of collecting assessment *for* learning information is to help inform decisions about how to teach next. In a differentiated classroom, the decisions that could be influenced include those identified by Dodge (2005):

- setting up groups
- pacing the activities
- framing and phrasing questions
- determining what kind of review will be required
- timing the assessments.

Before selecting an strategy, anticipate the results and consider the implications. For example:

- Will you change your plans for the learning activity if it emerges that half your students have not retained a necessary skill from the last activity?
- What will you do if all except two students have retained the skill?

Assessment *for* learning assessment results also can, under some circumstances, be repurposed to evaluate learning. For example, if students demonstrate their achievement of a learning outcome during the course of an activity, you may choose to make a record of this event as evidence of achievement.

2. Establish a focus

A busy classroom contains so much potential assessment information that even a full-time observer could not record it all. Decide what assessment information you need to help with your instructional decision making, and then select an assessment strategy that will focus on that in an efficient way. The following guidelines may be helpful.

- **Focus on learning outcomes.** Consider what students are expected to know and be able to do related to the specific learning outcome. For example, asking students the name of the interpreter from yesterday's social studies field trip does not form the basis of an assessment strategy. A question for ongoing assessment would be, "How is listening to a senior citizen interpret an historic site an example of research?"

- **Focus on sequential learning.** Identify any outcomes that act as a critical step in a sequence. In other words, students really should not proceed until they have achieved this outcome, or really need to proceed because they have achieved it. These outcomes should be the focus of an assessment *for* learning strategy.

3. Select and use the strategy

Consider the following guidelines when choosing an assessment strategy.

- **Choose a strategy that aligns with the purpose and focus for collecting the information.** Ensure that the strategy actually assesses what you are aiming to assess.

- **Pick a strategy that students enjoy**. Students often enjoy informal ongoing assessment strategies because they are quick, engaging and low risk. Varying strategies adds to the novelty and enjoyment.

- **Determine when the information is needed**. If the information is needed right away, then the strategy must provide student responses that you can use immediately, such as the "response cards" strategy used with one-word answers. If the information is needed for an upcoming learning activity, and if a more complex response is required from students, use the "exit slip" strategy or another strategy that allows you to read and interpret student responses after the activity.

- **Decide how much time can be afforded**. Assessment strategies do take time, and it is important to allow enough time to make them effective. Completing an "exit slip" may well take five minutes, and so the learning activity must wrap up in time to make it possible.

- **Decide how students could demonstrate understanding.** Many strategies can be used to tap into either knowledge or application, depending on the questions that are asked of students. For example, asking students to answer questions about a new concept demonstrates knowledge, but giving them an opportunity to apply the knowledge by solving a problem or creating an example provides richer information.

- **Vary the strategies used**. An ongoing assessment strategy should help each student quickly bring his or her understanding to the forefront, so that it is apparent to the student and to you. The means by which students demonstrate their understanding should not be an obstacle. For example, a student who has weak writing skills may not be able to quickly demonstrate his or her understanding by writing a response. To minimize this effect, rotate through assessment strategies that vary the way in which students respond.

4. Record the results

The high response nature of many assessment *for* learning strategies means that they generate information that tends to be rapid fire. Responses come quickly and from many or all students. This sudden splash of information has to be captured if it is to be used. However, the information gathered may have a short shelf life, in that it is used to make an immediate instructional decision and is then no longer useful. As a result, you may often simply capture and

53

hold the information in your working memory for the few seconds it takes to make an instructional decision. At other times, you may decide to retain the information, for any of the following reasons:

- to add to a formative assessment record; e.g., to help document a student's progress
- to plan differentiation strategies for upcoming learning activities; e.g., to set up groups
- to improve instruction for future students; e.g., to make a "note to self" about what to do differently next time you present these learning activities.

The most common formats for records of assessment *for* learning are notes, tallies and checklists.

5. Interpret the results and take action

Formative assessment is valuable only to the extent that the information is used. In this final step, go back to your original purpose and adjust your teaching based on the results you received.

The following vignette illustrates how a teacher uses a step-by-step process, ending in the interpreting of results and the plan for action.

Step 1–It's the end of a mathematics activity focused on multiplying values that have exponents. Ms. E would like to know if students are ready to move on to further work with exponents. She wants to check for understanding.

Step 2–Ms. E thinks that most students understand the concept but anticipates that possibly six or seven students still have some confusion. If this turns out to be true, Ms. E has decided that she will provide an in-class tutorial if there are five or more students who need more instruction, but will work one-on-one for 30-minute blocks at lunchtime if there are four or less students who need additional teaching.

Step 3–Ms. E selects the "exit slip" strategy that asks students to demonstrate their understanding and also to reflect on it. They will write down the solution to a problem, show their work, explain the thinking behind their answer in three to four sentences, and also note what they find hard or easy about this type of problem.

Step 4–Students take the last 10 minutes of class to complete their exit slips and give the cards to Ms. E as they leave. At lunchtime, she sifts through the cards and identifies four students who are still unsure of this concept. She uses a checklist to record her findings.

Step 5–On the cards of these students, Ms. E writes an invitation to make an appointment with her for extra coaching some time over the next week.

Individual assessment

In addition to strategies that allow a whole-class response, assessment *for* learning can occur through various strategies focused on the learning of individual students. Students can use this individualized information to reflect on their own progress, to understand themselves better as learners, to set goals, to make plans, to make choices and to prepare to demonstrate their achievement. Consider the following elements for individualizing assessment to support student learning.

- **Metacognition**—Assessment strategies that focus on metacognition encourage students to think about their own learning preferences and processes and to transfer new understandings and skills. They also encourage students to discuss and demonstrate their learning with peers, parents and teachers.

- **Strategic questioning**—Questions are at the heart of most assessments, and so your ability to ask good questions is critical. Black et al. (2004) note that questions should "raise issues about which the teacher needs information or about which the students need to think" (p. 13). Black et al. (2004) also stress the importance of allowing students time to answer questions, explaining that increased wait time gives students the time they need to think and shows that the teacher believes everyone will have an answer.

- **Varied assessment activities**—Students can demonstrate their learning by writing, making, doing and saying; within these four modalities there are many possibilities for different kinds of expression and production. Varying asssssment tasks will provide you and your students with a more accurate picture of student learning.

- **Student choice**—Providing students with options for assessment is an important way to increase their motivation, self-awareness and responsibility for their own learning. For more information on providing choice, see *Chapter 5: Differentiated Learning Experiences*.

- **Feedback**—Providing informative, corrective and timely feedback is an important way of supporting and guiding student development. To be most effective, feedback should refer back to learning outcomes, be specific and descriptive, and encourage self-correcting strategies.

What this can look like

Many strategies for individual assessment, such as learning logs and conferences, are differentiated by nature, because they are flexible enough to deal with the unique qualities of each student. Individual assessment strategies might include the following.

- Group or individual conferencing sessions in which students discuss their learning with the teacher.

- Peer-assessment and self-assessment tasks, including rubrics.

- Learning logs and journals.

- Small questions focusing on knowledge or a skill. For example, a unit or course reaches a point where it is critical for students to know the meaning of the term "The Renaissance", and so the teacher creates a question to check students' current ability to define it.

- Big questions focusing on an essential understanding. For example, it may be critical for further progress that students understand how Renaissance Europe formed the basis for the worldview of the western world, and so the teacher frames a question to check students' current understanding of this idea.

- A variety of options for student products, projects and learning tasks.
    - *Writing*—point form, outline, graphic organizer, sentence, paragraph, structured passage
    - *Making*—sketch, visual portrayal, model
    - *Doing*—performance, demonstration of skill, routine, procedure, decision making, problem solving
    - *Saying*—discussing, debating, conferencing, skit, role-play

- Varied assessment activities that use multiple intelligences as a framework; for example, asking students to:
    - discover and manipulate materials (bodily-kinesthetic)
    - present an oral story illustrating new information in context (verbal-linguistic)
    - introduce new terms in a graphic organizer (logical-mathematical)
    - complete a freewrite on a topic (verbal-linguistic)
    - turn to a partner and discuss (interpersonal)
    - draw a diagram to make the information memorable (visual)
    - write journal entries from a particular point of view (intrapersonal)
    - role-play a possible scenario (bodily-kinesthetic)
    - write a children's book about the topic (verbal-linguistic).

- "Tic Tac Toe" strategy—A number of individual assessment activities are displayed on a grid pattern, one task per box. Students select activities along a row, column or diagonal. The teacher ensures that each combination contains the variety of assessment activities needed to provide an accurate picture of student learning.

Assessment *of* learning

Assessment *of* learning (sometimes called summative assessment) is the process of collecting and interpreting information to judge student achievement against predetermined criteria for the purposes of grading and reporting. Assessment *of* learning occurs at benchmark points in learning, such as the end of a unit or chunk of learning.

Consider the following examples of differentiating assessment *of* learning.

- Some students in a class choose to demonstrate their learning by writing a report, while others choose to create a poster, and still others choose an oral presentation.

- A teacher provides text-to-speech software and a digital version of the test to a student who has significant difficulty reading the questions in a social studies test.

- A teacher discards some marks collected early in the semester for a student who got off to a bad start but subsequently made strong progress.

Differentiating the selection and use of assessment information

Differentiating assessment involves rethinking the standard practice of having all students do the same assessment tasks at the same time, regardless of their individual learning needs or the learning they have already demonstrated. Rather, in this new paradigm, teachers customize the selection and use of assessment information to reflect each student's highest level of achievement. For example, you might:

- review the evidence you have collected for each student and select a sample that best represents each student's achievement

- discard outlying information that conflicts with consistent evidence, as well as information from early assessments that has clearly been superseded by more recent information

- collect only as much information as needed regarding a student's achievement of a learning outcome; if you already have evidence to support the highest reasonable claim that can be made about a student's achievement, there is no need for the student to complete more assessment tasks related to this outcome

57

- postpone further assessment of a student if it is clear that further instruction related to a learning outcome is needed

- use a certain assessment activity as a formative assessment for one student and as a summative assessment for another student

- involve students in the collection, interpretation and communication of their own assessment *of* learning information whenever possible.

Consider the following examples of how teachers can differentiate the selection and use of assessment *of* learning information.

Example 1: A student has not had sufficient practice to achieve to her full potential related to the learning outcomes being addressed in an assessment activity; however, she is ready to use the activity as a practice assessment. The teacher will use the activity as an assessment *for* learning for this student and as an assessment *of* learning for the other students.

Example 2: A teacher uses a checklist to accumulate a record of the times he observes his students demonstrating the learning outcome "develop and justify own opinions and points of view" during discussion. The record for two students is as follows.

	Sep 14	Sep 21	Sep 28	Oct 5	Oct 12	Oct 19
Student A				✓	✓	✓
Student B	✓		✓			✓

The teacher concludes that Student A has reached consistent achievement of the learning outcome, and that Student B's achievement is inconsistent. By observing on more than one day, the teacher is able to see individual patterns of learning.

Example 3: A teacher uses scoring rubrics and rating scales as a means of identifying evaluation criteria and communicating achievement to students and their parents. He also uses rubrics and rating scales to provide specific feedback to help individual students improve their performance and understand where they are in the achievement of learning outcomes.

Example 4: A student's ability to problem solve in mathematics is quite strong; however, his ability to perform mental arithmetic is weak. The teacher lifts the requirement to use mental arithmetic when assessing problem solving, permitting the student to use a calculator. This allows the student to better demonstrate his or her problem-solving skills.

Assessing differentiated products

When assessment is differentiated only by product, the learning outcome remains the same for all students and a single rubric can be used to assess all forms of the product. It is often practical to design rubrics solely around the learning outcomes being addressed and not include criteria that are specific to any of the products. This practice helps students to focus not so much on the product itself (although this is always worthy of care and effort) but on the learning that is supposed to be demonstrated through that product. Rubrics can focus on a single learning outcome and related criteria or on a combination of different learning outcomes and criteria.

Careful analysis of learning outcomes will help you determine how much potential there is for differentiation by product. For example, a Grade 8 English language arts learning outcome on writing narratives from other points of view clearly indicates the type of product to be used (namely writing narratives) and, although the type of narrative can vary, there is not a lot of leeway to vary the type of product. In contrast, the learning outcome "compare and contrast the different perspectives provided by first and third person narration" has potential for differentiated products; e.g., students could present their comparison and contrast through writing, graphic organizers, dramatic presentations or other means.

For example:
Grade 8 social studies students are demonstrating that they can create a social message. The teacher develops a rubric that focuses on the communication learning outcome (shown in the partial rubric below.) Regardless of the type of product that students choose, such as a poster, an infomercial or a dramatic presentation, their achievement in terms of communication will be determined using the same rubric.

	Oral, written or visual literacy presents in a way that is engaging and purposeful
Wow!	presents in a way that is persuasive and engaging and has a purpose that is consistently clear
Yes	presents in a way that is credible and interesting and has a purpose that is evident
Yes, But	presents in a way that is logical and has a stated purpose
Not Yet	presents in a way that is vague and/or confusing and/or does not show purpose

Assessing differentiated topics

Sometimes you may have the opportunity to differentiate by topic, based on student interest. Assessment of content that has been differentiated by interest generally does not require different rubrics.

For example:
A teacher in a Grade 6 English language arts class creates opportunity for students to choose any topic of interest to demonstrate their learning of the outcome to "make connections between own life and characters and ideas in oral, print and other media texts."

Providing supports and scaffolds

In some cases, students need specific supports or scaffolding to demonstrate their learning. These supports allow students to demonstrate their best learning. Sometimes very minor supports, are all that is necessary to allow a student to be successful. Supports and scaffolds are considered to be part of differentiated assessment because they are matched intentionally with identified learning needs for a given student.

For example:
A teacher provides a student with extra time to complete a test, thereby relieving the student of some stress and making it possible for him or her to be successful.

Grading and reporting in a differentiated classroom

Grading is a measure of achievement and, in a differentiated classroom, it is important that understandings of what grading means are clear in relation to curriculum standards and the learning needs of students.

To grade effectively in a differentiated classroom you should:
- be selective; not everything that students do should be graded

- base grading on clear, specific criteria

- identify the indicators of student success, describe the criteria by which that success will be evaluated, and measure it accordingly

- use evidence that is directly linked to the learning outcome being evaluated and disregard other factors; e.g., if students are being evaluated on their understanding of a mathematical concept, factors such as neatness of the work should not reduce or inflate a student's grade

- identify and reduce factors that could prevent students from demonstrating their learning, such as difficulty with reading or slow written production; use strategies such as providing students with second chances to demonstrate their learning, or focusing on scores students earn later in a learning sequence so they have ample opportunities to practise

- consider what can motivate or, sometimes more importantly, impair motivation for learning; facilitate motivation to learn by supporting students in assuming responsibility for their own growth, ensuring tasks are clear and aligned with learning outcomes, and providing ongoing feedback and appropriate learning opportunities that are interesting, relevant and suitable for students' readiness and abilities.

Although assessment *of* learning focuses exclusively on student achievement relative to grade or course level expectations, your reporting also can include important information about students' work habits, progress during the course, strengths and needs, attitudes, the way they learn best, and/or suggestions for how they can improve their achievement. These aspects should not be combined or averaged into a score, but rather reported as separate, important elements. Consider strategies for reporting these aspects such as separate comments, attachments to the report card, separate communications, checklists or student-parent-teacher conferences.

Managing differentiated assessment

Consider the following tips to help you make meaningful, manageable decisions about how to differentiate assessment.

- **Be realistic.** Assessing differentiated content, process or product places demands on you as the teacher. In general, content differentiation tends to put the highest demand on teachers' understanding of the subject matter. Process differentiation tends to put the highest demand on teachers' classroom management skills. Product differentiation tends to put the most demand on teachers' planning skills because they will need to have choices laid out, materials available and general rubrics ready.

- **Create opportunities for students to experience a variety of ways to demonstrate their learning.** Varied experiences give student differences more of an opportunity to come to light. For example, by intentionally rotating students through tasks that focus on different multiple intelligences, you create opportunities for students to demonstrate their strengths and interests, while also revealing areas of need.

- **Consider what types and variety of assessment tools and strategies are best suited to the learning outcomes being addressed.** Student achievement of some learning outcomes can only be effectively assessed in a limited number of ways while others may lend themselves to a more diverse range of assessment methods. For example, the mathematics learning outcome, "Describe, orally and in writing, whether or not a number is rational" probably has less potential for differentiated assessment than the learning outcome, "Solve problems, using rational numbers in meaningful contexts."

- **Ensure students are equipped to deal with the choices they are offered.** In order to make sound choices for demonstrating their learning, students need:
  - a repertoire of products or strategies from which to choose
  - the critical thinking skills to identify, weigh and choose options
  - knowledge of themselves as learners
  - the maturity to choose the option that will let them best show what they have learned, not simply the option they think will be quickest.

- **Add to student repertoires of products and strategies.** Explicitly teach and then provide structured opportunities to demonstrate their learning in different ways. Include opportunities and tools for self-reflection and self-assessment.

- **Consider your own comfort level with various strategies and tools.** For example, when introducing a new assessment strategy, you may want to use it with the whole class, rather than attempting to deal with more than one strategy at once.

- **Address both strengths and challenges.** Sometimes helping a student to become well-rounded is in the student's best interest. As a result, you may ask students to work in a way that is not their preferred way in order to stretch themselves. At other times, you may decide that students should demonstrate their learning in the way that is most comfortable for them. For example, a student who would not choose to work independently might benefit from completing independent tasks on occasion. At another time, you may decide that it is important to collect the best evidence you can to support the highest claim you can reasonably make about a student's achievement and, therefore, you allow the student to use a graphic organizer rather than a formal essay to present an overview of a topic.

62

Differentiated Learning Experiences

5

Contents of this chapter

"In a diverse classroom, no single method can reach all learners. Multiple pathways to achieving goals are needed."
– From "Providing New Access to the General Curriculum: Universal Design for Learning" by Chuck Hitchcock et al., *Teaching Exceptional Children*, 35, 2002, p. 12. Copyright 2002 by The Council for Exceptional Children. Reprinted with permission.

Creating differentiated learning experiences involves proactively ensuring that students are engaged in a variety of meaningful activities and contexts. In an environment of flexibility and choice, classroom roles are altered. The teacher's role focuses on creating and selecting learning opportunities for students, guiding them and working with them to assess their progress. The student's role becomes one of an independent, self-motivated and confident learner.

Key elements of differentiated learning experiences include meaningful activities, flexible grouping, scaffolded instruction and choice.

Meaningful activities

Decisions about grouping, scaffolding and choice all must be built on a belief and a proficiency in designing activities that are meaningful for students. Meaningful learning activities are:
- developmentally appropriate
- connected and relevant to life experiences
- authentic
- engaging
- respectful and fair to all students.

Meaningful activities are built on an understanding of both individual students and good instructional practices. Activities should actively engage students in exploring, questioning, applying and reflecting on concepts and skills. This may include opportunities for:
- identifying similarities and differences
- summarizing and note taking
- using and creating visual representations
- generating and testing hypotheses
- using cues, questions and advance organizers to make sense of learning.

Implementing meaningful activities
Consider the following guidelines for creating meaningful, respectful activities:
- explicitly discuss the activity's purpose and importance with students
- provide clear directions and expectations to reduce uncertainty, surprise and disappointment
- challenge students of all ability levels to work to their full potential

- use learner profiles, pre-testing and other information to tailor activities and resources to student interests, backgrounds and learning preferences
- anticipate any challenges or barriers to learning and build in supports to reduce these barriers
- share or develop assessment tools with students (e.g., criteria, rubrics, exemplars) to clarify expectations
- provide learning resources students will need for the activity that are accessible, engaging and build understanding
- plan for efficient delivery to create momentum and keep the focus on learning
- assess and refine activities and tasks to maximize learning.

Best practices related to meaningful activities

Consider the following examples of what creating meaningful learning activities can look like.

- Use different types of materials and mediums when discussing and sharing ideas and information with students; e.g., visual, narratives, objects, music, literature, poetry.

- Provide students with multiple sources of information for their research activities and projects.

- Encourage the use of learning logs as a way for students to track their own learning, reflect on what they have learned and make connections, as well as apply and practise skills such as predicting, organizing and evaluating.

- Offer and model questioning strategies that address differing student abilities and readiness.

- Provide opportunities for students to apply what they have learned in contexts beyond the classroom setting.

- Provide problem-based learning contexts in which students actively solve problems in the same ways that professionals do in their jobs. Problem-based learning tasks can be structured individually, in small groups or as a class.

- Offer tiered activities to have students work on the same concepts or skills, but with varying degrees of complexity, abstractness and open-endedness.

- Model the use of graphic organizers to present information. For example, use a mind map to show and discuss connections between different ideas or concepts. Use a bubble map to present alternatives. Use a flowchart to discuss and work with sequence.

- Provide supports for recording and synthesizing information, such as guidelines for creating a summary, advanced organizers and templates for summarizing.

65

- Identify opportunities throughout the year for each student to take on the role of expert. The sharing of expertise builds both individual self-confidence and classroom community.

- At the start a new unit, find out about relevant student interests, then follow up on these during the course of the unit. For example, in a unit on classroom chemistry, a student might identify an interest in organic farming and the chemistry involved in certifying different kinds of food as organic. Follow-up activities might include:
  - having the student complete a unit project on organic certification and share the results in a presentation
  - forming a small study group of students interested in organic food and having them conduct research and report back to the class
  - inviting a guest speaker to talk to the class about organic products and discussing afterwards what was learned and how it connects back to the chemistry unit's learner outcomes.

Flexible grouping

In effectively differentiated classrooms, all students have opportunities to work in a variety of contexts through thoughtfully planned, flexible groupings that incorporate both student choice and teacher-assigned roles. Students are grouped and regrouped over the course of the school year according to their own learning and social needs, rather than just the needs of the task.

Flexible grouping:
- provides opportunities and supports for students to create and construct their own understandings and to actively develop skills
- allows for targeted instruction for groups with different needs, interests and preferences
- is based on a recognition of individual student differences
- promotes positive peer relationships and discourages cliques
- minimizes the negative social and emotional effects of homogeneous grouping strategies by ability
- promotes and develops social interaction skills
- promotes a sense of community, as students get to see their peers' strengths, not only their weaknesses, and this engenders respect for one another.

Typical types of grouping include:
- whole class
- small groups; e.g., three to seven students
- partners
- individual.

66

Groupings can be based on student learning preferences and interests, background experiences, academic level and readiness. These varying group structures provide options to target different learning outcomes for individual or specific groups of students.

Flexible grouping can include cooperative learning strategies, but does so in a way that emphasizes the individual needs of students who are placed into cooperative groups. All grouping structures have merit for all students as they can provide students with different experiences and contexts in which to work.

Implementing flexible grouping

Grouping decisions should consider learning outcomes, assessment data and student needs to determine how students will be moved in and out of different groups. Various types of assessment data should be used to determine how groups should be formed and what the purpose or task of each group should be. Specific understandings and skills can be established as a target or task that each group of students should accomplish at the time they need to.

It is important to consider student needs, interests and learning preferences, while also ensuring that all students have opportunities to work in group settings that they are comfortable with as well as those that challenge them to learn and grow.

Consider the following tips for managing flexible groups and moving students in and out of appropriate learning contexts and tasks.

Structure groups for success
- Limit group sizes. Smaller groups are easier to manage and encourage each member to contribute. Four to six members is often optimal for completing tasks.
- Promote classroom community by bringing students together for large group discussion or activities at the beginning or end of the learning activity.

Respond to student needs
- Establish an atmosphere that shows students that everyone's work is valued.
- Allot the time you spend with each group based on the group's learning needs. Time spent with each group does not have to be equal.
- Plan more independent activities for groups who are capable of working without close guidance; provide more structure and supervision to those groups that need it.
- Plan for ways to manage varying time-related needs of individual students.
- Provide students who finish early with additional meaningful and relevant activities. Discuss processes and steps for students who need extra time to complete their work.

Create structure

- Provide clear, focused directions. Checklists, menus and picture prompts can help groups manage tasks on their own.
- Make it clear what you expect of students. Provide rubrics, samples or examples to illustrate what quality work looks like.
- Make sure groups know that all members are expected to contribute and stay on task. Outline what evidence you expect to see of the groups' progress.
- Offer guidelines for student behaviour, including how to work in a group, how to ask for help and how to show respect for other groups in the classroom.
- Organize the classroom environment to facilitate group work. Designate accessible places for materials to be kept, work-in-progress to be stored and completed work to be submitted.

Best practices for flexible grouping

Flexible grouping involves varying instruction between individuals, partners, small groups, large groups and whole class. It also involves considering a variety of options within these basic groupings, such as whether to establish groups randomly or purposefully. The chart that follows describes each of these basic contexts and offers specific examples of instructional activities that make the best use of them.

68

Individual Learning Experiences

Best Practices	What This Can Look Like
• Provide structured opportunities for metacognition and self-reflection. • Individual learning experiences can be structured within other types of groups; e.g., small group, large group and whole class. • Provide clear directions to encourage independence. • Combine with larger group structures to emphasize collaboration and cooperation.	• **"Learning logs"** and **"journals"** are ways for students to track and reflect on their learning. Learning logs focus on more objective details of learning and encourage students to make connections, and practise skills such as predicting, organizing and evaluating. Journals, such as an opinions journal, encourage students to articulate their beliefs, attitudes and perceptions about what and how they are learning. • **"Interactive notebooks"** use a specific notebook format[1] to scaffold student interactions with information and text. On the right page of the notebook, students record notes during lessons, discussions, reading, viewing, group work and research activities. On the left page, they record their individual interactions with the information, including reflecting, processing, making connections, doodling ideas or posing questions. Teachers may provide suggestions but do not direct the content of the left page. • **"Agendas"** are personalized lists of tasks that students must complete in a specific period of time. Tasks can be assigned, negotiated with students or selected independently. Agendas should include both the task and the directions for completing it. • **"Think pad brainstorming"** is a strategy for combining independent and group work. Students brainstorm individually on paper before sharing their ideas with a partner, group or whole class.

1. The interactive notebook format was first introduced in the *History Alive* program produced by the Teachers' Curriculum Institute.

Paired Learning Experiences

Best Practices	What This Can Look Like
• Provide opportunities to develop and practise communication skills, make comparisons and share learning in a non-threatening context. • Assign partners based on learning needs, interests and preferences. • Consider when students should work with the same partner or switch partners for different learning contexts. • Encourage students to reflect and self-assess as a regular part of paired learning experiences. • Use paired grouping strategies to encourage students to challenge and support each other. Provide students with opportunities for peer teaching and mentoring. • Use paired grouping structures to introduce, teach and extend use of graphic organizers.	• **"Study buddies"** or **"learning partners"** can be established as a regular part of classroom routines. • **"Discussion breaks"** are an opportunity for students to discuss ideas, questions and information. Schedule three to five minutes into daily activities. Encourage students to record discussion points in their notebooks to help them stay on task. • **"Exit cards"** can provide opportunities to have students self-assess and reflect on their partnering activities and discussions by writing on an index card and handing it to the teacher as they leave the classroom. • **"Mind maps"** or **"bubble maps"** are a good way for partners to synthesize their understandings. Each student records ideas on sticky notes. Then together partners make connections, identify similarities and differences, and represent content by creating pictures and symbols. • A **"resident expert"** is a student who has received extra instruction in a topic or skill (or has expert knowledge and interest in a topic). Reteaching peers in a partner context can deepen the "resident expert" student's own knowledge and skills. • In **"team-pair-solo"**, students complete problems first as a team, then with a partner and finally on their own. • In **"say and switch"**, partners take turns responding to topics at signaled but unpredictable times. The person listening must pick up from their partner's train of thought before adding new ideas.

Small Group Learning Experiences

Best Practices

- Make intentional decisions about when and how to organize small groups.

- Structure focused tasks based on content or skill development, learning interests or preferences and readiness levels.

- Consider grouping students based on both similiarities and differences. Students benefit from opportunities to work with individuals whose interests and/or learning preferences differ from their own.

- Use cooperative mixed-ability groupings to provide students with opportunities to rehearse information, learn from one another, build individual accountability in a group, engage in a high degree of activity and receive support.

- Build in strategies to ensure that every group member is involved in tasks, including answering questions, solving problems or completing an activity.

What This Can Look Like

- Organize students into small groups for specific and focused instruction on concepts or skills they are experiencing difficulty with. The other students in the classroom can work on independent or paired groupings appropriate to their understanding or skill development. These groupings are fluid and change as student needs change.

- In the **"jigsaw strategy,"** students are organized into groups of four or five. Each student in the group is assigned unique material to learn and then teach to his or her group members. Students working on the same material get together to decide what is important and how to teach it to their small group. After practising in these "expert" groups, the original groups re-form and students teach material to each other. By assigning the same material to those students who are challenged with concepts or skills, you can spend additional, focused time with this group.

- **"Learning centres"** or **"stations"** allow students to work on specific tasks designed to target concept or skill development. Every small group does not necessarily have to complete all tasks at each learning centre. Time spent, tasks completed and degree of choice can vary for each group of students.

- In Spencer Kagan's **"numbered heads together"** strategy, each group member is given a number. The teacher poses a problem and all group members discuss it. Each group member is accountable for ensuring that every group member can complete the task. The teacher then calls a number and that student is responsible for sharing the group's solution to the problem.

What This Can Look Like (continued)

- In **"round robin brainstorming"**, the class is divided into small groups with one person appointed as the recorder. An open-ended question is posed and students are given time to think about answers individually. Then members of the group share responses with one another, going around the circle, one after another, and the recorder writes down the answers of the group members.

- In **"pass a problem"**, the teacher creates problems for teams to solve and writes or attaches them to envelopes. Teams read the problems, place their solution in the envelope and then exchange with another team to check their solutions and to determine if they solved the problems in different ways.

- In **"send a problem"**, one student writes a problem on a card and asks group members to solve the problem. Group members solve the problem and the question writer determines if they have come up with a good solution.

- In **"three stay, one stray"**, three group members work together to solve a problem, while one group member "strays" to another group to compare and discuss their ideas.

- A **"gallery walk"** encourages students to learn from each other in small group settings. Groups record their work on a piece of chart paper. Each group appoints a docent to stay with their work, while the remaining members rotate around examining other groups' ideas and asking questions of the docents. Members then regroup to discuss and add to their information.

- In a **"visible quiz"**, the teacher poses questions with multiple choice responses and students discuss the responses in a group. At a signal, each group displays its answer written on a large card. A group also can be called upon to explain the group's reasoning to the rest of the class.

72

Whole Class Learning Experiences

Best Practices	What This Can Look Like
• Provide students with opportunities to work collaboratively as a whole class. Encourage students to build on each others' ideas and strengths. This builds a sense of community in the classroom as students learn that everyone has something to contribute.	• Use a cooperative learning strategy such as Kagan's **"board share"** to involve student groups in a whole class activity. Each group brainstorms responses related to a question or task. One member of each group is the 'runner and recorder' and writes the group's ideas on the board. The class then discusses and reflects on the whole class effort.

Whole Class Learning Experiences (continued)

Best Practices	What This Can Look Like
• Use cooperative learning strategies to involve smaller groups in a whole class activity. • Model and teach skills through student interactions with each other. • Introduce different questioning strategies to help students learn to ask meaningful questions and understand what effective responses can provide.	• **"Think-pair-share"** and **"Think-pair-square"** encourage students to share their learning and thinking processes with the whole class. In think-pair-share, individual students think silently about a question posed by the teacher. Students share thoughts with a partner, then partners share responses with the whole class. In think-pair-square, partners combine into a small group before the whole class discussion. • In **"carousel brainstorming"**, the teacher posts charts on the wall with key questions or ideas at the top. Groups are formed and one person scribes for the group and adds to the chart as they brainstorm. Groups then rotate to a new chart, read the other groups' responses and then add to the chart. • An **"inside/outside circle"** strategy encourages interaction and conversation between all class members. Divide the class in half. One half forms a circle facing outward, the other half finds one person in the circle to stand opposite, so there are two circles of students facing each other. Students discuss a question or topic with the person facing them. On a signal, the outer circle moves one person and the conversation begins again. • Use a **"three-minute pause"** to stop at any point during an activity and encourage students to review what has been discussed, ask clarifying questions or reflect on their learning. • A **"socratic seminar"** poses a thoughtful question to students to help them understand ideas, issues and values in their text readings. Students develop questions for classmates in order to dig into a text they all have read. This strategy encourages involvement of all class members, develops critical and creative thinking, emphasizes respect for others and for differing viewpoints, encourages students to support their arguments with textual evidence, and reinforces effective communication skills.

73

Scaffolded instruction

Learning always proceeds from the known to the new. Good teaching recognizes and builds on this connection through **scaffolding**. Consider this construction metaphor, "A student learning new skills and concepts is like a carpenter building a house." The construction starts from the ground up, on the foundation of what is already known and can be done. The new is built on top of the known. The teacher has to provide this scaffold to support the construction .... The scaffold is the environment the teacher creates, the instructional support, and the processes and language that are lent to the student in the context of approaching a task and developing the abilities to meet it" (adapted from Wilhelm, Baker and Dube, 2001, p. 18).

Elements of scaffolded instruction

Effective scaffolding recognizes that students need to:
- learn in multiple and variable contexts
- engage in challenging, developmentally appropriate and concrete activities
- construct understandings based on prior experiences and knowledge
- be supported in learning what they cannot achieve on their own.

This type of supported learning occurs in what Vygotsky (1986) calls the zone of proximal development—the space between those contexts in which students perform tasks independently and those contexts in which students need adult or peer guidance and collaboration.

The Zone of Proximal Development[2]

Zone of actual development	Zone of proximal development		New zone of actual development
STUDENT	**TEACHER**	**JOINT**	**STUDENT**
What the student can already do independently	Assistance from teacher, peer or environment	Transition from receiving assistance to working independently	What the student can do independently or in peer-led groups
	Gradual release of responsibility to the student		
	Instructional Approaches		
Independent	**Modelled** **Shared**	**Guided**	**Independent**

2. Reproduced from Ontario Ministry of Education, *Combined Grades: Strategies to Reach a Range of Learners in Kindergarten to Grade 6* (Toronto, ON: Ontario Ministry of Education, 2006), p. 20 and adapted from Ontario Ministry of Education, *Guide to Effective Literacy Instruction, Grades 4 to 6: Volume One* (Toronto, ON: Ontario Ministry of Education, 2006), p. 79. © Queen's Printer for Ontario, 2006, 2007. Reproduced/adapted with permission.

Effective scaffolding strategies encourage students to continuously grow and develop to a level that is just above their current level of development. When you assign a task the students can already do, they are taught nothing. One way of thinking about the zone of proximal development is to consider the general rule that most people are comfortable with—a "10 percent stretch" when they are attempting a new task or learning a new skill. This means that for most learners, the optimal degree of challenge is provided by activities and materials that are about 10 percent beyond the current level of what they can do independently.

When planning for scaffolding, ask the following types of questions.
- What do students currently know and what can students currently do?
- What do they need to know and be able to do?
- How big is the gap?
- How do I ensure the gap is just right so that students are supported but also are challenged in a way that maximizes learning?

The process of scaffolding then becomes continual and cyclical, as new scaffolds are put into place to encourage students to continue to reach for new learning. When students are able to complete a task successfully, they are in, what Vygotsky calls, the zone of actual development.

Implementing scaffolded instruction

Implementing scaffolded instruction includes considering the ways that students recognize, process and engage with information. It involves providing options for supported group and individual learning, and opportunities to develop skills that are relevant and meaningful to the tasks at hand. It also involves planning multiple opportunities and options for students to use, apply and process the information they are working with.

The range of planned activities should reflect tasks that students can learn with the support of adults, peers and the instructional environment. The original concept of scaffolding was an interaction between a teacher and a student that provides support in learning. However, in recent years, the concept of scaffolding has expanded beyond just interactions between individuals. Scaffolding is now understood to include artifacts, resources and environments themselves. These scaffolding tools include technology and peer support and broaden the concept of scaffolding to address more complex and diverse learning environments. These resources and tools provide support to larger groups and help establish a learning environment in which peers can interact with and teach each other.

Effective scaffolding supports are continuously reviewed and replaced as student learning needs change. The design of scaffoldings considers that there are multiple levels of understandings, interests and learning preferences in the classroom, and incorporates the key elements of ongoing assessment and variable levels of support.

Consider the following questions.

- How can activities be designed to provide scaffolding that moves students from teacher-directed to student-directed learning experiences?
- How should activities provide a scaffolded sequence of instruction that starts with modelling or multiple examples?
- Does the sequence of planned activities have an explicit progression—from easy to difficult, concrete to abstract, personal to societal—that supports the learning needs and background of students?
- How can scaffolding activities help separate or organize information or processes into manageable chunks or steps?
- What types of modelled or guided examples should be included? When should these be provided?

Best practices in scaffolded instruction

The following chart summarizes best practices and sample strategies for effectively implementing scaffolded instruction.

Scaffolded Instruction	
Best Practices	What This Can Look Like
Develop shared learning goals to engage and motivate students. Shared learning goals must be accomplished on two levels. • Between individual students and teachers. Students need to see the point of the task, beyond simply following the teacher's directions. • Within the whole classroom environment. Scaffolding strategies should support the learning of groups of students working together. Such groups facilitate shared discussion and expertise, and collaborative discovery and inquiry, which builds the classroom as a community of learners.	**"Launcher units"** (Holbrook and Kolodner 2000) are introductory learning experiences that help introduce students to background knowledge, and build skills and processes that they need to engage in a larger, more independently or constructively structured unit of study. The launcher unit was originally designed for the Learning by Design™ curriculum (Kolodner et al. 2003), which approached science learning by engaging students in the design of a car to learn about the physics of forces and motion. Launcher units can focus on specific content or skills that prepare students for more independent study or project work.

76

Scaffolded Instruction (continued)

Best Practices	What This Can Look Like
	"Modelling" provides an opportunity for students to watch, to practise, and then to take responsibility for learning tasks. Teachers initially model and explain the learning task, and then share the process with students. Eventually, students take on nearly all or all responsibility for the task. Assessment strategies, such as observation and checklists, can assess student readiness and placement in the modelling process. Effective modelling includes thoughtful planning of the roles that teachers and students can take including: • teacher modelling of task and process • student imitation and practice • teacher moving away from instructional role • student guiding or leading others.
Recognize how different backgrounds and experiences influence and inform student understandings. Create structured opportunities to link prior knowledge with new learning.	**"Pre-assessment" strategies** such as pre-testing can help you to identify students who need additional help with concepts, terms and background information. **"Questioning"** that is used as a scaffolding activity provides support and assesses progress, and is adjusted according to student needs as they emerse in discussions or interactions. Questioning approaches can include cues, hints, prompts and partial solutions. The level of specificity in questions can be increased to provide additional support to students working their way through a process or problem, or decreased as students gain competence and skills.
Provide opportunities for students to develop decision-making and leadership skills.	**"Staging" activities** are investigations that prepare students by providing them with smaller or chunks of learning experiences early in the instructional sequence. These enable students to prepare to take on larger tasks or to understand complexities. Staging activities are sequenced in a process that moves from teacher modelling and proceeds with increasing transfer of the responsibility for learning to the student.

77

Scaffolded Instruction (continued)

Best Practices	What This Can Look Like
Make processes explicit and visible to students through activities such as: • visualization • role-play • simulations • analogies and comparisons • graphic organizers.	**"Structuring"** can provide students with tools and templates to help them structure and organize more open-ended tasks. **"Graphic organizers"**, such as Venn diagrams or flowcharts, can provide multiple formats to help students organize thinking and research. **"Think-alouds"** provide opportunities for students to engage in metacognitive activities while being provided with support and guidance. Think-alouds encourage self-talk within an interactive context.
Use flexible grouping structures as a means of providing scaffolding for students. As the learner becomes more capable, explicit support is reduced. This process is referred to as "fading."	**"Peer group structures"** can be used to provide scaffolding support that encourages dialogue, collaborative exploration of concepts, motivation and encouragement. Peer groups can be structured to provide **reciprocal teaching**, an interactive process that involves students in a teaching role. **"Small group instruction"** involves direct participation of the teacher and includes ongoing and continuous assessment and adjustment of scaffolding supports. **"Direct instruction"** is often an instructional component used in small groups. Direct instruction focuses on explicit teaching and modelling of skills and processes. **"Cooperative learning"** emphasizes the development of social interaction skills as well as cognitive development. Cooperative learning structures can incorporate scaffolding in heterogeneous groupings that focus on providing peer and resource supports. Cooperative learning processes also can move students in homogeneous groups through a learning environment that provides varying levels of teacher support.

78

Variety

Variety is an essential component of differentiated instruction. Using a range of teaching styles and activities allows you to reach more students. However, the goal is not simply variety-for-the-sake-of-variety. All learning activities need to be meaningful, manageable and directly support learner outcomes. For example, a puppet show might be a novel way to show learning about a particular science or social concept, but the logistics of finding or making the puppets, setting up a stage, developing a script and finding time to practise and perform for others might absorb inordinate instructional time and overshadow the actual learning related to the outcome it was intended to demonstrate.

Teaching to student strengths makes them feel more comfortable in the classroom and this translates into greater motivation. So, paying attention to the content's best modality and, at times, addressing student learning preferences will set the stage for greater achievement. At the same time, while individuals do have learning preferences with regard to modalities (sensory learning style), research shows that teaching all students in their best modality does not necessarily equal greater achievement. The content's best modality is often more important for achievement.

79

Sample strategies for creating variety
- Use the learning preference information that you identified in learner and class profiles to plan multiple entry points for each unit. Gardner (1993) suggests encouraging students to enter or explore a topic through a learning preference. He identifies five entry points:
    - narrative (presenting a story)
    - logical-quantitative (using numbers)
    - foundational (examining philosophy and vocabulary)
    - aesthetic (focusing on sensory features)
    - experiential (hands-on).

- Consider combining different pedagogical approaches to expand a learning activity. For example, Judith Dodge (2005) proposes linking multiple intelligence-based activities to higher levels of thinking, in what she calls "Gardner in Bloom." See the example below.[3]

Multiple intelligence-based activity	Expand to address critical thinking
Write three journal entries of a Canadian war bride in the 1940s …	… that compare three ways of life in London that were different from life in a rural community in Atlantic Canada
Write three headlines that you would find in the Renaissance Times …	… that show your understanding of how life has changed since the Middle Ages

- Use a grid to record and assess the strategies that you develop from student profiles. Each square in the grid can list an instructional strategy that responds to elements in a learner or class profile. Within a unit plan, aim to have one or two rows complete. Over a yearlong plan, aim to cover all or most of the instructional strategies.

Instructional strategies tracker

Unit _____ Date _____

Case scenarios	Current events	Debate	Drama	Field trip
Games	Guest speaker	Imagery	Internet search	Investigative interviewing
Lecture	Literature connection	Mapping	Music	Panel discussion
Picture study	Poetry	Problem solving	Role-playing	Small group work
Student presentations	Videos			

---

3. Adapted from Judith Dodge, *Differentiation in Action* (New York, NY: Scholastic Inc., 2005), p. 96.

Choice

Student choice is often thought of as the most obvious and straightforward aspect of differentiated instruction. To be effective, however, the choices provided must be thoughtfully and purposefully considered, and aligned with learning outcomes and learner needs, preferences, interests and readiness. Providing choice does not necessarily mean offering a wide menu of divergent options that students can select from. Rather, it involves carefully considering the alternatives that students can be offered in both the learning process and the ways they will demonstrate what they have learned. It includes considering when structured activities should be offered and when freedom of choice can be provided.

> In a differentiated classroom we address … needs by creating opportunities for students to express themselves individually or to work with others, by allowing students to choose activities of interest that are playful yet challenging and by empowering students through active learning and decision making. When you allow students the choice of working alone or working with others, you address their need for belonging. When you put students in charge of choosing which activity to complete, you address their need for power and freedom. When you offer students creative ways to show-what-they-know, you address their need for fun. The more we address these needs, the more we foster intrinsic motivation in learners (Dodge 2005, p. 51).

81

Implementing choice

The following guidelines can help you construct thoughtful, relevant and beneficial choices for students.

- **Provide authentic and meaningful challenges to students**. Every choice that is offered should take into account the ideas discussed in the Meaningful Activities section of this chapter.

- **Ensure that students have the skills needed to accomplish the choices you offer.** These skills may be taught through the process of exploring and learning content or as part of the process of making the choice itself.

- **Explicitly teach students how to make effective choices**. Learning how to consider alternatives and select options is part of becoming an independent learner. Learning skills of negotiation and compromise in selecting a product to complete with group members or how to consider pros and cons when making an individual choice encourages students to make meaningful choices.

- **Provide opportunities and strategies to help students get to know themselves as learners**. Building self-awareness allows students to take calculated risks, and to communicate their interests and preferences when asked to make a choice.

- **Teach students how to approach open-ended projects**. Provide students with strategies such as prioritizing, breaking choices down into tasks, organizing, sequencing and planning how to complete a project. These processes need to be modelled and guided as students learn how to judge what is involved in the choices they make.

- **Teach students how to evaluate their choices**. Evaluation of choices involves making decisions before committing to a project or path, as well as learning to reflect on what was done, how it was done, what worked and what could be changed and improved.

Students can be provided with choices in terms of the way they learn new concepts and skills (process) or the way they demonstrate that learning (product).

Choice board[4]

A "choice board" is an example of a skills-based set of practice tasks from which students can choose. All activities in the following example are designed to explore and to practise new skills related to a particular topic in a language classroom. Students choose an assigned number of tasks (usually three). Each task is completed in the language of instruction.

---

4. This section adapted with permission of SEDL. Theisen, Toni. "Differentiated Instruction in the Foreign Language Classroom: Meeting the Diverse Needs of All Learners." *Communiqué,* 6 (April 2002), p. 4.

82

Choice Board: Food Unit		
Choose three boxes to form a tic-tac-toe row. The boxes I choose are #_____, #_____, #_____ Signature _____ Class _____ Period _____		
1 **Verb Practice** Play a game of charades using 10 new verbs you learned this week.	2 **Question Practice** Develop a survey to find out favourite foods of your classmates.	3 **Vocabulary Practice** Write a 7–10 line composition using your new food vocabulary.
4 **Question Practice** Create 10 questions you can ask in order to get details about someone's favourite meal.	5 **Vocabulary Practice** Design a crossword puzzle using vocabulary related to food.	6 **Verb Practice** Design a 10-question quiz using the verbs in this unit.
7 **Vocabulary Practice** Watch a video clip and make a list of 10 key words used in the video.	8 **Verb Practice** Draw a picture to represent each of the new verbs.	9 **Question Practice** Create a song that will help you remember the question words.

Choice boards can be based on a specific activity, such as a "R.A.F.T assignment." It is designed around unit objectives and provides an effective, meaningful way to incorporate writing into content-area instruction. Four key ingredients are included in every R.A.F.T. writing assignment:

- R: Role of Writer (Who are you?)
- A: Audience (To whom is this written?)
- F: Format (What form will it take?)
- T: Topic + strong verb (What is your topic?)

Most R.A.F.T. assignments are written:

- from a viewpoint other than that of a student
- to an audience other than the teacher
- in a form other than the standard essay.

The choice board that follows provides samples of writing assignments students can choose from to demonstrate their understanding of the unit, "Travelling in France." Learners select one row and create that written product. What makes the R.A.F.T. such a popular activity with students is the variety and creativity involved. For each of these writing tasks the same scoring rubric can be used regardless of which row is selected.

R.A.F.T. Choice Board
(Travelling in France)

Choose one R.A.F.T. assignment. Pick up copies of individual tasks from the teacher. Use the Internet and other texts to research information you need to make your work authentic.

Role	Audience	Format	Topic
Customer	Hotel employee	Letter	Make a reservation for several nights. Include all details.
Hotel Employee	Customer	Reply letter	Confirm reservation details and include changes.
Customer	Hotel manager	Complaint	Demand compensation for problems and poor service.
Parisian real estate agency	Prospective renters	Real estate ad	Describe details of the apartments available for rent.
Students who want to study abroad	Study abroad organization	Application form for the program	Apply for a study abroad program.
Students who stayed with a family	Family members	Thank-you note	Thank the family for the home stay and tell them about your return back to Canada

84

Best practices to provide choice

Best Practices	What This Can Look Like
Provide options for students to create products based on their learning interests, preferences and readiness. Products should be related to real problems, concerns and audiences, and they should synthesize rather than summarize information.	Product choices could include: • a written report • an oral presentation • a group discussion on key concepts • a short book in which the key concepts are explained and described • a game centred around the characters and theme of a book • an event planned within a specified budget.
Combine choice with flexible grouping to let students explore concepts in a variety of ways. Students also can be provided with choices regarding the context in which they create the product; e.g., as individuals, with partners or in small groups.	Grouping strategies such as self-selected learning centres can accommodate student choice.
Structure choices within varying contexts, such as research, reinforcement, application and extension.	"All students listen to the same guest lecturer and take notes in the same style modelled by the teacher. For homework, students choose one of the five options for reflecting on the speaker's message …. They can write a poem, write and perform a skit, create a mind map of content, share the content with mom or dad and get their responses to it, or list the speaker's main points and categorize them according to similar attributes."[5]
Encourage students to use their choice of different tools to perform the same task.	Students could use paper and pencil, manipulatives or the computer to create a visual representation of a concept.
Use flexible pacing to allow for differences in student ability to master the key concepts.	Learning contracts provide an agreement between the teacher and student that focus on independent learning skill development. Goals are established collaboratively with the teacher and structures are provided to help students manage and organize their time and tasks. Students who complete certain tasks before classmates could be given time to work on projects in their learning contract.

85

5. From *Meet Me in the Middle: Becoming an Accomplished Middle-Level Teacher* (p. 70) by Rick Wormeli, copyright © 2001, with permission of Stenhouse Publishers.

Leveraging Technology

Contents of this chapter

6

87

"We should differentiate instruction when doing so would be the best means to solve a problem.
We should use technology in education when doing so would be the best means to solve a problem."
– Amy Benjamin in *Differentiated Instruction Using Technology: A Guide for Middle and High School* (2005) p. 9.

In today's classrooms, a wide range of technologies are creating new options for differentiated instruction and for the inclusion of students with disabilities. Technology can assist teachers in providing support, choice and flexibility to students. It also can directly support the learning of individual students with wide differences in their abilities to see, hear, speak, move, read, write, understand English, attend, organize, engage and remember.

In other words, there are numerous ways that technology in the classroom can be leveraged to address diverse learning needs. To do this efficiently and effectively requires careful selection, purposeful planning and thoughtful implementation. Not all technology is equally useful, for individual students or for educational purposes in general. Effective technology aligns with principles of universal design for learning (UDL) and provides multiple means of:

- *representation*—gives learners various ways of acquiring information and knowledge
- *engagement*—taps into learners' interests, offers appropriate challenges and increases motivation
- *expression*—provides learners with alternatives for demonstrating what they know.

This chapter provides information on planning for and using technology as part of a differentiated instruction approach. It offers strategies and ideas for using technology to enhance instruction, motivate and engage students, offer choice, ensure accessibility, create flexible groupings and scaffold instruction. Finally, recognizing that some students will need specialized technologies, this chapter provides guidelines for choosing assistive technologies for specific learning needs.

Planning for instruction

Technology should be used in natural and substantial ways and should be built into activities, rather than tacked on. The utilization of technology is only one part of any instructional solution. Thoughtful planning, ongoing monitoring and assessment and on-the-spot instruction and support will still be needed.

As you plan for instruction that will include the utilization of technology, consider the following questions related to students, learning environments, training and tasks.

- Why do I want or need technology in my classroom?
- What do I want technology to do (that I could not do without it)?
- What will this technology do for the students in my classroom?
- What skills and strategies will students need in order to use the technology?
- Do I have the skills and confidence I need to use technology effectively in the classroom?
- Is appropriate and effective equipment and software readily available and accessible for the students in my classroom?
- How will technology affect what I do (the way I plan, teach, assess and evaluate)?
- How will technology affect the students and their learning?
- Does everyone (e.g., students, parents, educational assistants, administrators) understand what is happening and why?
- Do I have access to ongoing support?

It also is critical to assess the value and usefulness of a particular technology, including the following factors:

- level of independent use by students
- unique capability and limits of the tool
- usefulness for task completion
- ease of use
- accessibly of equipment.

For many tools, it may not be so much a question of how to use the technology, but more of a question of knowing when and why to use it.

Enhancing instruction

A differentiated instruction approach incorporates a variety of instructional methods and materials. The use of speech, text and visuals are key to most instructional strategies, and these three modes of communication can all be enhanced by the use of technology.

Speech
Speech is the most frequent mode by which teaching happens. Studies have found that, on average, students spend 45 percent of their school day involved in listening activities.

Speech has two major advantages as a mode of teaching; it is inherently dynamic and it has the power of expression. Teachers can add information quickly and simply by saying more or saying it in a different way. Extra information also can be added through the tone, rate, inflection and volume of the speaker's voice.

The major limitation to speech as an instructional strategy is that it is transitory; i.e., once something is said, it is gone. This can create challenges for students, particularly students with disabilities. Students who do not hear well or who have attention problems may miss some of what is said. Students with processing or short-term memory difficulties may be unable to process or remember significant chunks of speech.

Technology can be leveraged to overcome speech-related barriers in a variety of ways. Consider the following sample strategies.

- **Investigate the feasibility of a sound field system.** This technology, which includes a microphone and speakers, ensures all students can hear what is being said in the classroom.

- **Pair speech with visuals or key words on an interactive white board or a digital slide show.** This extra support cues students to what is important, and reinforces the information, using another modality.

- **Use videos and audios clips that align with the learning activity.** Students can return to these links on their own to revisit and review the material.

- **Record key learning activities on digital recording devices.** Digital recordings create a permanent record of the speech. This digital recording can then be reviewed by or with students at a later time.

Printed text

Printed text is central to our culture and a key component of much of the instruction and many of the learning materials found in Alberta classrooms. Unlike speech, text captures information and ideas in a permanent way, so students can return to it as often as needed. However, text poses challenges to a number of students. Some students struggle with decoding text; others lack the background knowledge needed to manage new information presented in print.

Technology can be leveraged to overcome print-related barriers in a variety of ways. Consider the following sample strategies.

- **Provide digital versions of text.** These more flexible versions of a text allow teachers and students to change how information is displayed. Digital versions of texts also allow students to use software that reads the text aloud. Many electronic versions of textbooks and popular literature are available for free or for sale from many sources, including the following:

- WikiBooks: http://en.wikibooks.org/wiki/Main_Page
- Google Books: http://books.google.com
- Project Gutenberg: http://www.gutenberg.org/wiki/Main_Page.

These digital texts often include enhanced and additional materials such as glossaries, visuals and summaries.

- **Present text in flexible formats.** Digital text can be visually enhanced in numerous ways. The font size can be increased, the colour of the font and the background can be changed, and the contrast between the text and the background can be modified to suit the needs and preferences of individual readers. Also, the amount of information displayed at one time can be controlled.

- **Provide access to text-to-speech software.** Having digital text read aloud can benefit students with reading difficulties and students with vision loss. This technology may be a tool they use throughout their lives. For other students, including those students who are learning English as another language, text-to-speech software may be used to scaffold their learning until they develop stronger independent reading and language skills. For still other students, having material read aloud may be a preference (especially for students with attention difficulties).

- **Provide access to online dictionaries and glossaries.** Many students will benefit from using these supports on an as-needed basis.

- **Provide content in alternate formats.** Look for "considerate text" versions of popular novels (simplified vocabulary and storyline), synopses or outlines; these versions are often available online. Graphics novels are increasingly more available and can be engaging for students who struggle with print or just prefer the more visual medium. Video versions of key content also may be more engaging than print text for many students. Teachers have used video versions of books and resources for many years. Today's technology makes this option easier, faster and more accessible. There are many readily available videos, many of them free, that present various concepts, ideas and pieces of literature. Some of these videos also are captioned and a range of students can benefit from this technology, not only students with hearing loss. A list of alternate formats of authorized novels for the Alberta English language arts program is available at http://www.education.alberta.ca/admin/technology/atl/resources.aspx.

Images

Images can be a powerful and efficient way to communicate ideas and concepts. Many teachers use images to support teaching and learning in the classroom for these reasons. Consider the following picture.

To describe in words what is happening in this picture would take at least a few sentences. Even then it is doubtful that the listener or reader would get the full picture. This image elicits feelings and ideas in the viewer that are difficult to express in other ways.

At the same time, images, like other modes, have certain limitations. The use of images creates extensive barriers for students with visual impairments. As well, students who are colour-blind or have other sensory-processing challenges will be challenged by graphics in many instances. Even if students can all see equally well, they may interpret an image in many different ways, which may not be the way the teacher intends.

Technology can be leveraged to overcome image-related barriers in a variety of ways. Consider the following sample strategies.

- **Present digital images in flexible formats.** Enlarge images or modify the colour scheme to make them more visually accessible.

- **Use text information that is supported by visuals and visuals that are supported by text.** There are many digital resources and Web sites available that use multimedia to create interactive learning experiences (e.g., roll-over text to explain visuals, hyperlinks to background information that could include additional visuals).

Motivating and engaging students

Research suggests that a number of elements are essential to motivating and engaging students, including:
- positive relationships and school climate
- meaningful feedback
- hands-on, active work
- variety and attention to learning preference
- relevant and interesting learning tasks
- student voice and choice
- learning in context and making real-world connections.

Technology can be used to create engaging learning activities that address many of these elements. For example:
- **blogs and interactive Web sites** can enhance communication and build virtual communities that create positive relationships and a sense of belonging
- **digital learning objects** can provide immediate and nonjudgmental feedback for improving performance
- **web sites** can provide easily-accessed information for hands-on and active work
- **search engines** make it possible to locate information and activities that appeal to a wide range of interests
- **discussion boards, online communities and e-mail** make it possible for students to connect to learning and gather and share information and ideas in real-life contexts.

Specially selected technologies and tools can address diverse learning styles and preferences. The flexibility and availability of digital resources also enhances opportunities for student choice.

Offering choice

One of the hallmarks of a differentiated instruction approach is providing learners with choices in how they interact with new information and ideas, practise skills and demonstrate what they know. Many teachers provide students with choice in the types of materials they use, products they create and activities they do. Technology can expand and enhance this range of choices.

93

Ensuring accessibility

The term *accessibility* refers to how easily, how effectively and how independently an individual student can use a learning resource. Resources with flexible formats give students the choice, control and independence they need to be successful in their learning. Flexible resources also give teachers the tools they need to better meet the diverse needs of students in their classrooms.

Resources can enhance accessibility by:
- creating student engagement
- building student understanding
- displaying information.

The following three graphics illustrate the types of options and features that make learning resources more accessible and more responsive to a wide range of learning needs, preferences and strengths.

94

Creating student engagement

These types of options and features create multiple opportunities for students to explore, interact with, personalize and reflect on new skills, information and concepts.

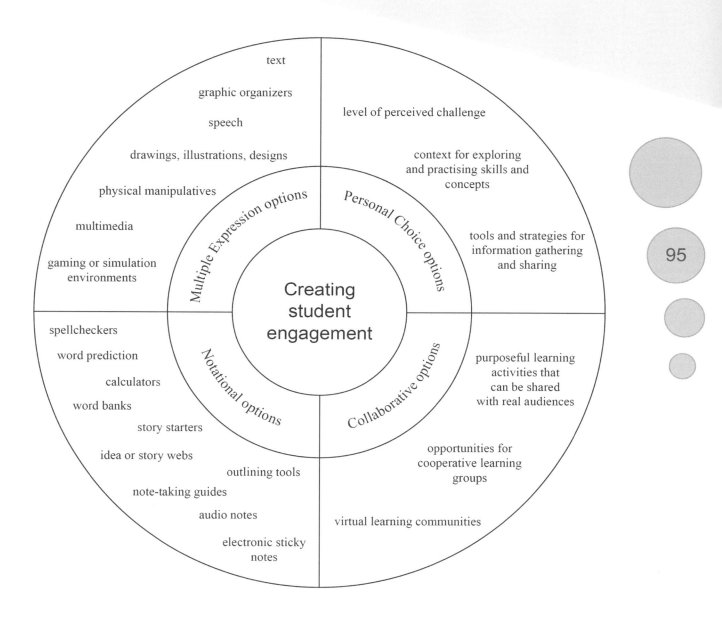

Building student understanding

These types of options and features create multiple means of providing instruction, explanation, illustration, summarization and feedback.

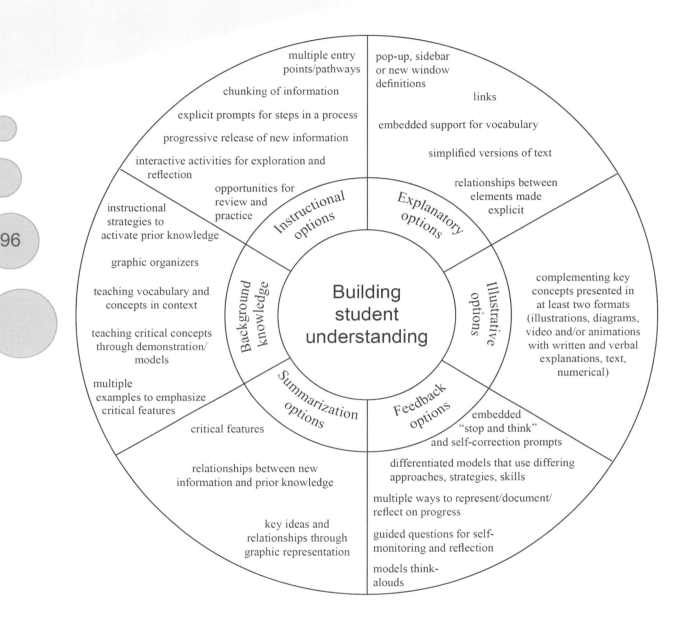

Building student understanding

Instructional options
- multiple entry points/pathways
- chunking of information
- explicit prompts for steps in a process
- progressive release of new information
- interactive activities for exploration and reflection
- opportunities for review and practice

Explanatory options
- pop-up, sidebar or new window definitions
- links
- embedded support for vocabulary
- simplified versions of text
- relationships between elements made explicit

Illustrative options
- complementing key concepts presented in at least two formats (illustrations, diagrams, video and/or animations with written and verbal explanations, text, numerical)

Background knowledge
- instructional strategies to activate prior knowledge
- graphic organizers
- teaching vocabulary and concepts in context
- teaching critical concepts through demonstration/models
- multiple examples to emphasize critical features

Summarization options
- critical features
- relationships between new information and prior knowledge
- key ideas and relationships through graphic representation

Feedback options
- embedded "stop and think" and self-correction prompts
- differentiated models that use differing approaches, strategies, skills
- multiple ways to represent/document/reflect on progress
- guided questions for self-monitoring and reflection
- models think-alouds

Displaying Information

These types of options and features create multiple means of representing and presenting information effectively.

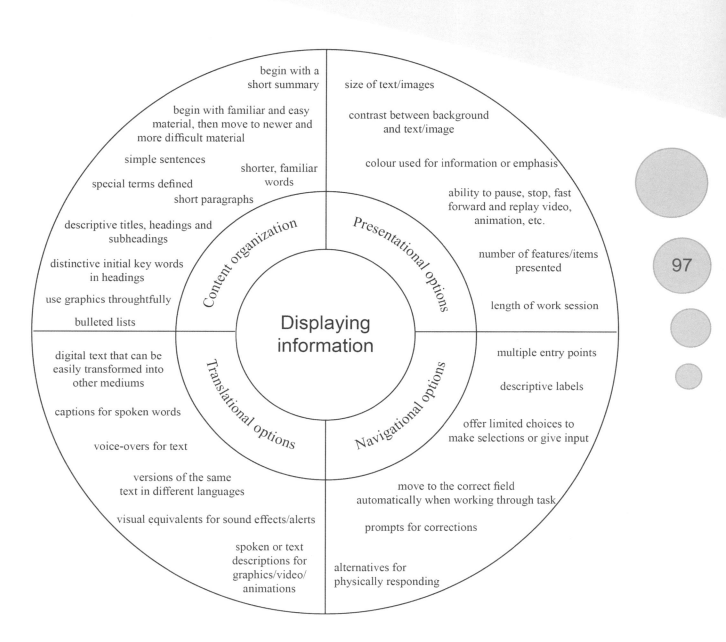

Creating flexible groupings

The utilization of technology can be integrated into activities with various groupings including:
- whole group (e.g., using interactive white boards to introduce new concepts, watching and discussing a video)
- small groups (e.g., completing WebQuests, developing a digital slideshow)
- partners (e.g., exploring Web sites, going on a virtual tour, playing an interactive game)
- individual (e.g., building an information web, reading a digital text).

Many technologies can be used in a number of grouping types, depending on the specific activity and student abilities, needs and preferences.

98

Scaffolding instruction

Technology utilization has the potential to provide flexible, unobtrusive scaffolds for learning. To do this effectively we need to:
- get to know the learner
- use this information to consider the implications for that student's learning
- match potential technology solutions to the student's particular abilities, preferences and interests
- build in supports and structures that will ensure the student is successful.

Learner and classroom profiles should include information about student comfort levels, preferences and current uses of technology. Many students today have spent their entire lives surrounded by and using computers, video games, digital music players, video cams, cell phones, and all the other toys and tools of the digital age. Matching student needs with potential technology solutions is a critical part of a differentiated approach.

Consider the following examples of five students who demonstrate learning abilities and needs that are becoming increasingly more common in Alberta classrooms. We need to understand these types of learners and their individual needs in order to provide them with the supports and choices they need to be successful in their learning.

Student characteristics	Implications for learning	Technology solutions that could provide potential scaffolds
Mary • quiet; seems shy • rarely speaks in class and never volunteers an answer • has difficulty hearing what others are saying, including the teacher's instructions	• misunderstands or makes mistakes because she didn't hear well • doesn't speak up because she is afraid of giving an incorrect or inappropriate response	• Investigate feasibility of sound-field system. • Pair verbal instructions with key words posted on board. • Create opportunities to answer in private; e.g., online journal.
Josh • has many great ideas and can tell you about them with great enthusiasm • shuts down when he has to put these ideas on paper	• struggles with printing and spelling • spends so much of his energy getting the words "right" that he loses his energy and his writing does not reflect those great ideas he can talk so easily about	• Provide instruction in keyboarding skills. • Investigate using speech-to-text software, digital recording and/or word prediction software. • Use storyboarding and mindmapping tools.
Jamila • recent refugee • limited classroom experience • has conversational English but has difficulty understanding the language of instruction	• often confused as to what she is being asked to do • has less background knowledge than most other students in the classroom • other students (and most teaching staff) assume she is fluent in English because of her conversational skills	• Use online tutorials to provide ongoing language instruction. • Provide access to online dictionaries and glossaries. • Use web links, photo galleries, simulations and other tools to help build background knowledge.

99

Student characteristics	Implications for learning	Technology solutions that could provide potential scaffolds
Susan • blind since birth • understands all concepts at or above grade level • reads Braille	• is frustrated that more novels and other print material are not available to her	• Provide timely Braille translations of core learning materials. • Consider specialized assistive technology including scanner, refreshable Brailler and screen reading software. • Do online searches for additional texts and literature available in Braille.
Taylor • has lots of great ideas • limited attention span of only a few minutes; is easily distracted (e.g., by a plane flying by or some random thought that pops into his head) • when playing games on his Wii he is focused, engaged and attends to many details at the same time	• starts many interesting projects but seldom finishes anything • minimal interest in most assignments	• Look for technology that will reduce distractions (e.g., sound-blocking headset, online work space with minimal extraneous information or features). • Develop customized online planning tools for planning and completing projects. • Find online games or simulations that are aligned with learning outcomes.

Choosing assistive technologies

Assistive technology is any technology that increases, maintains or improves the functional capabilities of an individual with disabilities. As the utilization of technology becomes more and more common place in learning environments, the line between educational technology and assistive technology is blurring. Many tools that are currently considered assistive technologies can offer benefits to all students.

The benefits of assistive technology for students with disabilities includes:
- building on individual strengths
- accomplishing higher rates of learning and improved achievement
- completing academic tasks independently, including tasks that they might not otherwise be able to handle unaided, leading to a greater sense of self-efficacy
- addressing a number of literacy and numeracy challenges.

When considering assistive technology, it is important to be aware of the following limitations.

- Assistive technology does not *replace* the teaching and learning process. It is tool that *supports* teaching and learning.

- Assistive technology is just one element in a student's educational programming. Students with disabilities may have a number of areas of need. Technology is only one of a number of tools that they may need.

- Not all assistive technology tools are appropriate for all students with disabilities. It is important to identify learning tasks and outcomes, evaluate barriers to accomplishing those tasks, and match the characteristics of technology with the student's individual learning profile.

- Some students will need basic keyboarding skills to maximize the effectiveness of assistive technology. Keyboarding instruction should begin when students are developmentally ready (typically around Grade 3) and instructional sessions should be short, motivating and incorporate real-life applications.

The following sections list some common assistive technology tools to support reading and writing, mathematics and communication. Many other tools may be available, depending on the needs of the individual student. A free, downloadable student handbook for choosing and using assistive technology, called *How Can I Try That?*, is available at www.wati.org or www.otap-oregon.org.

Tools to support reading and writing

There are a range of technology tools that support readers and writers of varying abilities.

Text-to-speech software (and screen readers) allows students to hear digital text read aloud by a synthesized voice. This technology requires digital versions of print, and may include a scanning capacity to convert print to digital text. On many programs students can control the pace of the reading and can choose to have the computer read individual words or whole passages. This type of technology is particularly helpful for students who can make sense of spoken language but have difficulty decoding text. This software can reduce frustration and allow for more complete comprehension of text. It allows students to access textbooks, assignments, books and literature independently and effectively. It may even increase the motivation to read, because for some students using this software provides their first opportunity to enjoy literature independently, successfully and comfortably.

Word processing software can address fine motor difficulties and increase legibility and quantity of written expression. Most word processing software also includes a number of standard features that can assist students with writing; for example:

- *spell-checking tools* can reduce some spelling difficulties
- *cut-and-paste* features can allow students to manipulate text more easily when editing, thereby saving time and physical effort
- *built-in thesaurus* can assist students who have difficulty finding the right words.

Word prediction software can be installed on computers that run word processing software. Current research identifies it as the single most effective technology tool for assisting written expression. Word prediction does not give the answer to any question, but it does provide students with an immediately available vocabulary list, speeding up the writing process by allowing writers to find the most appropriate word. This technology also can reduce spelling mistakes, increase motivation, and help students who have difficulty with the physical task of writing. It also can increase the quantity and overall quality of written work.

Planning and organizing software can help students organize their writing, a skill essential for high-quality written expression. Software programs that help students structure their writing are usually visual in nature, allowing students to:

- create webs that emphasize relationships between ideas
- manipulate categories of ideas and choose where to place them
- see an outline of the topics and subtopics of their writing
- easily manipulate and reorganize the text at any time
- use a built-in or teacher-created template as a basis for their work.

Speech-synthesis software can convert text on the screen into aural speech. For some students with cognitive and communicative disabilities, this software supports writing as well as reading. Hearing the text that they have produced can increase student independence and self-monitoring of their own writing. This software also will help students improve spelling skills.

Speech-recognition software is an affordable tool that works with most word processing systems. It allows students to use a microphone headset to dictate what they want the computer to type. Speech-recognition software has been used in many special education settings over the last 10 years, with varying levels of success. It requires that the user trains the computer to recognize his or her voice patterns and pronunciations by reading specific material repeatedly, for up to several hours. The more a student uses the program, the better the program gets at recognizing that student's voice, eventually reaching about 90 percent accuracy.

Speech-recognition software is designed for users with strong communicative or cognitive abilities and good visual vocabulary skills. Although most useful for individuals who are verbally fluent, with support, students who are less verbally fluent can benefit from the use of this tool.

There are a number of cautions to consider when matching this tool to an individual student, including the following.
- Initial training can be time-consuming, for both students and teachers.
- Even after successful initial training, the program will make some mistakes (students need to proofread and correct mistakes for accuracy to improve).
- There are a number of guidelines to learn when dictating, such as pausing the program to talk or ask a question.
- Visual fatigue can set in for some students, making the program less effective when it used for extensive periods of time.
- The technology may be distracting to other students in a large classroom setting.

Tools to support mathematics
There are a number of technology solutions that can support students in learning mathematics, including the following examples:
- calculators with special features such as large display screens and speech synthesis; e.g., "talking calculators" that vocalize data and resulting calculations
- mathematical overlays for specialized keyboards
- software that allows students to manipulate objects and geometric shapes
- text-to-speech software that assists in reading and writing for literacy-related tasks in mathematics; e.g., word prediction programs that can be customized to recognize mathematical terms
- online games for the development and practice of numeracy skills.

Tools to support communication

Software that encourages the use of language skills, including grammar and vocabulary development has the potential to help all students, particularly those with communication difficulties. This type of software may use a variety of techniques such as videos, audio, games and computer-assisted instruction.

Some students have difficulty with verbal communication, for both receiving and expressing information. Visual supports, such as picture symbols, can help these students make sense of verbal information and printed text. The primary purpose of these visual tools is to enhance student understanding. Visuals also can be used to support students with limited verbal abilities to communicate; e.g., ask for help, make choices, communicate needs.

Visual tools can be essential in assisting students with communication difficulties to become active, successful participants in the learning process.

Picture communication symbols also can be used by classroom teachers for creating materials to enhance language and literacy skills instruction for all students. Using a software program such as Boardmaker, picture word cards can be generated for a wide range of topics or student activities. Picture symbols are useful for making classroom charts, visual schedules, step-by-step instructions for task completion, materials for emerging readers, interactive storybooks, or big books with matching picture cards. The cards also can be used for vocabulary development and in reading comprehension and writing activities, for both whole group and individual learning activities.

A Schoolwide Approach

Contents of this chapter
Professional learning communities
Action research
A combined approach
       1. Identifying goals
       2. Working toward change
       3. Developing and maintaining staff capacity
       4. Assessing results

7

105

"... the biggest day-to-day repository of constructive power to improve schools is in the hearts, minds and hands of the people who work in them."
– Kenneth A. Sirotnik, in "Evaluation in the Ecology of Schooling: The Process of School Renewal"

By differentiating instruction in your classroom, you can make a tremendous impact on the learning of your students. By working collaboratively with other teachers through a schoolwide approach, you can have an even greater effect.

Although many teachers are aware of the benefits of differentiated instruction, they may *not* be implementing this approach for a variety of reasons. These include:

- a belief that differentiated instruction will be too difficult or time-consuming
- lack of exposure to differentiated instruction and strategies through preservice training or their own experience as a teacher or student
- lack of understanding of how to implement differentiated instruction in a substantive, planned and proactive way (Tomlinson 2005)
- a belief that they do not have the professional development or administrative support to start to initiate and implement differentiated instructional practices (Carolan and Guinn 2007).

These barriers can be overcome through a thoughtful, clearly articulated and collaborative schoolwide plan for implementing differentiated instruction including shared targets, professional development and indicators of success. Two starting points for building a schoolwide approach are through the complementary models of professional learning communities and action research.

Professional learning communities

Professional learning communities are created when teachers and administrators in a school purposefully share learnings and then act on what they learn. This process of sharing, reflection and improvement benefits students by helping staff enhance effectiveness as professionals.

Professional learning communities are based around seeking collaborative answers to the following three critical questions.

- What do we want each student to learn?
- How will we know when each student has learned it?
- How will we respond when a student experiences difficulty in learning? (DuFour and Eaker 1998)

The third question is a hallmark of what defines professional learning communities. It also is central to a school's commitment to differentiation. If students are not learning through current methodology, educators work together to explore thoughtful alternatives.

Action research

Action research is a form of applied research that draws on a range of designs and methodologies to examine a practical problem or issue and generate solutions to institute a change. Action research has the potential to greatly enhance school improvement initiatives by providing educators with a systematic process to reflect on issues, consider options, implement solutions and evaluate results (Alberta Teachers' Association 2000). Action researchers focus on constructing a detailed, coherent, useful understanding of what was intended, and of what actually happened and why.

For more information on action research:

- Action Research Network in Alberta
  www.uleth.ca/edu/research/arnia/

  This Web site, developed by David Townsend of the University of Lethbridge, provides an overview of action research in the Alberta context. It includes references to projects undertaken by teacher-researchers in recent years.

- Alberta Initiative for School Improvement (AISI)
  www.education.gov.ab.ca/k_12/special/aisi/

  This Web site contains an annotated bibliography of print materials that support action research aimed at school improvement.

A combined approach

The remainder of this chapter describes a framework for building and sustaining a schoolwide approach through four overlapping steps, which combine elements of professional learning communities and action research.

1. Identifying goals
2. Working toward change
3. Developing and maintaining staff capacity
4. Assessing results

Throughout these steps, change is planned *with*, rather than planned *for* teachers. Change usually occurs through the work of a small, committed team of teachers and the school administrator, with input from other staff members throughout the process. This cyclical process includes ongoing discussion about teaching and learning and about the school's values, relationships, procedures, current realities and priorities.

1. Identifying goals

Early in the planning process, educators discuss their sense of the current reality of the school related to differentiation, including strengths, concerns and values—what the school stands for and what it would like to be. These preliminary discussions of vision lead to the establishment of specific shared goals for improving differentiated practice. To be most effective, groups should focus on a few specific, achievable goals, such as improving learning through effective flexible groupings and conferencing practice.

Consider the following questions.
- What are the key elements of differentiated instruction that we want to see in place in the school?
- What are our current goals for differentiating instruction and improving the learning for all students in our school?
- What specific learning outcomes are a priority? How will these be measured?
- What strategies will be implemented to help students achieve the outcomes?
- How will implementation be monitored?
- How will results be shared and with whom?
- What are good sources of information about differentiated instruction?

The following checklist presents desirable programming features related to differentiated instruction. School staff can begin by reviewing the checklist to add, delete and modify criteria to suit their school's needs. Individuals respond to the survey according to their sense of reality in the entire school, not just in their own classrooms. In discussion following individual completion of the survey, team members select goals which they will focus on over the next specified time frame.

Differentiated Instruction Checklist

	Program Strength	Program Need
• We devote time to collegial discussions about our students' learning needs and interests.		
• We reflect regularly on how our school's program enhances the learning of all students.		
• We regularly offer students a variety of human, print and media resources for learning.		
• We regularly offer students a variety of learning activities to learn and to demonstrate learning.		
• We frequently employ observational and formal assessment information about individual students to plan appropriate instruction for all students.		
• We regularly challenge students to determine preferred personal strategies to complete learning tasks.		
• We regularly employ varied instructional formats—full class, small groups, independent learning and peer learning.		
• We consider individual student interests and background knowledge in the planning of instruction.		
• We frequently challenge students to self-assess their learning and to set related goals.		
• We offer choices in projects, resources, learning activities and display of learning.		

	Program Strength	Program Need
• We provide students with extra time and additional adult or peer support to complete assignments.		
• We employ resources with a range of challenge (e.g., levelled books) and in a variety of formats (e.g., taped readings) as well as manipulatives (e.g., blocks, sentence strips, sticky notes).		
• We regularly model strategies and challenge students to identify strategies that work best for them to complete specific learning tasks.		
• We regularly make exemplars of student work available to show students what is possible and what is expected.		
• We modify assessment tools including rubrics for individual students completing tasks.		
• We inform parents about differentiation strategies and invite parents to be meaningfully involved in their children's learning.		
• We consider ongoing assessment of work-in-progress as well as culminating assessments and standardized assessment of student progress to guide our planning.		
• We regularly offer individual students positive feedback and encouragement as well as focused, specific suggestions for improvement.		

110

2. Working toward change

Once you have established clear goals, it is critical to develop a detailed, practical action plan to work toward change. Planning includes consideration about roles, time lines, resources, and how individuals will implement and assess selected strategies. Consider the following ideas.

- Read relevant literature, consult colleagues and talk to experts and others with experience.

- Assign roles and responsibilities related to practical, organizational matters. Who will arrange meetings? How often? Who will be involved?

- Create a reasonable time line, with clear, specific milestones.

- Plan for assessment. How will we know if we have achieved our goals?

- Determine how the core team and additional teachers will work to achieve goals. Will they work alone or in teams or groups? How will they assess progress; e.g., individually or collegially? How will they report results? How will colleagues celebrate and publicize? Are mentorship and peer feedback appropriate for the project? Will teams work together on projects, perhaps to differentiate resources, activities and assessment techniques? Will they collaborate to plan learning activities and assessments? Will individuals engage in a research project, perhaps exploring two or three instructional strategies to assess which works best with individual students? What professional development and other support will teachers need along the way?

- Dedicate time for ongoing discussion and planning, often focused on what to do about students who are not learning to their potential.

- Ensure the necessary resources are committed to the initiative. Many Alberta schools and districts have employed Alberta Initiative for School Improvement (AISI) funding to support projects.

- Identify obstacles and plan strategies to overcome these. Regularly invite all stakeholders to voice concerns related to goals and plans. As concerns are voiced, professional development presentations and discussions should address these concerns honestly and directly.

- Maintain open communication throughout the process. In addition to communication among staff members, sharing goals and progress with parents and students can increase understanding and support for differentiated instruction.

111

3. Developing and maintaining staff capacity

Students are not the only learners in a school. Teachers and adminstrators also are learners, who need opportunities to develop new skills and knowledge for their own enrichment as well as for the benefit of the school community. Independent professional development opportunities may help you to better understand and implement differentiated instruction in your classroom. Collegial professional development, in which teachers plan and engage in learning together, will further support and align with a schoolwide approach to differentiated instruction. Professional development, like a schoolwide approach in general, is most effective when learning opportunities are spread around and there is distributed teacher leadership at the grass-roots level. In addition to professional development related to instruction, teachers also need opportunities to develop leadership skills in order to support and sustain the initiative.

Staff development that best supports differentiated instruction encourages teachers to:

- develop skills to reflect on, identify and respond to students' individual needs
- stay informed on current best practices for teaching and learning
- use effective classroom managment strategies
- explore and choose a range of flexible instructional approaches
- collaborate with other school staff and specialists to create responsive caring classrooms.

When planning professional development opportunities, select from a variety of approaches that best meets the needs of teachers and other staff at your school. Professional development may involve presentations by school staff, outside experts, study groups, or reading and discussion of selected professional literature. In general, teachers who engage in professional development that focuses on effective classroom practices are more likely to use those practices in their classrooms (InPraxis Group Inc. 2006). Some common characteristics of effective differentiated instruction that can be supported through professional development include:

- offering personalized scaffolding
- using flexible means to reach defined ends
- developing subject-area expertise
- creating a caring learning environment in which differences are seen as assets.

Whatever methods are used, professional development should always include follow-up discussion to presentations. How applicable are the contents to our goals and strategies? What follow-up resource might be helpful?

112

4. Assessing results

The ongoing collection of appropriate assessment data helps to answer two critical questions: Is our approach enhancing student learning? What can we do to enhance the benefit for all students?

Assessing results involves evaluating two separate things—how thoroughly and effectively the initiative is being implemented, and what effect the initiative is having on students and the school community. Practical evaluation strategies for school-based initiatives include:

- pre- and post-tests
- surveys
- interviews
- school records
- observation data.

The assessment of teacher perceptions should certainly be considered. For example, the checklist included in the previous section can be employed throughout the project to document perceptions of progress. However, meaningful and appropriate assessment of student progress is the most important measure of success, since student learning is the central focus of all projects.

Outcomes in Alberta's programs of study require ongoing observation, pre-specified response, performance assessment and student self-assessment, as represented in the following chart.

113

	Observation	Pre-specified Response	Performance Assessment	Student Self-assessment
DEFINITION	Informal assessment of students, often rotationally scheduled and focused on specific outcomes.	Assessment which requires students to approximate a predetermined answer.	Formal assessment which demands the use of criteria which are communicated directly to learners and used as guidelines by both students and teachers.	Assessment completed by students about their own work and that of classmates. The assessment is usually observational or a performance assessment.
EXAMPLES	Anecdotal records; observations of students working in groups; checklists.	Multiple choice; short-answer; true-false; matching.	Analytical or holistic marking forms for writing; debate; readers' theatre; representation; rubrics.	Instructional application of criteria to final product; self-assessment of writing; goal-setting activities; portfolios.

The implementation of differentiated instruction is an ongoing process. Analysis of assessment data will help you identify and celebrate successes, refine practices and set new goals to continue to enhance learning for all students.

Students with Disabilities

8

Contents of this chapter

"We need to be clear that diversity is an essential part of the human condition and needs to be anticipated and celebrated."
– Dr. Dave Edyburn, Associate Professor, University of Wisconsin, Milwaukee

Diversity has become one of the defining features of Alberta's schools. All classrooms today include a growing number of students with diverse learning needs, including students with disabilities. Ensuring that these students can be successful requires teachers to not only understand the unique learning needs of individual students but to be willing to plan for and create optimal learning opportunities and supports throughout the school day and across subject areas. In a diverse classroom, no single method can reach all learners.

How a differentiated approach supports students with disabilities

The 2005 *Differentiated Instruction: A Research Brief for Practitioners*, conducted by University of Alberta, found that of all groups of students, those with disabilities and/or at-risk of academic failure experience the greatest gains through a differentiated approach. According to this research, the key component that made the difference was explicit and targeted instruction (e.g., small group and one-to-one interventions) that increased intensity of instructional time.

Other research findings from that study identified the importance of:
- a supportive, caring learning community, including positive relationships with trusted adults
- early intervention and targeted instruction
- collaboration in the development of individual learning goals with students, parents, administrators, counsellors and subject teachers
- development of self-advocacy for students at-risk of academic failure.

Differentiated instruction benefits students with disabilities because it creates and promotes an environment in which learning differences are not just tolerated, they are expected and valued. A differentiated approach supports an inclusive education system in which all students have the best possible learning opportunities.

The range of instructional options and supports in place in a differentiated classroom will address many of the unique learning needs of students with disabilities. In addition, teachers who use a differentiated approach may be more willing and able to further adjust instruction to meet the needs of students with more intensive learning difficulties.

116

Finally, the process of ongoing assessment *for* learning, which is embedded in a differentiated instruction approach, also benefits students with disabilities. It allows teachers to more quickly and naturally identify which types of instructional strategies and supports individual students are responding to positively or not responding to.

Response to instructional supports and interventions

Students with disabilities have a continuum of needs that can be met to varying degrees by differentiated instruction. One way to consider the differing levels of needs of students is based on their response to instructional supports and interventions. For some students with disabilities, differentiated instruction may be enough to meet their learning needs; for others, differentiated instruction is the starting point for building individualized programming. This is illustrated in the model below.

Multi-tiered Response to Intervention Model

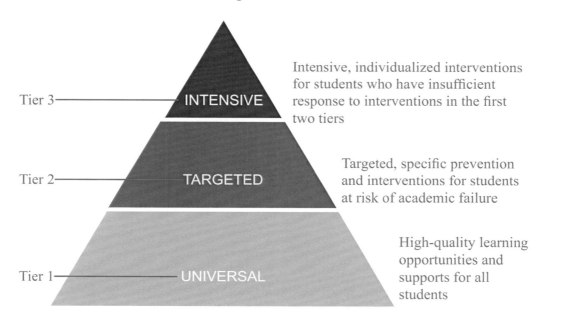

Tier 3 — INTENSIVE
Intensive, individualized interventions for students who have insufficient response to interventions in the first two tiers

Tier 2 — TARGETED
Targeted, specific prevention and interventions for students at risk of academic failure

Tier 1 — UNIVERSAL
High-quality learning opportunities and supports for all students

The base of the pyramid is made up of students whose disabilities have a mild to moderate impact on their learning. These students will respond positively to many of the strategies and supports typically used in a differentiated classroom, including accessible learning resources, explicit strategy instruction and structured opportunities.

The next and smaller tier is made up of those students who will benefit from differentiated instruction but who also need more targeted supports and interventions such as levelled learning materials, small group and/or individualized instruction. Without these supports and interventions, this group of students is at risk of school failure, early school leaving and additional difficulties such as behaviour problems. Some of the students in this group will need different levels of support at specific points in their schooling while, for other students, the level of support needed may flucuate throughout the grades.

At the top of the pyramid is a small group of students who need intensive individualized supports and intervention that go well beyond differentiated instruction. These students will need specialized supports and services. Differentiated instruction may provide some social benefits but the learning needs of this group of students go beyond what a differentiated instruction approach alone could provide.

It is essential that all students with disabilities, no matter where they might be on this pyramid, have high academic expectations set for them. The starting point of programming for all students in Alberta, whatever their particular ability or need, is the programs of study.

A team approach

All students with disabilities, particularly students with more specialized needs, require a collaborative and supportive team approach. This team, often called the learning team, is made up of people with various types of expertise who work together to:

- support the student
- support the classroom teacher
- share information, insights and questions to identify strategies and supports, that will increase the student's learning success.

At a minimum, the learning team includes the classroom teacher (who is the key educator) and parents of the student. It also may include a school-based learning supports teacher (sometimes called a special education coordinator, a resource teacher or a learning coach), a school administrator and other school staff. This group should be informal and collegial.

Parents have essential information and important perspectives about their child's learning needs. The support of parents has positive and pervasive effects on a student's success in school, and parents should be encouraged to feel that their contribution is a valuable part of the learning team process.

Some learning teams also include specialists that provide support and programming advice to the classroom teacher. These specialists could include speech pathologists, physiotherapists or occupational therapists, psychologists, mental health therapists, vision consultants or audiologists, and educational consultants with expertise in particular areas such as deaf education, Autism or behaviour.

As much as possible, students also should play an active role in their own learning teams. When appropriate, students should participate in meetings, contribute to plans and provide feedback on what is working and what is not.

Learner profiles and assessment

Creating a learning profile for a student with disabilities is an opportunity to get to know that student and to see beyond the student's disabilities. It is an opportunity to identify strengths, abilities and interests and gain a better understanding of the implications disabilities have for the student's learning and social participation. This information will help teachers choose supports that are responsive and meaningful.

Accurate assessment *for* and *of* learning are critically important to ensure all students are successful. The goal of assessment is to better understand the needs of the learner. Parents are an important source of information and insight about their children and should be involved in the assessment process. For example, they can provide information about their child's strengths and needs and wishes and dreams for the future.

The assessment process is multi-tiered, multidisciplinary and occurs in a continuous cycle—from planning through to final assessment and evaluation. The assessment process begins at the classroom level, with the teacher using informal techniques such as observation, reading inventories and other diagnostic tools to explore how the student is learning and to identify areas of strength and concern.

At the school level, it may be helpful to do more formal academic assessment, as well as screenings for sensory or other issues that could interfere with learning. School-based assessment should provide initial information for identifying and trying out various strategies, supports and interventions to see if they make a positive difference for the students.

For some students with disabilities, it may be necessary to go beyond the school to arrange for other types of assessments such as emotional-social needs, speech/language, fine and gross motor or sensory functioning such as hearing and vision. This type of specialized assessment should be used to inform educational programming and decision making.

119

For some students with a disability, a diagnosis can be a protective factor. A specific diagnosis may have important implications for a student's educational programming, social and emotional learning and overall well-being. This knowledge can help teachers align supports and strategies with students' unique needs. A knowledge of the disability also can help teachers know what to look for in ongoing functional assessments of what the student can do (rather than what he or she cannot do) and identify potential barriers to learning in the classroom that require supports and creative solutions.

For more information on specific strategies for teaching students with specialized learning needs, see the following Alberta Education publications.

- *Unlocking Potential: Key Components of Programming for Students with Learning Disabilities* (2003) at http://education.alberta.ca/admin/special/resources/unlocking.aspx.
- *Teaching Students with Autism Spectrum Disorders* (2003) at http://education.alberta.ca/admin/special/resources/autism.aspx.
- *Teaching Students with Fetal Alcohol Spectrum Disorder: Building Strengths, Creating Hope* (2004) at http://education.alberta.ca/admin/special/resources/fasd.aspx.
- *Focusing on Success: Teaching Students with Attention Deficit/Hyperactivity Disorder* (2006) at http://education.alberta.ca/admin/special/resources/adhd.aspx.

Understanding a student's unique needs also will help teachers plan for learning needs that may go beyond the programs of study. For example, students with vision loss, in addition to the regular curriculum, require an extended curriculum to learn skills related to mobility and manage materials and technology to support literacy (e.g., learning to read Braille or use magnifiers for large print). Students who are deaf and hard-of-hearing, as well as some students with physical disabilities, also may need extended curricula. This will require working collaboratively with district and regional specialists and developing a system of supports to respond to the unique needs of these students and their families.

For more information on programming for students with specialized learning needs see the following Alberta Education publications.

- *Essential Components of Educational Programming for Students who are Blind or Visually Impaired* (2006) at http://education.alberta.ca/media/511690/ecep_blind_or_visually_impaired.pdf.
- *Essential Components of Educational Programming for Students who are Deaf or Hard of Hearing* (2007) at http://education.alberta.ca/media/511693/ecep_deaf_or_hard_of_hearing.pdf.
- *Essential Components of Educational Programming for Students with Autism Spectrum Disorders* (2006) at http://education.alberta.ca/media/511684/ecep_autism_spectrum_disorder.pdf.

120

- *Essential Components of Educational Programming for Students with Behaviour Disabilities* (2006) at http://education.alberta.ca/media/511687/ ecep_behaviour_disabilities.pdf.

Flexible groupings

Flexible grouping is a hallmark of differentiated instruction and all students, including students with disabilities, need to be part of many different learning groups, including:
- large group instruction
- small group instruction
- one-to-one instruction
- cooperative small group learning
- partner learning
- peer teaching pairs
- independent learning activities.

It is essential that group membership is flexible and ever-changing to allow students to work with a diversity of peers. Group membership can be based on multiple factors including interest, previous knowledge and experience, aptitude, social compatibility, student choice and random assignment. Flexible grouping prevents students from being labelled or pigeonholed (e.g., the helper versus the helped).

Students need an accepting, safe learning environment that encourages them to take risks and ask for help. Teachers should provide explicit instruction, cueing and prompts, guided practice and feedback. They also have to monitor the social behaviour in groups on an ongoing basis to ensure the groups are providing the safe and accepting learning environment for all students involved.

All students need to learn the social rules and roles in each type of grouping so that they can contribute to this safe environment. Some students with disabilities may need coaching to gain the social skills necessary to function successfully in different types of groups. Other students in the class also may need to learn specific strategies to facilitate successful communication and group work. For example, it may be helpful to teach the class about the importance of eye contact and direct language when working with a peer with a communication difficulty. Small groups and partner work can provide authentic and motivating opportunities for all students to develop stronger social and communication skills.

121

Flexible and accessible learning resources

Many students, including students with disabilities, will benefit from learning resources that are flexible and accessible. For example, digital versions of print-based text can be used by students with low vision who need to adjust the size of print, by students with reading difficulties who use text-to-speech software or by students with physical disabilities who need computer-assisted technology to manipulate pages. Digital text also can provide other accessibility features such as alternate ways of displaying or organizing information, translational options (such as Braille translation), or additional features that support learning such as built-in dictionaries or glossaries, links to additional background information or opportunities to see additional samples or do additional practice.

Accessible resources also can be print-based resources. Varying reading levels, including organizers at the beginning of chapters, and visuals that support and enhance text are all ways to make resources more responsive to diverse learning needs.

Digital versions of authorized Grades 4 to 12 student basic textbooks for English language arts, mathematics, social studies and science are available through the Digital Repository for Students with Disabilities. For more information see: http://www.lrc.education.gov.ab.ca/pdf/Digr-Info-Flyer.pdf.

Essential instructional components

Research identifies several essential instructional components that are particularly important for classroom instruction to be effective for students with learning difficulties.

Duration and intensity of instruction
Students with learning difficulties may require interventions of longer duration and intensity than other students in order to achieve mastery of both foundational and higher-level skills and to be able to apply their learning to new situations. They may need more learning opportunities distributed over a longer time. In addition, these students may need instruction that is of greater intensity (e.g., more small-group or guided-practice learning activities). Teachers can make decisions regarding the intensity and duration of instructional components by carefully assessing the individual student's understanding and progress in order to gauge his or her response to instruction.

Cumulative review of important concepts and skills
Cumulative review of previously mastered content promotes retention. Early in the learning of a new skill, many students tend to be error-prone, not very fluent, and inconsistent in their application of skills to new situations. Students with learning difficulties generally take longer to move past this stage than other students. These students need more opportunities to practise their skills and to

review prior learning. Cumulative review needs to be targeted (e.g., reviewing key skills and concepts that are not fully mastered) and should incorporate a wide range of activities. For example, students who struggle with learning letter–sound relationships may need to continually review previously learned sounds and sight words. These reviews can be a combination of quick oral reviews (e.g., "Tell me the following sounds for these letters."), short activities and structured games targeting the skill.

Guided practice and explicit instruction in transferring knowledge

Students with learning difficulties often have difficulty transferring knowledge. They are particularly in need of guided practice and specific instruction that helps them transfer their skills to new problem-solving contexts and to situations that present new content but require previously taught skills. Teaching also should make explicit connections across previous and current content areas.

Language tailored for instruction

The oral and written language you use for instruction and for providing feedback to students has a direct impact on the learning of students. Monitor yourself to ensure you are using:

- appropriate level of language; e.g., simple, direct, unambiguous language
- appropriate level of explicitness
- concrete examples
- appropriate level of description and detail
- feedback that guides student thinking
- explicit error correction
- positive feedback that motivates and encourages students.

Vary the complexity of language of instruction (oral and written), via the number/amount, sequence, and/or complexity of instructions or information. For instance, explicitly state themes rather than have students infer them, vary pacing, and elaborate and review key ideas. For example, teachers may need to:

- simplify and shorten instructions (often visual reminders/cues are useful)
- provide concrete examples of more abstract concepts
- present new information with an emphasis on main ideas and provide clear conceptual links between key ideas and supporting details.

Sometimes, these students will need to hear ideas restated in different ways and will benefit from multiple opportunities to listen to the teacher. Teachers can provide important tips, cues and explicit feedback in the form of interactive dialogue, thus acting as the students' coach.

Language of instruction also includes the print-based materials used in the class to communicate content and instructions. There are a number of strategies for modifying or expanding upon the language of instruction in materials, such as adding visuals (e.g., picture charts, symbols, photos), providing definitions for specialized language and adjusting reading levels so students with less-developed reading skills can read and understand the text.

Concurrent instruction in foundational skills and higher-order processes
Students need systematic instruction to master foundational skills such as computation and decoding if they are to achieve proficiency in higher-order skills. At the same time, they need instruction that also targets higher-order skills such as problem-solving and comprehension strategies. Students need clear instruction on basic skills and concepts as well as on the use of higher-order strategies and metacognitive principles that promote and consolidate learning. For example, a student with limited word-recognition skills needs targeted instruction in this area while at the same time learning comprehension strategies for understanding text. To do this, the teacher could model the comprehension strategies when reading aloud from a more advanced text.

Scaffolding instruction

There are a variety of specific teaching strategies that are especially effective for supporting students with learning difficulties. Scaffolding is the overarching strategy that is most effective for these students, and specific types of scaffolding include:

- modelling
- guided practice
- memory prompts and supports
- strategy instruction
- use of graphic organizers.

Specific strategies can overlap and can also be used in tandem. For example, when working with higher-order cognitive thinking processes, modelling, guided practice and memory prompts could all be used to support student learning.

Scaffolding is a key component of a differentiated instruction approach and is especially important for students with learning difficulties. Scaffolding is a way to:

- move the student from one place to another in terms of learning
- gradually transfer the responsibility for learning from the teacher to the student, thereby fostering a more independent learner.

Teachers can provide scaffolds in a variety of ways, such as activating background knowledge, providing prompts or think sheets, or facilitating guided practice. Collaborative and supportive interactions between a student and a more knowledgeable other (the teacher, a parent, or another student) help students bridge the gap between what they know and what they do not know. Scaffolding support also can be created by technology or written material that provides prompts and other needed material.

Effective scaffolded instruction:
- involves intentional planning
- considers student strengths, needs and current level of knowledge and skill (as identified in individual learner profiles and other in-class assessment strategies)
- focuses on a specific learning goal or type of skill
- provides tailored assistance that is adjusted on an as-needed basis
- provides emotional support (e.g., praise and encouragement)
- provides specific feedback that highlights student progress and identifies specific behaviours that contributed to success
- controls for frustrations and risk by creating learning environments that are safe and learning tasks that are within what a student can do
- helps students begin to generalize and internalize learning
- helps students become more confident and independent learners.

Accurately determining a student's current level of functioning is key to planning and implementing scaffolded instruction. For many students with learning difficulties, scaffolding will be adjustable but ongoing. To maintain a reasonable level of competence, many students with learning difficulties will require scaffolding for the long term. The degree of scaffolding needed may change across subject areas, types of learning task and contexts and environments for learning. Teachers can help students generalize their learning by identifying other contexts where they can apply the process and by actively encouraging the students to practise the task or process in these contexts.

For more information on scaffolded instruction, see *Chapter 5: Differentiated Learner Experiences*.

125

Modelling[1]

"Modelling" can take on a number of forms for a number of purposes. Some common examples include the following.

- **Thinking aloud.** The teacher overtly verbalizes the thought processes used to complete a particular activity. Teachers can use "think-aloud" techniques in a number of instructional contexts including modelling how a reader processes text and demonstrating writing techniques such as planning an essay or revising a piece of writing.

- **Modelling learning strategies.** For example, by modelling good reading strategies the teacher makes explicit those skills that cannot be readily perceived by students. Students also can be invited to think out loud and model their strategies for decoding words, making predictions, summarizing and evaluating text.

- **Demonstrating the task.** The teacher may, for example, demonstrate all the steps in completing a graphic organizer or show the steps that students need to take to solve a specific type of math problem.

Guided practice[2]

In "guided practice," the teacher provides students with support and guidance as they initially learn new information or tasks, and then gradually phases out this support as the students become more proficient. Guided practice is critically important to many effective instructional programs, including those targeting mathematical problem solving, written expression and word recognition skills.

Guided practice is an important way to prevent students from forming misconceptions. Some students may come to the task lacking in prior knowledge and may be overwhelmed by the complexity or amount of new information. Other students may have limited working memory capacity or poor language skills and, thus, also will struggle to process the information that is presented. Guided practice helps students understand and clarify task expectations and facilitates their ability to link new knowledge with existing concepts.

1. This section adapted from Expert Panel on Literacy and Numeracy Instruction for Students with Special Education Needs, *Education for All: The Report of the Expert Panel on Literacy and Numeracy Instruction for Students with Special Education Needs, Kindergarten to Grade 6* (Toronto, ON: Ontario Ministry of Education, 2005), p. 63. © Queen's Printer for Ontario, 2005. Adapted with permission.
2. Ibid., pp. 64, 65.

Guided practice can include different levels of support. For example:

1. *The students and the teacher work together* on a particular learning task. Students can contribute to the task (for instance, solve a particular step of a math problem or complete a section of the graphic organizer), but they are not required to perform the entire task by themselves. As the teacher guides the practice she offers verbal directions as well as demonstrating the task. The teacher also may provide written and/or pictorial directions that students can use independently for reference.

2. *Students work in small groups or with a partner*. When students have the preliminary skills and confidence to begin to practise the task more independently they work on the task collaboratively with a partner or small group. The teacher continues to provide supportive feedback.

3. *Students practise independently*. Practising new skills and concepts on their own, and in various contexts, promote mastery and automaticity. The teacher continues to provide supportive feedback and helps students develop strategies to begin to self-evaluate and generate their own feedback.

Memory prompts and supports

Memory difficulties often go hand-in-hand with learning difficulties. Common difficulties related to short-term or working memory include problems:
- recalling information despite repeated instruction and review
- keeping track of their belongings
- remembering daily routines despite regular exposure
- recalling facts and procedures, such as new vocabulary words, specific content information or mathematical procedures.

Most students with learning difficulties will benefit from instructional practices such as the following, which prompt and support memory.

- **Present concepts concretely.** Real-life examples add meaning and relevance that aid learning and recall. Concepts presented in familiar or authentic contexts are easier to learn and retain.

- **Use familiar language to introduce new concepts.** Encourage students to connect their previous knowledge to new learning.

- **Present the same information more than one way.** For example, when presenting new information orally, write the main points on the board.

- **Incorporate hands-on learning experiences and demonstrations.** Students learn more effectively when they try out new information and skills in a variety of settings.

127

- **Provide multisensory memory cues.** For example, to teach new reading vocabulary, include auditory, visual and kinesthetic cues. Review sound-symbol associations by:
  - saying the name of the letter
  - looking at the letter paired with a picture that starts with the letter
  - tracing the letter on the desk, in the air or on your arm.

- **Use visual cues to introduce new concepts or review content.** For example, use colour-coding, a sequence of photos or drawings, or a flowchart.

- **Use auditory and kinesthetic cues in combination.** For example, combine songs with movement. Music and physical routines linked to learning facts can help students memorize faster and act as a cue for retrieving specific information.

- **Provide regularly scheduled reviews of procedures and concepts.** For example, start each day by reviewing previously learned skills and ideas. Then present new skills and ideas. Before students leave for the day, review the new information.

- **Teach students to make lists of reminders regularly.** Note dates and assignments on a posted calendar. Build procedures into the day for recording information in daytimers and homework agendas. Tape simple cue cards of daily class routines on student desks.

- **Provide memory aids for frequently used information.** For example, high-frequency spelling words can be written on a file card and taped inside a binder. Schedules should be posted on the board and students can have personal copies in their desks or notebooks.

- **Teach students strategies for memorizing specific pieces of information.** For example, the **"fold-over"** strategy below can be used to learn second-language vocabulary or spelling words.

Fold-overs
1. Fold a paper to make four columns.

2. In the first column, copy target vocabulary words in English.

3. In the second column, write the French words for each of the vocabulary words.

4. Check your answers in the text. Correct any answers you got wrong and fill in words you did not know.

5. Fold back the first column so the English words are not visible. Now, practise translating the other way. Look at each of the French words you wrote in the second column and write the English translation in the third column. Check your answers against the original words in the first column.

6. Repeat this process to translate the words back into French in the fourth column. A complete practice page might look like this:

mother	la mère ✓	mother ✓	la mère ✓
father	le père ✓	father ✓	le père ✓
brother	le frère	brother ✓	le frère ✓

Strategy instruction

Independent and successful learners tend to use a broad array of strategies to solve problems and monitor their own learning. Most students with learning difficulties do not have effective learning strategies or do not know how or when to use these strategies. Providing students with instruction in "how to learn" enables students to become more efficient learners.[3]

Research suggests that instruction in the use of strategies is most effective when it is explicit, especially when working with students with learning difficulties.[3]

Consider the following guidelines for teaching a new strategy (Gaskins and Elliott 1991; Woloshyn, Elliott and Kaucho 2001).[3]

1. Create and post a step-by-step visual to introduce the specific strategy.
2. Provide information about when and where to use the strategy.
3. Provide students with a convincing rationale for using the strategy, including a personal story of how you have used the strategy in your own learning.
4. Model using the strategy. Verbalize your thought process as you work through each step.
5. Provide students with multiple opportunities to practise using the strategy, guiding their attempts to do so until they can carry out the strategy independently.
6. Provide students with feedback and evidence of strategy success.
7. Cue students to transfer the use of the strategy to other contexts.

---

3. These paragraphs adapted from Expert Panel on Literacy and Numeracy Instruction for Students with Special Education Needs, *Education for All: The Report of the Expert Panel on Literacy and Numeracy Instruction for Students with Special Education Needs, Kindergarten to Grade 6* (Toronto, ON: Ontario Ministry of Education, 2005), p. 65. © Queen's Printer for Ontario, 2005. Adapted with permission.

This type of step-by-step strategy instruction provides an organizational structure that helps the student focus on carrying out the task rather than trying to think about what to do next while also trying to complete the task. With repeated practice and instruction that uses other effective instructional supports (e.g., teacher modelling, cueing), a student will begin to internalize the steps of the strategy and become a more independent and strategic learner.

To generalize the use of a particular strategy, it is important to help students understand how the strategy works for them. Encourage students to ask themselves the following types of questions.
- What parts of the strategy help me the most and why?
- What parts of the strategy are the hardest to do and why?
- How could I change the strategy to make it work better for me?
- How can I use the strategy for different kinds of tasks and in different kinds of situations?
- In what kinds of situations would this strategy *not* work?
- How can I remind myself to use this strategy?

In addition:
- have students give themselves feedback on their use of the strategy
- help students develop positive self-talk, which acknowledges that success is a result of effort and correctly using the strategy
- teach students to cue others to use the strategy and to give reinforcement when peers apply the strategy effectively.

Learning how to use strategies effectively requires time and motivation. Initially many students will require substantial time and extensive guidance and support to learn how to use the strategies effectively. With experience, including guided practice and feedback, students can learn to use strategies faster and more competently. Over time and with the gradual introduction of multiple learning strategies, students can develop repertoires of effective learning tools.

There are a wide variety of cognitive strategies to choose from, especially in the areas of reading comprehension, problem solving and test taking. Teachers need to choose appropriate strategies based on student learner profiles and student responses to instruction.

For sample strategies that are effective for students with learning difficulties, see the following Alberta Education resources.
- *Unlocking Potential: Key Components of Programming for Students with Learning Disabilities* (2003), pages 53–71, available at http://education. alberta.ca/admin/special/resources/unlocking.aspx.
- *Teaching Students with Fetal Alcohol Spectrum Disorder: Building Strengths, Creating Hope* (2004), pages 27–49, 51–71, 73–109, available at http://education.alberta.ca/admin/special/resources/fasd.aspx.

130

- *Focusing on Success: Teaching Students with Attention Deficit/ Hyperactivity Disorder* (2006), pages 63–88, available at http://education. alberta.ca/admin/special/resources/adhd.aspx.

Graphic organizers

"Graphic organizers" (also called "key visuals") are tools for gathering, organizing and displaying information in a visual format. Graphic organizers use words, pictures and graphic cues to help students generate ideas, record and re-organize information and see relationships. Venn diagrams, story boards and webs are all examples of types of graphic organizers.

Graphic organizers are not fill-in-the-blank exercises. They are interactive tools for constructing knowledge and generating understanding and new ideas. Graphic organizers:

- demonstrate not only what students are thinking, but also how they are thinking as they work through learning tasks
- provide a visual link between language and content
- organize information and explicitly develop ideas and the underlying relationships among those ideas
- lower the language demands for students who have difficulty with reading and writing
- reduce the load on short-term memory, allowing the student to focus on the information.

Many examples of graphic organizers can be found on Web sites such as http://www.eduplace.com/graphicorganizer.

Consider the following seven steps for teaching students how to use specific graphic organizers.

1. Introduce a new organizer by showing an example and describing its purpose and form.
2. Model how to use the organizer with easy or familiar material. Show your thinking by discussing the steps and how you decide which information to use aloud. Model the kinds of questions you would ask yourself.
3. Create opportunity for guided practice with relatively easy new material and have students complete the graphic organizer with a small group or with a partner. Stop the class at different points in the process and give feedback.
4. Build in time for reflecting by showing final products and discussing what worked and what did not work. Give students an opportunity to revise the information they are working with.
5. Give students multiple opportunities to practice using the graphic organizer. Some students may find it easier to work on a larger version of the tool; try enlarging the size by photocopying it on to 11x17 paper.

131

6. Encourage students to consider how the tool can be used in a variety of situations. Look for opportunities to use the tool with different types of materials and tasks and in different subject areas.
7. Encourage students to modify the organizers and construct their own variations for the tool.

Effective supports

The goal of instructional supports is to give students with disabilities the same opportunity to succeed as other students. Typically, supports will span all subject areas and instructional settings that the student is engaged in. They help ensure that the student can successfully access the curriculum and demonstrate knowledge, skills and concepts to the best of his or her abilities.

There are three general types of supports:
- **Environmental**—related to the resources, materials the student uses as well as the layout and use of classroom space (e.g., preferential seating, adaptive devices such as ramps or computer technology)
- **Instructional**—related to the way information and concepts are presented or practised (e.g., providing alternative reading materials, copies of notes, small group instruction)
- **Assessment**—related to how students demonstrate their knowledge and understanding in the classroom and in testing situations (e.g., extra time to complete tasks, option of providing oral response, rest breaks, assessment materials in alternate formats such as Braille).

There can be an overlap in these types; for example, it is possible that a specific support could be both environmental and instructional, and also could affect assessment. Tools 1 and 2 at the end of this chapter provide organized lists of effective supports.

The process of selecting effective supports is grounded in good instructional decision making. Teachers play a key role in helping students identify and use supports effectively. Similarly, parents, students and other members of the learning team have a role in selecting, monitoring and evaluating the use of supports. Choosing appropriate supports involves asking systematic questions about individual students, such as the following.
- What helps this student learn or perform better?
- What does this student say about what helps him or her learn or show what he or she knows?
- What do this student's parents say about how their child learns?
- What gets in the way of this student demonstrating skills and knowledge?
- What supports and strategies has this student been taught to use? What is working successfully for this student now? What is not working or failed to work in the past?

132

Understanding some of the common barriers to the effective use of supports (sometimes called *accommodations* in the literature) is an important starting point. Common barriers include the following.

- **Misunderstanding the purpose**
  Parents, students and school staff (and sometimes other students) can perceive that particular supports give students with disabilities an unfair advantage over other students. In reality, appropriate supports give the student the same opportunity as other students. Parents and school staff also may believe that supports replace the need to acquire or develop basic skills. It is important to balance the use of supports with the teaching and practise of basic literacy, numeracy and study skills so that students can develop these skills to their fullest potential.

- **Selecting supports that are not appropriate**
  School staff often report having difficulty translating information from specialized assessments into selecting appropriate supports. As a result, there is a tendency to overrely on the same basic supports for all students with particular kinds of disabilities, rather than individualizing the supports to match the specific learning needs and strengths of the student. Different students benefit from different kinds of supports.

- **Not involving the student in the process**
  School staff often report difficulty knowing how to meaningfully involve students in the decision-making process. However, research indicates that students benefit most from supports when they participate in the selection process. Often a student, who would benefit from support, does not make full use of it because he or she is self-conscious about doing things differently than peers. In a differentiated classroom, with all students using varied supports, there is likely to be less stigma surrounding individual supports, even if no other students are using a particular support.

  Involving students in the selection process provides opportunities for them to learn about and become comfortable with how they learn. It also will help them become better advocates for themselves in future learning situations.

- **Using supports inconsistently**
  When supports are not used consistently, it is difficult to determine if they are helping students. Also, students need time and opportunities to learn how to use supports and strategies effectively in a variety of situations, not just on major assignments or exams.

133

- **Overusing supports and possibly reducing expectations**
  When too many supports are used, particularly at the elementary level, it can reduce expectations for student learning. For example, always providing a scribe might limit opportunities for the student to develop skills and confidence in writing.

There are several important considerations related to the selection, use of and monitoring of effective instructional supports.

- **Base decisions on an understanding of student strengths and areas of needs**
  In addition to identifying student needs, identify student strengths and learning preferences to determine appropriate supports. Talk with students about what helps them learn better. Consult with parents about what they do to help their child complete tasks at home. The following chart shows an example of how learning strengths could be used to select supports for students with memory difficulties.

Sample supports for students with memory difficulties	Consider those supports for students who learn best by:		
	seeing	hearing	doing
• Give one instruction at a time.		X	
• Build routines into the day for recording information in daytimers or assignment books.	X		X
• Provide written memory prompts for frequently used information such as high-frequency spelling words or schedules.	X		
• Use visual cues, such as colour-coding, photos, flowcharts or charts	X		
• Use auditory and kinesthetic cues in combination. Combine songs with movement.		X	X
• Provide regularly scheduled reviews of procedures and concepts (e.g., review previously learned skills and ideas at the start of each day, review new information at the end of the day).		X	

Sample support for students with memory difficulties	Consider those supports for students who learn best by:		
	seeing	hearing	doing
• Make lists of reminders regularly, and note dates and assignments on a calendar.	x		x

Select supports and strategies that are the least intrusive for students. If possible, avoid supports that isolate students from peers or draw unnecessary attention.

- **Use a collaborative approach**
  Educate parents and students about the benefits of using supports and how the supports may be adapted for use at home and in the community.

  Involve relevant specialists in selecting appropriate supports based on their knowledge of student strengths and needs, and the demands of the setting.

  Ask students about their preferences regarding supports; respect their opinions and attitudes. If the student is not comfortable with a support, it is important to revisit his or her strengths and needs, and then brainstorm alternate supports that the student will commit to trying for a period of time.

- **Use support consistently and monitor student performance**
  Prioritize the introduction of support if more than one is to be used. Let students become familiar with one support before introducing another.

  Consult with students about the use of supports after they have tried them for a period of time. Compare student performance before and after.

135

Assistive technology

"For people without disabilities, technology makes things easier. For people with disabilities, technology makes things possible."
– National Council on Disability

Assistive technology for learning (ATL) is the devices, media and services used by students with physical, sensory, cognitive, speech or learning disabilities to actively engage in learning and to achieve their individual learning goals. ATL assists students in performing functions related to learning that would otherwise be difficult or impossible to accomplish independently.

ATL is different from educational or instructional technology. Educational technology is generally used by all students; ATL is more specialized and allows access to learning for students with barriers due to their disabilities. However, the technologies may overlap. Some ATL is beneficial for all students. For example, text-to-speech software could benefit all students who are learning to write. Likewise, students with disabilities may benefit from educational technology such as reading instruction software, but they also may need assistive technology such as a specialized keyboard or touch screen to successfully access these programs.

Areas where ATL may reduce learning barriers for students with disabilities include, but are not exclusive to:
- printing and handwriting
- reading
- expressive writing
- studying
- mathematics
- computer access
- vision
- hearing
- communication.

ATL has a continuum of tools ranging from low-tech to high-tech. Some examples are listed below. There may be an overlap between what is typically considered education technology and what is considered assistive technology.

Low tech options:
- raised-line paper
- alternate writing tools; e.g., magnetic letter, alphabet stamps, magnetic words
- materials to support memory and organization; e.g., highlighting pens, sticky notes

136

Mid-tech options:
- voice recorders
- calculators
- talking spell checkers
- dedicated word processors.

High-tech options:
- specialized software such as word prediction, text-to-speech
- dedicated communication devices
- specialized computer hardware such as touch screens, refreshable Braille display.

Many students with disabilities require both low-tech and high-tech solutions to be successful learners. The general rule is to begin with the lower-tech solutions and progress to more complex technologies, only if the low-tech options do not adequately reduce barriers to learning. For example, the best solution for a student whose handwriting is difficult to decipher might be a portable word processer with memory, rather than the more costly laptop computer.

Choosing which ATL solution would be most appropriate for an individual student is an ongoing process that involves exploring alternatives, gathering information and setting up opportunities for students to try potential ATL solutions across learning environments. A standard set of questions, such as the "SETT framework",[4] developed by Joy Zabala, can be a helpful tool for gathering and organizing information. The SETT framework considers the student, the learning environment, the learning tasks, and then the tools needed by the student to address the tasks.

The **student**
- What does the student need to do (that he or she is unable to do now and that ATL may be able to support)?
- What are the student's unique learning needs?
- What are the student's current abilities and strengths?

The **environment**
- What materials and equipment are currently available in the learning environment?
- What is the physical set-up?
- What is the instructional arrangement? Are there likely to be changes?
- What supports are available to the student?
- What resources are available to the school staff working with the student?

137

---

4. Adapted with permission from Joy Zabala, "The SETT Framework: Critical Areas to Consider When Making Informed Assistive Technology Decisions," *The 2Learn.ca Education Society*, November 1995, http://www.2learn.ca/institute/institute2006/handouts/SETTshortpaper.pdf (Accessed March 9, 2009).

The **tasks**
- What activities take place in the environment?
- What activities support the student's learning?
- What are the critical elements of the activities?
- How might the activities be modified to accommodate the student's unique learning needs?
- How might technology support the student's active participation in those activities?

The **tools**
- What low-tech, mid-tech and high-tech options should be considered for a student with these needs and abilities doing these tasks in these environments?
- What strategies might increase student performance?
- How might the tools be tried out with students in the environments in which they will be used?

For more information on using the SETT framework, evaluating ATL solutions and creating an implementation plan see "Chapter 9: Infusing Assistive Technology for Learning into the IPP Process" in Alberta Education's *Individualized Program Planning* (2006) at http://education.alberta.ca/admin/special/resources/ipp.aspx.

For additional information on assistive technology see *Chapter 6: Leveraging Technology*.

138

Tool 1: General Supports for Students with Disabilities

Name _____   Date _____

Completed by _____

Environmental
- ❏ Seat student near teacher
- ❏ Seat student in an area with minimal distractions
- ❏ Seat student near a positive peer model
- ❏ Stand near student when giving instructions
- ❏ Use a sound-field system
- ❏ Provide access to study carrel
- ❏ Use a desktop easel or slant board to raise reading materials
- ❏ Allow student to move around the classroom
- ❏ Make materials self-correcting
- ❏ Highlight important concepts and information and/or passages
- ❏ Prepare recordings of reading/textbook materials, tasks
- ❏ Provide an extra textbook for home use
- ❏ Provide graph paper or large spaced paper for writing
- ❏ Allow use of personal word lists, cue cards
- ❏ Increase use of pictures, diagrams, concrete manipulators
- ❏ Increase print size in photocopying
- ❏ Provide a visual summary of the daily schedule
- ❏ Other _____

Instructional
- ❏ Vary difficulty of instructional material
- ❏ Vary amount of material to be learned
- ❏ Vary amount of material to be practised
- ❏ Vary time for practice activities
- ❏ Use advance organizers and graphic organizers
- ❏ Provide an outline or study guide
- ❏ Use assignment notebooks or homework checklists
- ❏ Repeat directions or have student repeat directions
- ❏ Shorten directions
- ❏ Highlight instructions
- ❏ Pair written instructions with oral instructions and/or visuals/picture cues
- ❏ Reduce number of tasks required in assignments
- ❏ Break long-term assignments into shorter tasks and develop a schedule for completing each task
- ❏ Use strategies to enhance recall; e.g., cues, cloze
- ❏ Accept dictated or parent-assisted homework assignments
- ❏ Provide extra assignment time
- ❏ Provide models of written work or other assignments to guide students; e.g., sentence, paragraph, book report, short story, poem, essay

139

Tool 1: General Supports for Students with Disabilities (continued)

Instructional (continued)
- ❏ Permit student to print
- ❏ Provide a student buddy for reading
- ❏ Provide access to peer- or cross-aged tutoring
- ❏ Provide time with a teacher assistant to assist with organizing or reviewing information and concepts
- ❏ Provide nonverbal reminders for student to stay on task
- ❏ Provide immediate positive reinforcement for behaviour; e.g., verbal praise, tangible reinforcers, notes home, progress charts
- ❏ Implement self-monitoring systems so student takes responsibility for own behaviour
- ❏ Other _____

Assessment
- ❏ Adjust the appearance of the assessment tool; e.g., margins, spacing
- ❏ Adjust the type of tasks (T/F, multiple choice, matching)
- ❏ Provide additional cues or prompts such as cloze and word lists
- ❏ Vary how assessment is administered; e.g., small groups, individual
- ❏ Record test questions
- ❏ Reduce number of items or select items specific to current ability level
- ❏ Give extra time
- ❏ Permit rest breaks during tasks
- ❏ Adjust readability of text
- ❏ Allow alternative formats such as webs or key points in place of essays or long answers
- ❏ Read questions aloud
- ❏ Allow oral response
- ❏ Practise taking similar questions or assessment tasks
- ❏ Other _____

Tool 2: Sample Academic and Instructional Supports for Students with Disabilities

Name _____ Date _____

Completed by _____

Reading Difficulties	Written Expression Difficulties	Fine and Gross Motor Difficulties
❑ Use less difficult/ alternative reading material ❑ Identify/define words prior to reading ❑ Reduce amount of reading required ❑ Allow alternative methods of data collection (dictation, interviews, fact sheets) ❑ Enlarge text of worksheets, reading material and tests ❑ Limit words on a page ❑ Extend time to complete assignments ❑ Read directions several times at start of assignments ❑ Emphasize important terms and clarify meanings ❑ Provide additional repetition and guided practice of directions, skills and concepts ❑ Use assistive technology; e.g., text-to-speech software	❑ Reduce volume or requirements for written work; e.g., by accepting an outline or point-form notes ❑ Break long-term assignments into manageable tasks with a schedule for completing tasks ❑ Extend time lines for completing assignments ❑ Offer alternative assignments ❑ Allow student to work on homework at school ❑ Encourage use of word processor ❑ Waive spelling, punctuation and paragraphing requirements ❑ Use assistive technology; e.g., word processor, spell check device, grammar check device, text-to-speech software	❑ Use assistive and adaptive devices (slant boards/desktop easels) to display written material – pencil or pen adapted in size or grip diameter – alternative keyboard – portable word processor ❑ Set realistic and mutually agreed-upon expectations for neatness and organization ❑ Reduce or eliminate the need to copy from a text or board – provide copies of notes – permit student to photocopy a peer's notes – provide carbon/NCR paper to a peer to allow a duplicate copy of notes to be made ❑ Extend time to complete assignments ❑ Alter the size, shape or location of the space provided for answers ❑ Accept keyword responses instead of complete sentences ❑ Allow student to type answers or to answer orally instead of in writing

This tool adapted from Calgary Learning Centre (Calgary, Alberta, 2002). Used with permission of the Calgary Learning Centre.

Tool 2: Sample Academic and Instructional Supports for Students with Disabilities (continued)

Attention Difficulties	Memory Difficulties

❑ Provide alternative seating
  – near teacher
  – facing teacher
  – at front of class, between well-focused students, away from distractions
❑ Provide additional or personal work space (quiet area for study, extra seat or table, "time-out" spot, study carrels)
❑ Permit movement during class activities and testing sessions
❑ Provide directions in written form
  – on board
  – on worksheets
  – copied in assignment book by student
❑ Set time limits for specific task completion
❑ Extend time to complete tests and assignments
❑ Use multiple testing sessions for longer tests
❑ Use place markers, special paper, graph paper or writing templates to allow student to maintain position better or focus attention
❑ Provide cues; e.g., arrows and stop signs on worksheets and tests
❑ Provide a quiet, distraction-free area for completing assignments and tests
❑ Allow student to wear noise buffer device such as headphones to screen out distracting sounds
❑ Provide checklists for long, detailed assignments
	❑ Provide a written outline
	❑ Provide directions in written form
	❑ Provide a specific process for turning in completed assignments
	❑ Provide checklists for long, detailed assignments
	❑ Read and discuss standard directions several times at start of exam
	❑ Provide cues; e.g., arrows and stop signs on worksheets and tests
	❑ Allow student to use reference aids such as dictionaries, word processors or vocabulary cue cards

142

English Language Learners (ELL)

9

143

In teaching students who are learning English as another language, the big picture is the same as it is for all students. Teach every student based on his or her developmental and language proficiency level and identify and address the needs of each student.

English language learners have an immediate need to communicate with their English-speaking peers and teachers, and to do this they need to achieve fluency in the language. However, for most of these learners, basic interpersonal communication skills take about two-to-three years to develop, while academic language proficiency can take five-to-seven years. During that time, English language learners need additional support to access content while developing their language skills. This chapter provides information and strategies to help you support the learning of English language learners, as well as other students in the classroom, by differentiating instruction.

Purposeful planning

Effective instruction for English language learners needs to both support achievement of grade-level learning outcomes and promote language acquisition. All teachers, in all subject areas, share the responsibility for language development, out of both necessity (because students need to learn English to learn content) and best practice (because students learn English more easily and fully within an authentic context). Providing such instruction begins with the planning described in *Chapter 2: Purposeful Planning*. As you work through this planning process, consider how the following ideas may affect your instruction.

- **Culture and communication are inextricably bound**
  English language learners are not only learning a new language they are learning a new culture. You can support English language learners by providing opportunities to learn the cultural beliefs and practices of their English peers within authentic communication contexts. At the same time, English language learners also need to know that their own language and culture are valued. Providing opportunities for students to use their home language maintains a valuable link to the family and community.

- **Students' emotional well-being can affect their learning**
  Providing a safe and welcoming environment for English language learners is essential to their success. English language learners need to know that they are contributing members of the class. They need to know that their ability, prior lived experiences, and areas of interest and expertise are recognized and valued in the classroom and school community. Taking time to learn an English language learner's name (some names are written surname first) and how to pronounce it, as well as learning a few words in the student's language, are important first steps in making the student feel welcome. Also, consider ways to reduce stress for

English language learners, particularly in contexts when they are expected to participate in discussion; e.g., keeping group sizes small, allowing students time to prepare their contribution.

- **All learners need the opportunity to work from their strengths**
As with all students, English language learners are most motivated and engaged when they have opportunities to show their expertise, explore topics of interest and choose preferred learning modes. Experiencing success will increase student confidence and willingness to participate, which in turn promotes language development.

  It also is important to promote continuing development of the student's home language. Allowing students opportunities to read, write and speak in their home language gives them better access to their existing expertise and skills and allows their ideas to flow. Translating into English afterwards helps students begin to see the connection between their first language(s) and English. As students enhance literacy skills in their first language, those skills will eventually transfer to English.

- **Context-specific social language usually develops more quickly than academic language**
English language learners benefit from interactions with fluent English speakers. Through these interactions, they have the opportunity to negotiate meaning, communicate ideas and receive corrective feedback. Social acceptance is a motivator for learning a new language and can be fostered through a variety of activities and opportunities to interact with English-speaking students. For meaningful social interaction to occur, limit the amount of time that English language learners spend working in isolation with audio books or on the computer. Provide opportunities for students to work coperatively in partners and small groups.

Learner profiles

Like all students, English language learners are each unique, with their own experiences, abilities, knowledge and learning preferences. However, their shared experience of learning English as a second or third language is an important and useful starting point for differentiating instruction. In addition to the common elements of learner profiles, it is important to include English language learners' current level of English language proficiency.

145

Level 1	At this level of proficiency students may:
	– be self-conscious and confused
	– smile hesitantly
	– benefit from support of peer buddies
	– observe surroundings carefully
	– be silent for periods of the school day
	– use one- or two-word utterances in English
	– use pictures and gestures to support communication
	– rely on first language
	– read or write limited number of high-frequency utility words (e.g., exit, open, a bus #, etc.)
	– need support for writing
	– copy without understanding.
Level 2	At this level of proficiency students may:
	– begin to understand social norms such as eye contact and personal space
	– understand basic classroom activities with visual support
	– increase confidence in familiar classroom situations
	– respond to yes/no questions
	– label and use pictures to communicate
	– increase use of high-frequency utility words
	– begin to compile words and phrases for daily living (e.g., food, clothing)
	– know some subject-specific words and phrases
	– name letters and know most corresponding sounds
	– imitate and copy phrase and sentence patterns
	– increase sight word vocabulary
	– begin to write short sentences independently
	– use some writing conventions such as capital letters and periods.
Level 3	At this level of proficiency students may:
	– be confident enough to initiate conversations with English-speaking peers
	– begin to act as buddies to others
	– communicate competently in the classroom environment
	– respond to basic questions using simple sentences
	– use vocabulary competently for daily living
	– increase subject-specific vocabulary
	– experiment with synonyms and antonyms*
	– write simple sentences with minimal errors
	– experiment with longer sentences and basic paragraphs*
	– begin writing for academic purposes*
	– improve their use of writing conventions
	– be more comfortable expanding friendships beyond peers who speak their first language
	– understand most social conversations without support.

Level 4	At this level of proficiency students may: – adjust language depending on the communication context – be more comfortable expanding friendships beyond peers who speak their first language – understand most social conversations without support – understand most academic language with some support – contribute information on a variety of topics – respond to hypothetical questions – use subject-specific vocabulary in context – use specialized vocabulary associated with the subject area* – write a variety of texts independently* – experiment with sentence variety to develop personal style and voice* – use conventions more accurately.
Level 5	At this level of proficiency students may: – be confident and competent when communicating with teachers and peers – use English language to self-advocate – use English confidently and competently for academic purposes and to solve problems – may fluently switch between their first language and English – have fluent speech, which may be influenced by first language – transfer subject-specific vocabulary to a variety of contexts* – understand humour and figurative language* – write a variety of well-organized and unified texts* – vary sentence structure and use complex sentences to achieve a variety of purposes* – establish voice and style in writing* – use conventions consistently and with minimal errors – select specific words to achieve purpose.

* Characteristics of students of junior/senior high age.

The strategies presented throughout the rest of this chapter can be used to differentiate instruction and support English language learners as they move through these stages.

English as a second language proficiency benchmarks

Alberta Education has developed proficiency benchmarks for English as a second language. The benchmarks provide:

- the foundation for developing a common understanding of English language proficiency levels and English as a second language programming needs across the province
- descriptions of the English language abilities that students typically demonstrate at each of the five proficiency levels: Kindergarten, grades 1–3, grades 4–6, grades 7–9 and grades 10–12.

The benchmarks help teachers:

- support the initial identification of language proficiency levels
- guide appropriate programming for English language learners

- monitor, track and report language progress
- plan for language instruction within everyday classroom situations
- communicate with students and parents about language acquisition and set appropriate language learning goals.

A PDF version of benchmarks is available at http://education.alberta.ca/program/esl/resources.aspx. An interactive online version of the benchmarks is available on the LearnAlberta.ca Web site. Type keyword "ESL."

Assessment

Effective assessment strategies provide students with the opportunity to show what they know and can do. For English language learners, even more so than their classmates, this requires differentiating assessment through the use of supports and alternative assessment strategies. Assessment of English language learners should:
- remove language-related barriers as much as possible
- gather information from a variety of sources
- align with instructional practices used to teach the content
- document individual growth over time
- take into account student age and developmental level, grade level, learning preferences, language proficiency, cultural and educational backgrounds.

Sample assessment strategies that are often appropriate for English language learners include journals and learning logs, nonverbal communication strategies, and differentiated products.

Journals and learning logs
Journals and learning logs serve as valuable tools for assessing growth in English language proficiency. They also are places where English language learners can access their background knowledge, make connections between old and new learning, and reflect on what they have learned. Journals and learning logs can be used to consolidate and represent knowledge and ideas in a variety of ways. Differentiate for English language learners by allowing them to record their ideas using their first language, English words and phrases and/or illustrations.

Nonverbal communication strategies
Nonverbal assessment strategies are one way to allow English language learners to show what they know. Nonverbal assessment strategies allow students to give a physical or pictorial demonstration of their understanding. For example, teachers may have students:
- use gestures; e.g., respond to statements or scenarios with a thumbs up or thumbs down
- point to information or answers
- perform hands-on tasks; e.g., use manipulatives to demonstrate how to solve a math problem
- act out vocabulary, concepts or events

- produce drawings, models, graphs or charts
- manipulate visual information; e.g., place ready-made labels on a map, web or other graphic organizer.

Consider the following examples of differentiated products.

Grade and outcome	Typical product	Differentiated product
Mathematics, Grade 1 *Pose oral questions in relation to the data gathered.*	Gather and graph data and then pose questions to peers to test comprehension.	Create a pictorial graph to analyze a set of objects, then complete questions using stems or cloze provided by the teacher; e.g., _____ out of _____ blocks are red.
Language Arts, Grade 4 *Recognize how words and word combinations, such as word play, repetition and rhyme, influence or convey meaning.*	Explore fun uses of language in picture books and poetry and practice playing with language in their own writing.	Complete some basic rhyme recognition activities; e.g., circle the rhyming words in a poem and then think of more rhyming words.
Science, Grade 8 *Select and integrate information from various print and electronic sources or from several parts of the same source; e.g., summarize information on a river basin.*	Complete a written summary based on research in the library or computer laboratory.	Complete a cloze activity using facts from reading and their own science knowledge, then follow up by making a drawing or graphic representation of each fact.
Social Studies, Grade 7 *Recognize the positive and negative consequences of political decisions.*	Complete a "cause-and-effect graphic organizer."	Paste ready-made basic text with pictures into a "cause-and-effect graphic organizer."

149

Supports

English language learners benefit from a variety of supports in order to learn new skills and concepts. These same types of supports can be used in assessment situations to support English language learners and allow them to best demonstrate understanding. Examples of supports that can be used when learning new content include:

- providing models
- adjusting language level of content
- providing study notes (with visuals)
- providing extra practice
- assigning a reader buddy or peer tutor.

Supports that can be made to assignments and also used in assessment situations include:

- adjusting the length of material or the types of questions to be answered
- providing extra time
- allowing for an oral or visual product versus a written product
- providing extra assistance to read the material.

English language learners should be working toward the same learning outcomes as their same-aged peers; finding ways to support this is a major goal of differentiated instruction. Consider the following ideas.

Modified presentations

Aim to present new concepts in such a way that all students gain an appropriate degree of knowledge. This may include the following strategies.

- Begin instruction at the individual student's current level of functioning.
- Stand close to students who need extra help.
- Modify the pace of instruction.
- Give clear, simple directions.
- Speak at a slower pace, taking care to enunciate words.
- Write instructions, key ideas and vocabulary on the board with visuals to support understanding.
- Repeat and/or paraphrase concepts that are important or difficult, or ask students to do this.
- Demonstrate, model or act out instructions.
- Complete the first example with students.
- Ask students to retell and explain in their own words.
- Use different coloured chalk and pens to break up or categorize information.
- Break information and directions into small steps.
- Provide additional background information or context for learning activities.
- Provide additional time to preview materials or complete tasks.
- Use idioms carefully and explain them in simple terms.

- Use visuals, including maps, graphs and charts.
- Provide many examples. Look for examples that will be clear and relevant to students.
- Check for understanding on a regular basis.
- Teach important vocabulary. Identify common words that can appear in a variety of contexts (such as "left" in mathematics as in "after you subtract x, how many are *left*?").

Differentiated products

Differentiating the product means varying the type and complexity of the products that students create to demonstrate their learning. For example, graphic organizers are a useful way to assess student understanding without requiring extensive writing. Parts of the organizers can be completed in the student's first language or with illustrations. Allowing students choices for demonstrating their knowledge also can accommodate differing student abilities, interests and learning preferences.

Reading supports

It is essential to provide English language learners of all ages with reading supports to clarify and interpret written content. The ability to access content within their grade-level range and to be more independent readers contributes significantly to their success. Examples of reading supports include:
- partner reading
- guided reading in small groups
- recordings; e.g., books on tape, podcasts
- text-to-speech software
- bilingual dictionaries and software translation tools.

Nonlinguistic representations

Students create meaning through not only the spoken and written word but many other channels of communication. English language learners, in particular, require nonlinguistic representations, including hands-on experiences, demonstrations, real objects, body language, manipulatives and physical models, to supplement the verbal information they are receiving. English language learners can use nonlinguisitic representations to explore concepts. For example, using base-ten blocks in math, puzzles in social studies or building blocks in science. They also can use these modes to represent their knowledge. For example, after reading a story or novel in English language arts, students can create a drawing of the setting, a character or the conflict to demonstrate their understanding without having to reply only in words.

Using a variety of nonlinguistic representations allows English language learners to form mental images related to what they are learning and to elaborate on their knowledge. They can then access the information and connect it to prior experience and new learning. Nonlinguistic representation also can include artistic activities such as dance, mime, drawing, painting, masks and other art forms.

151

Artistic activities can be powerful modes of communication and allow students to use abstract, creative and other levels of thinking, even if knowledge of English is limited.

Advance organizers

Advance organizers help students make sense of new information they will be learning by focusing on, organizing and connecting important ideas.

- **"Expository organizers"** use a combination of words and visuals to provide students with a description of the new content they will be learning.
- **"Narrative organizers"** introduce new content about a story.
- **"Skimming strategies"** such as Survey, Question, Read, Recite, Review or SQ3R are a way for students to preview texts. This strategy is best taught through direct instruction, modelling and guided practice of each step. A textbook chapter organizer that combines pictures and words is another way to engage English language learners in the process of skimming.

Graphic organizers

Graphic organizers such as "K-W-L charts", "P-M-I charts", "mind maps" and others can be used across grades and subject areas to support English language learners in developing a deeper understanding of key concepts or ideas. Organizers allow English language learners to draw on prior experience and knowledge, form connections, and see relationships among ideas, while limiting the amount of text students have to deal with. Graphic organizer also provide a constant visual reference so students can focus on comprehension and language development rather than memory.

Using graphic organizers to teach new concepts is an effective way to engage students in discussions and have them learn the essential vocabulary in a meaningful context. At the beginning of a unit of study, give students a graphic organizer with main ideas included and ask them to add to the organizer as new information is gathered. Alternatively, at the beginning of a new topic, students can use their background knowledge and experience to organize what they already know about a topic and record it using words and/or pictures. Use this information to identify areas of strength and interest, as well as misconceptions related to the topic, and to plan learning activities with this information in mind.

Graphic organizers also can be used to summarize discussions, review key information and plan writing assignments and other projects.

The following sample idea builder shows how English language learners can complete graphic organizers using a combination of words and pictures. For more examples of graphic organizers to use with English language learners, see *English as a Second Language: Guide to Implementation, Kindergarten to Grade 9*, at http://education.alberta.ca/teachers/com/English language/resources.aspx.

Idea Builder[1]

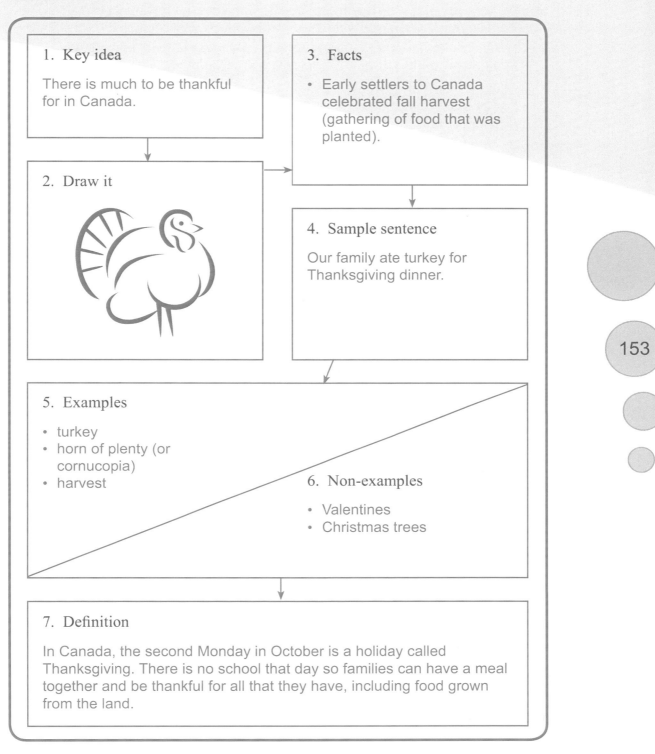

1. **Key idea**

There is much to be thankful for in Canada.

2. **Draw it**

3. **Facts**

- Early settlers to Canada celebrated fall harvest (gathering of food that was planted).

4. **Sample sentence**

Our family ate turkey for Thanksgiving dinner.

5. **Examples**

- turkey
- horn of plenty (or cornucopia)
- harvest

6. **Non-examples**

- Valentines
- Christmas trees

7. **Definition**

In Canada, the second Monday in October is a holiday called Thanksgiving. There is no school that day so families can have a meal together and be thankful for all that they have, including food grown from the land.

153

---

1. Form reproduced with permission from Edmonton Public Schools, *Thinking Tools for Kids: Practical Organizers* (Edmonton, AB: Resource Development Services, Edmonton Public Schools, 1999), p. 178.

Students need to be explicitly taught how to interpret graphic organizers, as well as how and why to use different organizers. Consider the following tips.

- Use graphic organizers to plan and introduce your lessons.
- Choose organizers that best represent the ideas or texts under study.
- Show examples of new organizers, and describe their purpose and form within the context of the lesson.
- Use easy and familiar material to model how to use organizers.
- Model organizers on the board, overhead or chart paper, using a "think-aloud" format.
- Give students opportunities to practice using the format with easy material, coaching them at various points in the process.
- Share final products, discuss what worked and what did not, and give students an opportunity to revise information.
- Provide students with many opportunities to practice using graphic organizers.
- Use graphic organizers with a range of topics and issues.
- Encourage students to evaluate which organizers work best in which learning situations.

Record keeping

Keeping track of the supports successfully used with English language learners provides valuable information to next year's teachers. Knowing what works for each student, and in which situations or courses, can support consistency, transfer of skills and a smooth transition from one year to the next. A sample record-keeping system follows.

Assessment supports for _____

Assessment Support (check each subject in which the accommodation is used)	Language Arts	Math	Social Studies	Science
Extra time				
Modified or adjusted questions				
Bilingual dictionary or word list				
Text-to-speech software				
Word processor with spell check				
Oral or visual presentation versions				
Reading buddies/peer tutors				
Exemplars, models and templates				

Meaningful and respectful activities

It is important to recognize that language ability is only one facet of a student's abilities. English language learners need the same opportunities for challenging, engaging, developmentally appropriate activities as other students. The activities you choose and how you differentiate these activities should communicate to students that they are capable of:

- becoming bilingual and biliterate
- using higher-order thinking
- using creative and imaginative thinking
- creating literature and art
- generating new knowledge
- thinking about and finding solutions to problems.[2]

Consider the following starting points.

Authentic contexts

Language acquisition requires the opportunity to use language in a way that is expressive, functional, personally relevant and representative of the way language is used in everyday settings. As you plan for instruction, seek ways to embed language instruction within authentic subject-area content and group interactions.

Relevant connections

It is important to use a variety of ways to activate students' background knowledge and to help them link what they are learning in English to that prior knowledge. For example, students may not have studied the influence of the new immigration on Canadian society, but they may have experienced the influence of another culture in their homeland and be able to talk about that.

English language learners benefit from opportunities to connect their prior lived experience to the things they are learning and the texts they are reading. For example, students studying Eva Ibbotson's *Journey to the River Sea* in Grade 8 English language arts have an opportunity to connect their own journey to Canada with Maia's journey to Brazil.

Provide English language learners with opportunities to use their first language, words and images to represent their connections. Double entry journals offer one framework in which to organize student connections between the text they are reading and their own experiences.

155

---

2. Adapted with permission from Jim Cummins, "Teaching and Learning in Multilingual Ontario" (webcast), *Curriculum Services Canada*, December 7, 2005, http://www.curriculum.org/secretariat/december7.shtml (Accessed January 2008), 52:40–54:12.

Areas of interest

Tapping into student interests is a key aspect of differentiating instruction. Helping English language learners connect learning to their areas of interest offers another way to build vocabulary and oral fluency in English. Focusing on areas of interest encourages motivation and purpose for learning correct grammatical form and new vocabulary.

"Silent periods" and "time outs from English"

Part of being respectful is not requiring new English language learners to speak before they are ready. Allow for a silent period during which these students will begin to acquire language by listening and understanding English. If possible, continue to allow periods of "time out from English" during which the English language learner can spend time talking with other students who share their native language. This provides an opportunity for them to ask questions and process what is going on in the classroom.

Differentiated resources

An integral component of differentiated instruction for English language learners is providing resources at varying reading levels. These resources can include a variety of text types, such as news articles, picture books, journal entries and web pages. Making a variety of resources available allows for differentiation and choice for all students, including English language learners. Providing English language learners with content-specific material at a level they can read successfully allows them to gain information and key vocabulary that may provide the scaffolding necessary for them to read a more challenging text. If possible, provide books in the first language of the English language learner to further support learning and making connections to the English content.

To help English language learners choose appropriate reading materials, teach strategies for selecting a book that is at their reading level. The five-finger rule is one way to test whether a book is the right level of difficulty for reading independently. Students read the first page of the book. Whenever they come to a word they do not know or are unsure of, they put up one finger. If all five fingers are up by the end of the page, the book is probably too challenging to be read independently at this point.

Look for opportunities to plan and share resources with other teachers who teach the same subject. Work together to find or create resources, or divide the core units for the year and then create and share resources. Examples of ways to simplify resources include:
- reducing the amount of text
- increasing the number of explanatory graphics such as pictures
- changing a paragraph to a diagram or chart.

Note-taking strategies

Note taking requires students to synthesize information and record it in their own words and, in turn, increases their understanding of the information. A variety of different note-taking formats may be used, depending on the task and the student.

- **"Webs" or "mind maps"** allow students to represent information using both words and pictures, making them a good starting point for English language learners.

- **"Informal outlines"** are more structured notes that organize information into main ideas and related details.

- **"Split page notes"** are one way to combine both the outline and visual representation in an organized way. This format allows students to record the main ideas and related details, together with a visual representation of the information.

To teach note-taking strategies, begin by providing English language learners with teacher-prepared notes as a model of good note taking. Have them engage with the information by finding or creating graphics to illustrate the notes. Ask students to add to and revise the notes as new information is learned, providing guidance and feedback as needed. As students improve their language fluency, move to teacher-prepared notes in a cloze format with key words missing, eventually progressing to student-created notes. Include space on a note-taking organizer for students to record a summary of the information and questions they have, providing further opportunities for them to consider and respond to the new information.

Flexible learning groups

As with other students in the class, English language learners will benefit most when you use a variety of criteria for organizing groups. Consider the following points for grouping students.

- Organize small groups containing both English language and native English speakers, to increase the opportunity for peer tutoring and support. This kind of grouping assists English language learners in negotiating meaning while presenting natural opportunities for English-speaking peers to scaffold language development. Assign roles and tasks for group members.

- Consider grouping English language learners who have the same first language as one group when it is necessary to clarify content and discuss concepts at a deeper level.

- Keep learning groups small when possible. Small groups of three or four increase the amount of talk time for each student and allow the English language learner to feel more comfortable contributing to the discussion.

- Use cooperative learning groups intermittently. Varying instruction to include explicit instruction and structured application gives English language learners time to practice skills and processes independently.

The following sample strategies support comprehension and language development within flexible grouping structures, including partner work, independent work and working in small groups.

"Say something" strategy

"Say something" is a partner reading strategy in which English language learners practise both reading text material aloud and responding to material that is read to them.

Partner 1 – reads a short section of text material
Partner 2 – says something about what Partner 1 read; for example:
- summary of the ideas
- a question about the material
- a prediction of what will come next
Partner 2 – reads the next short section of text material
Partner 1 – says something about what Partner 2 read.

"Do now" activities

Establish activities that students are expected to do immediately upon entering the classroom. "Do now" can be used across grades to reinforce self-directed behaviour and provide natural opportunities for individuals or small groups of students to do targeted learning activities. Examples of "do now" activities include:
- reading
- journaling
- drawing
- problem-solving activities
- vocabulary activities.

"Do now" activities provide English language learners with an opportunity to focus on skill development. They also can provide the teacher with time to work with an individual or a small group of English language learners while the other students are working independently.

Learning centres

Learning centres are organized, self-contained collections of resources and materials that complement curricular topics. English language learners can use learning centres to work on language skills and to engage in social interaction with their peers. Examples of learning centres include:
- skills-based games; e.g., spelling, basic math facts, matching
- content review; e.g., crossword puzzles, flash cards
- manipulatives; e.g., fraction puzzles, models.

Cooperative learning

Cooperative learning groups foster language acquisition by creating authentic and supportive opportunities for English language learners to use language and

158

interact with fluent English speakers. They provide a motivating, developmentally appropriate and feedback-rich context. Students working in cooperative learning groups naturally adjust their language to make sure other group members can understand them. There is a common goal to be achieved and doing so requires students to negotiate meaning.

Given the less formal, more expressive use of language in the cooperative group, English language learners have an opportunity to use language that they are comfortable with. They also receive more feedback. In a typical 20-minute, whole-class interaction, a student may have one feedback opportunity. In a 20-minute cooperative interaction, a student may receive as many as six feedback opportunities, all of them in a natural context that reduces self-consciousness and anxiety. In this way, they are supported in moving beyond the language they can use independently to using more complex and challenging forms. Finally, in cooperative learning groups, English language learners hear the same information discussed using a variety of phrases. This improves understanding and allows students to move the learning from short-term comprehension to long-term acquisition.

Think-pair-share

"Think-pair-share" is a cooperative learning strategy that provides opportunities for students to participate, learn from others and make connections. In "think-pair-share", you pose a topic or question. Students think about the question on their own for a given amount of time (usually one-to-three minutes), and then discuss their thoughts in pairs. Finally, each pair has an opportunity to share their answers with the whole class.

Literature circles

A "literature circle" is a student-centred reading activity that can be used at any grade level. Small groups of four-to-six students are organized based on book choice, with different groups reading different books. Forming groups based on text choice allows for shared interests and varied achievement and ability levels. Each member is assigned a role (e.g., illustrator, questioner, recorder, etc.), which helps guide the group in a discussion of the book they are all reading. Students then share their thoughts, concerns and understanding about the novel. Literature circles:

- allow English language learners various entry points into the discussion based on the roles they are assigned (for example, the illustrator role offers students the opportunity to contribute nonverbally, while still giving them the option to describe what they draw or explain how it connects to the text)
- foster and deepen reading comprehension, motivation and interest
- encourage English language learners to use English to inform, describe, explain, clarify, generalize, synthesize, and compare and contrast
- provide supportive opportunites to practise the planning, modelling and

scaffolding required during conversation

- offer a wide range of literature options, differing in readability, interest, genre and content, as well as opportunities to tie-in directly with content and vocabulary from other curricular areas
- allow for the use of supports such as audio books, reading with a partner, choral reading, reading at home and re-reading to improve fluency and, in turn, comprehension.

Scaffolded instruction

Once you know a student's current stage of language development, it is possible to work at a level *between* what the student is capable of at the moment and the point you want the student to reach next. By modelling correct grammar or pronunciation, asking challenging questions or providing direct instruction, you can scaffold the language development of English language learners. For example, if a student is using nonverbal communication, such as pointing and circling responses, scaffolding occurs when that student is supported in his or her attempts to answer yes/no questions, give one word responses or complete a sentence starter.

Simple sentence starters, like the examples below, are a good way to scaffold English language learners in moving toward the next level of English language fluency.

I live in …
I am in Grade …
At recess, I like to …
My new friends are …

Language experience approach
A "language experience approach" uses dictated language of students to create a learning context to explore reading and writing.

For example:
1. The teacher creates an opportunity for students to recount personal experiences.
2. The teacher records the students' stories word-for-word.
3. The teacher and students review the word-for-word transcripts focusing on vocabulary and syntax, and revise content as needed.
4. The students copy the revised stories and draw pictures to illustrate the content.
5. The students revisit these revised stories for both instruction and independent reading.

The language experience approach creates opportunities for students to experience what it is like to express themselves with enhanced clarity.

Tiered assignments

Tiered assignments are made up of different sections, or alternate assignments that allow students to address the same content but with different levels of support, challenge and complexity. For example, instead of answering questions in complete sentences, some students complete a cloze activity. Tiered assignments offer English language learners an entry point into the content being learned and an opportunity to successfully demonstrate their understanding of that content.

Tiered questions

Tiered questions are meant to allow all students the opportunity to be successful responders. The questions should be based on the language stages of various students in the class and phrased to maximize the ways students can respond. A progression of tiered questions may look like the following.[3]

Language stage	Sample type of question
Level 1: Pre-production	Show me … Point to … Circle the …
Level 2: Early Production	Yes/no Either/or One- or two-word answers Lists Labels
Level 3: Speech Emergence	Why …? How …? Explain … Phrase or short sentence answers
Level 4: Intermediate Fluency	What would happen if …? Why do you think …?
Level 5: Advanced Fluency	Decide if … Retell …

Choosing the right level of questions requires an understanding of an individual student's current level of language proficency. Decide which level a particular student can respond to successfully and plan the questions to be asked accordingly. Ask questions frequently throughout the learning activity, maximizing the English language learner's opportunity to respond and, in turn, gain confidence. Wait at least six to 10 seconds after asking the question to give students sufficient time to formulate their response and to think about how they are going to say it in English.

---

3. Chart adapted from Jane D. Hill and Kathleen M. Flynn, *Classroom Instruction that works with English Language Learners* (Alexandria, VA: Association for Supervision and Curriculum Development, 2006), p. 15. © by Mid-continent Research for Education and Learning (McREL). Adapted with permission.

Frequent feedback

Timely, relevant, corrective feedback is an important way to help English language learners move to the next stage of language development. Modelling correct English is some of the most valuable feedback English language learners receive. Formative feedback about how the English language learner is progressing in using correct grammar and pronunciation is more effective than providing a numerical mark reflecting correctness. As English language learners develop their language skills, they can begin to reflect on and assess their own progress in both academic and language learning. Rubrics provide one way for this to happen as rubrics outline expectations and allow English language learners to assess their performance against these expectations.

Language and literacy instruction

As well as the language instruction provided to the class as a whole, English language learners also need strategies, tools and supports specific to their individual language and literacy needs.

"Word banks" and "word walls"

Creating "word banks" or "word walls" of frequently used or subject-specific vocabulary provides English language learners with an easy-to-access reference. When possible, pair words with a related picture. Create a word wall to reflect the English language learner's developing vocabulary. Post the words in a way that allows them to be removed for reference or reorganization. Organizing word banks and word walls by topic (e.g., trees and forests, fractions, Renaissance Europe) helps students understand the relationships between and among words and ideas.

Use the word wall as part of regular language learning activities. For example, add a word whenever a student asks for the meaning of an unfamiliar word or seeks a word to help express himself or herself. Organize and reorganize the wall based on instructional focus (e.g., organize by spelling pattern, phonemes, rhyme, meaning, usage) over time.

Create portable word pockets (by creating an extra copy of each word posted on the word wall) and storing the words in an envelop or pouch under the appropriate heading. The words are then available for students to take for sorting activities or to use for spelling reference during writing activities.

Bilingual dictionaries

An English/home language dictionary is an important tool for English language learners to access when reading and writing in a variety of contexts. Student-created bilingual dictionaries allow English language learners to draw on their first language and prior experience to connect background knowledge with new learning.

162

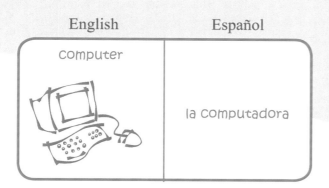

English   Español

computer

la computadora

Vocabulary and key concepts

Direct vocabulary instruction, including word analysis and instruction of essential vocabulary, improves reading comprehension for English language learners (Carlo et al. 2004; McLaughlin et al. 2000). Select key vocabulary related to the topics being studied and provide opportunities to teach that vocabulary and to use the vocabulary in a variety of contexts in order to deepen student understanding of the word meanings.

Teach student strategies for dealing with unfamiliar vocabulary in the texts they are reading. One such strategy is "read around."[4]
1. Skip the word and read to the end of the sentence.
2. Go back and read the whole sentence again.
3. Look at the beginning of the word for letter-sound clues.
4. Think, "What word would fit here?"
5. Try out the word in the sentence: Does the word *sound* right? Does this word make *sense*? Does this word match the *letter clues*?
6. Look at the picture for a clue.
7. Ask someone.

Cloze

"Cloze" activities involve the omission of letters in words or words in sentences where students have to figure out what letters or words are missing. Cloze activities promote sense-making skills and reflection on the rules of language. They also are a great tool for reinforcing content-area learning in a way that reinforces the related language. Cloze passages can be differentiated to meet the language-level needs of various English language learners in the class.

To create a **"letter-level cloze"**, select high-frequency words from students' oral vocabulary, classroom word walls or from reading material and reproduce them with key letters missing. Begin by following a consistent pattern; e.g., remove the short vowel sound from single-syllable words, remove the ending consonant.

---

4. Adapted with permission from Dana Antayá-Moore and Catherine M. Walker, *Smart Learning: Strategies for Parents, Teachers and Kids* (Edmonton, AB: Smart Learning, 1996), p. 16.

163

Students should know what word they are trying to make either because it has been vocalized or because it is within a familiar context; e.g., a sentence from a story. As students become more adept, focus on English words that are easily confused; e.g., "then" and "than." This strategy works well as part of a "mystery message" written on the board each morning as a "do now" activity.

"Word prints" are spatial representations of missing letters that can help students progress from letter-level to word-level cloze activities. Word prints are sets of boxes that represent the shape of each letter and, together, represent the shape of the word. Word prints allow students to become familiar with using visual strategies to assist with spelling. Small square boxes that "sit on the line" represent vowels and squat consonants, rectangular boxes that "hang below the line" represent descending consonants, and rectangular boxes that "stand tall" represent ascending consonants.

To create **"word-level cloze"** activities, select sentences from student reading or language-experience stories (short pieces of writing dictated by the student) and reproduce them with key words missing. Begin by following a consistent pattern; e.g., remove adjectives. Students should be able to use the context of the sentence to figure out a word that makes sense. Early on, it is advisable to provide students with a bank of possible words to choose from and to have no distracters (words that will not be used) in it.

"Cloze passages" also can be used to model question-answer techniques and to summarize information learned. In both cases, it is important to ensure the cloze passage has direct correlations to original text or learned material; for example, that information is presented in the same order and the same vocabulary is used.

Guided writing
Students should be taught to write in a variety of forms, especially those that may be needed in later life, such as letters and expository text. Assist English language learners in developing an effective and repeatable process they can use to create each form. Within that process, provide them with strategies to ensure that they consistently apply the rules of language, including grammar.

Begin with language experience stories where students write about personal experiences or topics of interest. Then, have them branch out into new and more creative topics, such as writing in response to reading. By working through the process of planning, drafting, revising and editing, you can address vocabulary and grammar concerns specific to each student within the context of real writing. This is especially important for students with limited instruction in writing in their first language.

164

Correction and revision

Initially, all students need to get their intended message down on paper without being overly concerned about mechanics. Teacher-student conferencing during several rewritings then can help the student communicate more clearly in developing a product that can be a source of pride. With English language learners, it is important to limit the focus of error correction to one or two points at each stage of the revision process. Too much correction will be overwhelming and students will not retain explanations. Once the organization and intent of the writing is clear, attention can be given to grammar, especially verb tenses, which take a long time to master. Selecting the most appropriate vocabulary may be the next priority, followed by refining the use of articles and prepositions. Spelling errors can be left until the final stages. It may be helpful to explain this process to older students so they understand that they will be gradually correcting and revising errors.

Most of students' explicit learning about grammar and spelling arises from writing-conferencing time. This also is the best time to point out the positive aspects of each student's work.

When marking errors in written work, differentiate the level of support based on English language proficiency. The support strategies below move from much support to minimal support.

1. Circle or underline each error and write the correction symbol above it.
2. Highlight the error without supplying the symbol.
3. Write only the symbol in the margin of any line with this error.
4. Put only a check in the margin indicating that there is an error of some sort.[5]

Spelling

Spelling is best taught within the context of real writing tasks. Students who are older and already know the rules of their first language also may benefit from direct instruction in the general rules of English spelling along with related strategies.

Individualized spelling lists can be pulled from:
- students' personal lists of spelling words
- words that students are using in their daily writing
- content words that are being used in different subject areas
- a teacher-written passage that includes many examples of a specific spelling pattern or rule
- high-frequency word lists.

5. Adapted from Susan Earle-Carlin, "Providing Language Feedback in Writing 39," *Program in Academic English/English Language, University of California, Irvine*, n.d., https://eee.uci.edu/programs/English language/feedback.html (Accessed June 2009).

165

Invented spelling

Asking a beginning English language learner to use "sounding out" as a strategy to find the spelling of a word is often very frustrating, because a sound in the student's first language may not have a corresponding sound in English. It takes time for students to learn to hear the difference, so that they can eventually use sounding out as a spelling strategy.

English language learners can use invented or temporary spelling approximations quite successfully with some initial support from the teacher and their peers. It may be necessary to work closely with students during several writing sessions, including scribing dictated stories, so that they understand the process and trust that their invented symbols and spelling are accepted.

Students may be encouraged to use a straight line or a wiggly line when there are whole words or parts of words that they cannot spell, or they can be encouraged to write one letter for a sound they can hear. They also may want to write the word in their first language or use drawings or symbols.

166

Spelling folders

Make and laminate individual folding cards. Inside each card, students write words they are having difficulty with, then practice with the "look-say-cover-write-check" strategy.

Must spell lists

Have individualized "must spell" lists for each student. Posted on the desk, this list of eight to 10 high-frequency words are words that the student is responsible for spelling correctly in his or her daily writing. A must spell list might include a list of high-frequency words students tend to use in their writing, such as:

about	are	because	been	does
felt	from	girl	heard	here
just	know	like	little	looked
make	next	now	our	said
saw	there	they	their	write

Best try

When English language learners ask how to spell a word, encourage them to give it their best try to spell the word on their own. This "best try" approach encourages ownership for learning and active problem solving. If the spelling attempt is incorrect, the best try allows the adult editor to see the approximate spelling and comment on the parts of the word that are correct. It also may give clues about the writer's specific spelling difficulties, and common patterns that are causing problems may become obvious. When giving the correct spelling, write it down and spell it out loud;

e.g.,   student writes "ntelligent"
          teacher writes "intelligent."

Technology for learning

Technology for learning can provide English language learners with support in reading, writing, clarifying and interpreting written content, and enable them to better access content that is within their grade and language proficency level range. When choosing and implementing technology, consider students current comfort and skill level with technology, and whether support may be needed.

Technology for Learning for English Language Learnerss	
Multiple Means of Representation (acquiring knowledge and information)	
Audio supports	Audio tools (e.g., digital books, talking books, e-books, books on tape, music CDs, radio, sound files, podcasts, telephone) allow English language learners to practise listening to a wide range of voices and to develop an ear for the language. It also can provide opportunities for the student to replay and review content.
Video supports	Video tools (e.g., television broadcasts, movies, video files, documentaries) allow English language learners to experience speakers with different styles of nonverbal communication. Video images give context to the audio, making it easier to decipher meaning.
Transcripts and captions	Transcripts, captions and audiovisual descriptions provide access to content for students with limited English because they are able to read along for better understanding or further clarification.
Text-to-speech software	Text-to-speech software programs, such as *Read, Write & Gold*, read text and often include other assistive features such as word prediction and dictionaries. Some text-to-speech software programs have built-in scanning functions to convert print into a digital format. Students are supported by having the text highlighted as they listen to it being read. Other supports often built into text-to-speech software programs include speech feedback, screen reading, a phonetic spell checker, word prediction, a thesaurus, study skills and research tools.

167

Graphic supports	Content can be presented with picture symbols to support reading development. *Boardmaker* is a communication and learning tool containing over 4500 picture communication symbols (PCS). It is a tool teachers can use to enhance the language and learning process for students of all levels. This software enables the creation of printed, symbol-based educational materials with PCS and other pictures and graphics in 42 languages.

Multiple Means of Expression (demonstrating what they know)

Word processing	Word-processing tools allow English language learners to create organized, easy-to-read documents. Word-processing tools help writers focus on: • generating and clarifying meaning • managing ideas and information • structuring texts in a variety of ways • revising, editing and improving style • targeting presentations for particular needs and audiences. Some word-processing programs provide additional supports, such as customized word or sentence banks. Some provide the opportunity for teachers to add graphic supports to these banks. These programs allow students to see and hear words and phrases prior to choosing them for their writing. These supports may allow students to use vocabulary at a complex level.
Blogs	Blogs allow students to share their thoughts and ideas and meet and interact with people around the world, exposing them to authentic uses of the language.
Spell checkers	Several tools that can help English language learners, who have difficulty spelling, include hand-held devices and software applications or features within writing software programs. Some programs with spell checking offer additional supports such as: • homonym support • talking spell checkers • spell checkers linked to a dictionary • phonetic-based spell checkers.

168

Multiple Means of **Expression** (demonstrating what they know) (continued)	
Word prediction	Sometimes students know what they want to write but have difficulty forming the words or thinking of new words to use. Word prediction programs are used with word processors to provide an efficient way to produce written work. These programs predict what words users intend to write, based on the first letters typed, rules of English grammar and frequency of use. Rather than typing a whole word, users can type the first letter or first few letters and choose from a list of predictions. Other features of these programs may include spell checking as students type and spoken feedback.
Visual organizers	Software applications allow students to organize information in a variety of ways. Students can add interests and further information, and convey meaning with fewer words, by incorporating graphics, charts and diagrams. Technology can play an important role in making connections for understanding. For example, graphic organizers constructed with *Inspiration* serve as a visual tool to help students see the relationships among concepts and how they connect to one another. Visualization allows students to become active researchers and comprehend abstract concepts. One of the advantages of using technology is the opportunity to provide visual context.
Electronic dictionaries	Electronic dictionaries are written especially for English language learners. The two types are online dictionaries (with helpful illustrative sentences and extensive definition entries) and pocket automatic bilingual dictionaries that are completely portable. Some electronic dictionaries reference grammar, pronunciation and common errors and allow students to: • click on a word or phrase to have it repeated • see related pictures or video clips • read related texts. Electronic dictionaries are faster to use than print dictionaries and also have helpful features, such as cross-referencing and word and spelling games.

169

Multiple Means of **Engagement** (tapping into interests and preferences)	
World Wide Web	The World Wide Web allows students to access culturally relevant information, such as stories translated from students' first languages and news articles related to cultures. For example, *Bookbox.com* offers children's digital books in more than 21 languages. Download of stories are available for purchase and can be previewed for free online. Some Web site content may not be appropriate or may be at reading levels that are too advanced. Teachers should follow the Internet protocols of their schools and need to be selective when choosing web content for their students. Text-to-speech software can support students using Web sites.
E-mail pen pals	Students can practise their writing and communication skills with e-mail pen pals. Several Web sites help to connect students and support use of this medium.
Multimedia	Using digital photos and video editing programs, students can create multimedia projects. When students are engaged in activities like these they are constructing their own knowledge, with the teacher acting as a facilitator.
	Software that provides an avenue for artistic expression (e.g., drawing programs, music-creation programs, graphic-design programs) also may be helpful in supporting students with diverse learning preferences.

For more information and strategies for teaching English language learners, see:
- *English as a Second Language: Guide to Implementation, Kindergarten to Grade 9* (2007), http://education.alberta.ca/media/507659/English languagekto9gi.pdf
- Chapter 6 of the language and culture 9-year program guides to implementation for grades 4, 5 and 6; e.g., *Spanish Language and Culture 9-year Program Guide to Implementation, Grades 4–5–6* (2008), http://education.alberta.ca/teachers/program/interlang/spanish/spanlc4to6.aspx.

Students who are Gifted

Contents of this chapter

10

171

"To make forward progress from what they know to what they don't know yet, students who are gifted need differentiation. For these students, differentiation may mean different tasks and activities than their age peers—rich and meaningful tasks that lead to real learning."
– David Harvey, Consultant for Gifted Education

Many students who are gifted require differentiated programming and supports to meet their exceptional learning needs. The strategies and information in this chapter are based on findings from the research on giftedness and gifted education.

For a summary of research completed by the Centre for Gifted Education at the University of Calgary, visit Alberta Education's Web site at http://education. alberta.ca/apps/aisi/literature/ and click on Student Groups, then choose Understanding Giftedness, 2005.

Purposeful planning

With thoughtful planning, the provincial, standardized grade-level programs of study can be the beginning point for differentiating instruction that will provide appropriate challenge and support for students who are gifted. Students who demonstrate that they already know some content or are able to learn the content in much less time than their classmates, will benefit from content differentiation. Differentiating content for students who are gifted means creating opportunities within specific learning outcomes to explore a concept or skill in greater depth or breadth. The goal of differentiating for students who are gifted is to more deeply engage these students and maximize their learning potential.

Students who are gifted may demonstrate high ability in a single subject, more than one subject or in certain parts of several subjects. If what the student needs to learn, relative to his or her area of strength, is not within the instructional plans for the class then, without differentiation, that student may be the one in the class who learns the least.

There are a number of ways to differentiate content for students who are gifted, including making content and related learning activities more:
- abstract
- complex
- interrelated
- constrained (Harvey 2000, pp. 70–71).

These strategies also may be used in conjunction with flexible pacing.

Making content more abstract

Abstract content focuses less on specific, factual information and more on concepts and generalizations. Building on abstraction means encouraging students to consider ideas in general terms, and to move more fluidly between facts and broad understandings. For example, a student who is gifted in math could quickly move beyond manipulatives into identifying patterns and relationships. Artistic representations can challenge students to explore and synthesize concepts in abstract terms. For example, students could identify patterns and relationships through a dance, song or theatrical presentation. Thinking in more abstract terms can provide greater challenge and complexity for students.

Making content more complex

Content can be made more complex by introducing additional variables, other considerations, different sources and alternate viewpoints to a learning task. The original content remains, but is compared, contrasted or combined with other information or concepts. For example, a basic learning activity of surveying the class to find out how many students come to school by walking, biking, bussing or car could be made more complex by asking students to gather additional information in the survey and use this to compare distance from school with various modes of transport.

Making content interrelated

Students who are gifted often spot the potential for applying ideas or methods from one field of study to others. Build on this ability by looking for potential connections from one subject to the next, and challenging students to use knowledge, processes and skills in different combinations. For example, students could take science knowledge about weather and climate, and use it in a social studies inquiry about how people adapt to their environment.

Interrelatedness also can be explored across space or time. For example, students could be challenged to think about how humans adapt to their physical environments across geographic regions or what meaning humans have ascribed to weather conditions throughout history.

Making content more constrained

Interestingly enough, making content more constrained can sometimes present as many worthwhile challenges as making it more complex. By lessening the degrees of freedom in an activity, it is possible to concentrate students' focus and encourage them to go more deeply into a particular aspect of a learning outcome. For example, a basic assignment to write a poem about traffic during rush hour could be channeled into a more constrained assignment of writing the poem only about the traffic sounds during rush hour.

173

Flexible pacing

Often students who are gifted may benefit from moving through grade-level learning outcomes at a different rate than classmates. Flexible pacing can take a variety of forms, including:

- allowing students to complete some outcomes more quickly in order to spend additional time on more challenging outcomes and related activities
- allowing students to do a deeper exploration of specific learning outcomes that are especially meaningful to them
- moving students to an appropriate starting point in the program of studies based on pre-testing
- streamlining how a student moves through the program of studies to eliminate repetition of previously learned materials.

The goal of these flexible pacing strategies is to provide opportunities for students to spend more time on outcomes and activities that will enrich their learning.

Consider the following approach.

1. Identify learning objectives for the whole class according to the program of studies.
2. Pre-test the entire class to identify students who would benefit from an opportunity to work at a faster or more independent pace or at a deeper, more abstract level.
3. Plan appropriate enrichment or challenging activities for those students who require them.
4. Eliminate unnecessary review and practice activities for those students who have mastered the material.
5. Keep accurate records of activities and assessments to ensure individual students have the opportunity to explore and apply all learning outcomes.

For more information on planning, see *Chapter 2: Purposeful Planning*.

Learner profiles

Each student who is gifted has an individual profile of abilities, needs, interests and learning preferences. However, there are a number of general characteristics and developmental issues that often are associated with giftedness and that have important implications for learning. Common intellectual characteristics of students who are gifted include:

- advanced intellectual achievement
- high motivation and interest
- verbal proficiency
- problem-solving ability
- logical thinking
- creativity.

Some of these characteristics appear in students at all ability levels, but they are more prevalent and more pronounced in students who are gifted. Being aware of these characteristics can help you develop a more accurate and relevant learner profile for each student. Other elements that may be particularly important for the learner profiles of these students are developmental issues, learning difficulties and strengths. For more information on learner and class profiles, see *Chapter 3: Developing Learner Profiles*.

Developmental issues

Typical developmental issues faced by all students also are experienced by students who are gifted. These issues may be complicated by the exceptional learning needs and characteristics many students who are gifted demonstrate, particularly during adolescence. Students who are gifted may face a variety of challenges, including perfectionism, underachievement, uneven or asynchronous development and learning difficulties. For some students who are gifted, a combination of characteristics may lead to difficulties with peer relations, avoidance of risk taking or excessive self-criticism.

Students who may be more at risk emotionally, socially and academically include:
- divergent thinkers who suggest ideas that are logical to them but unusual to classmates
- creative high achievers, particularly those with artistic gifts, who may experience feelings of isolation or depression, and, as a result, may be subject to anxiety, insomnia, feelings of worthlessness, loss of energy or decreased ability to concentrate.

For more information and sample strategies that teachers and parents can use to help students who are gifted manage common developmental issues, see *The Journey: A Handbook for Parents of Children who are Gifted and Talented* (Alberta Learning, 2004), available at http://education.alberta.ca/admin/special/resources/journey.aspx.

Perfectionism

Perfectionism is a pattern of characteristics and behaviours that includes compulsiveness about work habits, over concern for details, unrealistically high standards and rigid routines. Perfectionism can develop at various stages of development for various reasons, but for many students it is simply a part of their personality, not necessarily the result of parental pressure or any other outside influence. Perfectionism can be thought of as part of the experience of being gifted, which can be used in a positive way to achieve excellence.

However, perfectionism can become a serious issue for some students. To monitor the effects of perfectionism, teachers and parents need to ask questions like, "Are these attitudes and behaviours barriers for this student?" and "Do they prevent this student from experiencing success and happiness?"

175

Perfectionism may be creating problems if the student:

- feels like he or she never does things well enough
- sets unrealistic standards based on his or her advanced reasoning ability even though other skill areas may not be as well developed
- feels inferior or defeated if he or she does not meet these high standards
- becomes so terrified of doing something wrong, he or she refuses to try new things and actually accomplishes very little
- in extreme cases, develops compulsive behaviours that require professional medical or psychological assistance.

Use patience and understanding to positively channel a student's perfectionism. Other considerations include the following.

- Be aware of expectations that you create for the student. Ensure they are reasonable and allow the student to be an individual, to express himself or herself and to make mistakes.
- Help students set reasonable and reachable goals and expectations.
- Help students develop time management skills.
- Help students develop an understanding of perfectionism and how it affects others.
- Create a safe environment in which mistakes are part of learning and students feel supported, no matter what.

Underachievement

In relation to giftedness, the term underachievement describes the performance of students whose achievement level at school falls far below their cognitive ability. This discrepancy is not caused by an underlying learning disability, attention deficit/hyperactivity disorder or any other disorder that may be affecting their achievement. Rather, students underachieve in school for a variety of social and emotional reasons. Some specific causes of underachievement in students who are gifted include:

- poor self-image
- lack of a future vision or dream to work toward
- problems within the family that divert student thinking and effort
- feelings of anxiety
- the desire to fit in with their peer group
- the desire to rebel
- the desire to avoid participating in special programming
- feelings of stress based on the need to please others or their own unrealistic expectations
- disinterest in subject-area topics and related learning activities
- work that is too easy or too difficult
- work that is meaningless and repetitive to the student
- fear of failure.

Underachievement can manifest in various ways in the classroom. Students who underachieve can be disruptive or withdrawn. They may engage in power struggles with their teachers or they may become apathetic, surrendering their passion for learning and not completing tasks. One of the most serious consequences of underachievement is early school leaving. A common assumption is that boredom with schoolwork is the cause of underachievement, and that the solution is to increase the difficulty and workload for the student. However, this approach can be counterproductive for students who are already disengaged. It is important that students have meaningful and challenging work to do at school and receive appropriate guidance and support at home.

To help students overcome underachievement, consider the following:
- provide ongoing support and encouragement
- help students understand the connection between effort and results
- involve students in setting realistic and meaningful goals for learning.

Asynchronous development
Asynchrony is uneven development in the rates of intellectual, emotional and physical development. Asynchronous development can be a characteristic of students who are gifted. This means students may:
- feel out-of-sync with same-age peers and age-appropriate learning activities and topics
- demonstrate different maturity levels in different situations, which could result in difficulties adjusting emotionally and socially.

These tendencies can increase with the student's degree of giftedness, and can make students vulnerable to feelings of frustration and social isolation. Students who experience asynchronous development respond best to a sensitive and flexible approach to instruction. The greatest need of students who experience asynchronous development is a caring and supportive learning environment where it is safe to be different.

Learning difficulties
Some students who are gifted also may have learning difficulties such as specific learning disabilities, attention deficit/hyperactivity disorder or Asperger's syndrome. These twice-exceptional students often have difficulty reaching an academic level that matches their measured potential, and their giftedness may go unrecognized or be ignored.

Students who are simultaneously gifted and have a disability can pose a special challenge for both teachers and parents. It is important to recognize and understand this dual exceptionality and collaborate with parents, other teachers and the student to ensure that instruction addresses both their exceptional strengths and their exceptional needs.

177

Identification of strengths

For students who are gifted, learning needs often are related to strengths rather than defects or weaknesses. A need can be an extension of a strength or can involve learning to use a strategy to support that strength. It is essential to use multiple sources of information to identify an individual student's strengths and areas of need. As much as possible, involve students in the process, so they begin to identify and understand their own strengths and interests. Look for ways to identify not only academic needs but also social, emotional and psychological needs that affect learning.

Consider the following types of questions.
- What strengths and talents does this student demonstrate?
- What is happening now in the student's educational programming?
- What led to this student being identified as gifted?
- What kind of data will give a fuller picture of this student; e.g., academic, social, emotional, psychological?
- What do this student's particular interests and accomplishments tell us about this student's learning needs?
- How can information about the student's abilities, interests and motivation inform differentiated instruction?

There are a wide variety of tools and strategies that students can use to identify and assess their own strengths, needs and areas of interest. Creating opportunities for students to explore their own strengths will help students learn about themselves and advocate for their own exceptional education needs.

Assessment

Students who are gifted require differentiated assessment strategies in order to accurately demonstrate what they know and can do, and to allow you to make effective decisions about future instruction. These students need assessment tasks that generate rich, dynamic and valid data to gauge progress and inform programming decisions for individual students. For information on assessment, see *Chapter 4: Differentiated Assessment*.

Assessment for instructional planning

Students who are gifted often have pre-existing knowledge that overlaps with learning outcomes in the provincial grade-level program of studies. Assessing students at the start of a new term or unit allows you to determine their background knowledge, existing understandings and readiness related to new content. This information is vital in making decisions about whether and how to differentiate content and instruction.

Assessment *for* learning

Differentiating assessment for students who are gifted often involves making these students more active partners in their own assessment process. Consider ways to involve students in developing and using criteria or rubrics to reflect on their own work and make adjustments throughout the learning process. Learning logs, journals, portfolios and other interactive strategies also can be used to differentiate the assessment process.

Information used for assessment *for* learning should be descriptive and framed in the context of coaching, self-assessment and reflection. The main purpose is to help students learn and grow, so they can keep themselves motivated and challenged.

Assessment *of* learning

Students who are gifted often require opportunities to create differentiated products in order to fully demonstrate their thinking and learning. Differentiated products may include written, oral, manipulative, discussion, display, dramatization, artistic, graphic representation and service learning. For example, writing assignments may not be the best way for some students to show their learning. Some students may think quicker than their hands can write. An action product, such as a multimedia slide show, or a dramatic performance, could be a better type of learning experience for these students.

Students who are gifted often benefit from producing "real-life products" for real audiences. These products go beyond the typical research paper or report to alternatives that develop individual students' talents and curiosities, and can be shared and used by others. Consider ways that alternate products could be used to:
- broaden the range of student experiences
- expand students' ways of learning and of expressing themselves
- challenge students in their areas of strength
- create opportunities for students to explore hidden talents and use gifts they might not otherwise use
- allow students to learn in a deeper and more advanced way through their preferred learning style.

Whatever products students develop, think carefully about the role of grading for these students. Be cautious using test or term marks as main indicators of growth. Many of these students may already have high averages and there is little benefit in focusing on moving a mark up only one or two points. Futhermore, if you already have evidence to support the highest claim that can reasonably be made about a student's achievement, there is no need for the student to complete more assessment tasks related to a particular learning outcome.

Assessment *of* learning information should provide summary and, hopefully, celebratory descriptions of learnings and achievements.

179

Differentiated learning experiences

Differentiated instruction for students who are gifted means enhanced opportunities for thinking and learning, not just more work to do. Students who are gifted benefit from learning environments in which they have opportunities to:

- gain understanding of self and others
- explore their own learning strengths and needs
- learn and practise coping skills that assist in their growth and development
- take risks and see mistakes as learning opportunities
- practise leadership and service within the school community.

For most students, an enriched learning environment can be provided within the regular classroom by substituting or adding activities that foster higher-level thinking skills and problem solving. Many instructional strategies and learning activities that challenge individual students can benefit other students in the class as well. For example, activities such as debates, which involve students in creative and challenging learning, may be connected directly to learning outcomes in a variety of subjects.

For more information on differentiated learning experiences, including scaffolded instruction, flexible grouping and choice, see *Chapter 5: Differentiated Learning Experiences*.

Meaningful activities

A useful starting point for identifying meaningful activities for students who are gifted is to consider how individual student characteristics are linked to specific learning needs. The following chart illustrates sample characteristics and the type of learning needs that may be associated with them.[1]

1. Chart adapted from the Department of Education, Employment and Training, State of Victoria, *Bright Futures Resource Book: Education of Gifted Students* (Melbourne, Australia: Department of Education, State of Victoria, 1996), p. 30. Copyright owned by the State of Victoria (Department of Eucation and Early Childhood Development). Used with permission.

Characteristic	Learning Need
• unusual retentiveness …	• exposure to quantities of information
• advanced comprehension …	• access to challenging learning activities
• varied interests …	• exposure to a wide range of topics
• high level of verbal skills …	• opportunities for in-depth reflection and discussion
• accelerated pace of thinking …	• individually paced learning
• flexibility of thought processes …	• challenging and diverse problem-solving tasks
• goal-directed behaviours …	• longer time spans for tasks
• independence in learning …	• more independent learning tasks
• analytical thinking …	• opportunities for higher-level thinking
• self-motivation …	• active involvement in learning
• emotional sensitivity …	• opportunities to explore and reflect on affective learning
• interest in adult issues …	• exposure to real-world issues
• holistic thinking …	• integrated approach to learning
• avid reader …	• access to diverse materials

181

Goal setting

An important way to ensure activities are meaningful is to involve students in setting learning goals and monitoring their own progress as much as possible. Participating in their own goal setting helps students who are gifted to practise higher-order and metacognitive thinking. It also encourages them to take ownership for their learning, to set realistic expectations and to celebrate and value their progress.

Student involvement in their own goal setting can be promoted in a variety of ways and contexts, including:
- in learning logs, journals and communication books
- through individual student–teacher conferences
- during class time, within specific subject areas or types of learning activities (e.g., spelling, keyboarding, study skills, mathematics, research projects, physical education, music) or in areas of personal growth (e.g., leadership skills, self-management, organization)
- in classroom discussions and celebrations of individual and group accomplishments
- by teachers and other adults modelling how they use the goal-setting process in their own work and personal lives.

You can support students in setting effective goals by teaching them strategies such as the following "SMART" acronym.

Specific: written in clear language. Work with students to ensure that the wording of goals specifically and accurately expresses want they want to achieve.

Measurable: provides information for assessing progress and achievement of the goals. For example, help a student transform a vague goal such as "I will be fast at keyboarding" into a more measurable goal such as "By January 30, I will keyboard at 25 words per minute on three trials on *Superkey*." Progress toward measurable goals can be monitored through graphs, log books and other data-recording strategies.

Achievable: realistic for the student. Students who are gifted benefit most when their goals are both realistic and optimistic. High achieving students sometimes strive for excellence or goals that may not seem reasonable from another person's perspective but may be entirely possible for that student.

Relevant: meaningful for the student. Encourage students to identify goals that are relevant to their immediate and future plans. Emphasize that worthwhile goals can be set in many areas of life, including personal, athletic, financial and organizational.

Time-limited: can be accomplished in a specific time period. Goals may be short- or long-term. Long-term goals can be broken down into short-term objectives, as in plans for a long-term research project.

Once these goals have been set, look for ways that activities and instruction can support students in achieving their goals. Work with students to monitor their progress and adjust goals as needed. Providing opportunities for group as well as individual goal setting can help students see the function and process of goal setting in a variety of contexts.

Tiered assignments
Tiered assignments are parallel tasks that have varied levels of complexity, depth, abstractness and support. Students in the class all focus on the same learning outcome but work on different *levels* of activities related to the outcome. These types of assignments allow students who are gifted to work at a more challenging level. Tasks from one tier to the next should differ in level of complexity, not simply be more or less work.

182

Designing a tiered assignment involves selecting a skill or concept, developing basic learning activities and then creating higher-level variations by changing variables such as using advanced materials, moving toward a more abstract concept, reducing support, making it more open-ended, and/or making it faster paced.

For example, a tiered assignment for a Grade 2 science class studying communities might offer the following types of activities.

Tier 1		Tier 2
• Describe an ant community in pictures or words.	*or*	• Describe an ant community using at least three sentences with at least three describing words in each sentence.
• Use a Venn diagram to compare an ant community to your community.	*or*	• Make an electronic slide show explaining how what you learned about ant communities helps you understand living and working together in a human community.

Questioning techniques
Questions that draw on advanced levels of information require leaps of understanding and challenge student thinking. Open-ended questions invite critical and creative thinking, and nurture the development of students' capacities to frame their own questions.

Anomalies and paradoxes
Presenting anomalies and paradoxes also can stimulate the interest of students who are gifted. Glitches in logic upturn a tidy view of the world and create opportunities for students to enter into a deeper inquiry, become immersed in the principles and build a clearer understanding of a particular aspect of a field of study (Harvey 2000, p. 70).

Independent projects
Independent projects can offer challenge and engagement for many students who need academic enrichment. Such projects let students identify issues or topics of interest, plan an investigation and synthesize the findings.

183

Components of an independent study project include:
- identifying and developing a focus
- developing skills in creative and critical thinking
- using problem-solving and decision-making strategies
- learning research skills
- developing project management strategies
- keeping learning logs
- reflecting on and evaluating the process and product
- sharing the product with an intended audience from beyond the classroom
- keeping a portfolio of results.

Independent studies help students move from being teacher-directed to student-directed. With teacher support and coaching, students learn how to decide on a focus, develop a plan of action and follow it through, and monitor the process. Students take part in developing criteria for assessment and work collaboratively with the teacher. It is important to recognize that students may need to be explicitly taught the skills to do this kind of independent work. They also need to be clear on the product, processes and behavioural expectations. Some students may benefit from an independent study agreement that outlines learning and working conditions and lays out basic expectations.

Possibilities for independent study could include such activities as:
- writing and recording a script
- creating a magazine or picture book on a topic of interest
- developing a slide show presentation on a topic of interest and presenting it to other students
- writing a story and sharing it with younger students
- creating a display about a story read or topic researched
- writing a new ending to a story or movie.

Higher-order thinking

Bloom's taxonomy (Bloom 1956) provides a useful framework for designing learning activities that promote higher-levels of thinking. Bloom proposes that at the most basic level of thinking, we acquire knowledge and comprehension. At higher levels we learn how to apply principles and to analyze, evaluate and synthesize. Assuming that students have no background in a topic of investigation, they would move from knowledge and comprehension to application before working with the higher-order skills of analysis, evaluation and synthesis. The latter three levels are associated with critical thinking. Consider how the following chart of this taxonomy of thinking can be used to plan for differentiating products and processes for students who need additional challenges.

Taxonomy of thinking

Category	Definition	Differentiated processes	Differentiated products
Synthesis	• Rearrange and/or alter individual parts to create an original concept, idea or product	Compose • Design • Invent • Create • Hypothesize • Construct • Forecast • Rearrange parts • Imagine • Adapt	Organize event • Song • Poem • Story • Advertisement • Invention • Other creative products
Evaluation	• Judge value of something • Create standards or criteria • Support judgement	Judge • Evaluate • Give opinion • Give viewpoint • Prioritize • Recommend • Critique • Prove	Decision • Rating • Editorial • Debate • Critique • Defence • Verdict • Judgement
Analysis	• Understand how parts relate to a whole • See relationships • Find uniqueness	Investigate • Classify • Categorize • Compare • Contrast • Solve • Take part • Simplify	Survey • Graph • Questionnaire • Plan • Solution to problem or mystery • Report • Proposal, position paper
Application	• Make use of learned knowledge • Transfer knowledge from one situation to another	Demonstrate • Use guides, maps, charts, etc. • Build	Recipe • Model • Artwork • Demonstration • Craft • Illustrate
Comprehension	• Demonstrate basic understanding of concepts and skills • Paraphrase in own words	Restate in own words • Give examples • Explain • Summarize • Translate • Show symbols	Drawing • Diagram • Response to question • Translation • Retelling
Knowledge	• Ability to remember specific facts, ideas or vocabulary	• Match • Recognize • Tell • Recite • List • Memorize • Remember • Define • Locate • Recall • Label • Define	Quiz • Skill work • Vocabulary activities • Facts • Matching activities

185

Mentorships

Mentorship is an effective strategy for facilitating the differentiated learning needs of students. Mentorships give students opportunities to develop relationships with adult experts who share their passion for a specific area of interest. In a successful mentorship, the mentor and student will have compatible learning and communication styles. Mentorships provide opportunities for students to engage with adults for a variety of purposes, such as interviews, individual projects, connection to the local community and exploring career options.

The following steps may help you organize successful mentoring relationships.

1. Identify what (not whom) the students need.
2. Discuss with the students whether they would like to work with a mentor and, if so, what they would like to gain from the relationship.
3. Identify appropriate mentor candidates. Explore contacts from the local community. Do the appropriate reference checks as directed by school jurisdiction policy.
4. Interview and screen the mentors. Be explicit about the goals, learning strategies and potential benefits for both the student and mentor. Provide training as required.
5. Match mentors with students.
6. Prepare students for the mentorship. Ensure they understand its purpose, benefits, limitations and commitments and put this in writing so it can be referenced throughout the relationship.
7. Monitor the mentor relationship to ensure that it is achieving its goals. Renegotiate the relationship, as needed, and seek new mentors if students are not benefiting.

Other learning environments

In addition to differentiated experiences in the classroom, some students will benefit from programming that involves one or more alternative learning environments such as the following.

*   Cluster grouping: Small groups of students receive advanced instruction in reading, mathematics or other content, or work on alternate assignments.
*   Out-of-grade placement: Students are placed with a higher grade for certain subjects such as language arts, mathematics and/or science.
*   Online courses: Students use web-based e-mail, digital content, videoconferencing and direct linkage with teachers.
*   Seminars and special projects: Students participate in interdisciplinary studies, special interest groups or other projects.
*   International Baccalaureate (IB): Students participate in special academic programs that are internationally developed and recognized for academic rigour.

186

- Advanced Placement (AP): Students participate in senior high school courses that follow the prescribed AP program and students who successfully complete examinations in the program may apply for advanced credit or placement at post-secondary institutions.

187

Tool 1: Differentiated Learning and Teaching Strategies for Students Who are Gifted

Mathematics	Language Arts	Science	Social Studies		Content
✓	✓	✓	✓	✓	Content
					Make activities more complex; e.g., comparative studies, more variables
					Accelerate activities from concrete to abstract, move quickly
					Modify outcomes from a higher grade level
					Extend activities beyond the program of studies
					Increase range and variety of topics available
					Increase quantities of information available
					Increase the variety of information available
					Use tiered assignments according to student readiness
					Investigate related themes or ideas from various disciplines
					Explore related ethical issues
					Do an in-depth study of a related self-selected topic
					Develop expanded library research skills
					Develop expanded Internet research skills

This appendix adapted from the work of David Harvey, Elk Island Public Schools Regional Division No. 14 (Sherwood Park, Alberta, 2005).

Tool 1: Differentiated Learning and Teaching Strategies for Students Who are Gifted

(continued) page 2/6

Mathematics	Language Arts	Science	Social Studies		Process
✓	✓	✓	✓	✓	
					Use pre-testing to reduce or eliminate unnecessary learning activities
					Decrease the amount of review
					Decrease the amount of repetition
					Organize mini-tutorials
					Develop a learning contract
					Use computer-based instruction; e.g., digital resources, web-based instruction
					Create opportunities for higher-level thinking skills
					Increase time span for assignments to allow depth
					Increase opportunities for primary research and data collection
					Increase opportunities for in-depth discussion
					Increase opportunities for in-depth reflection
					Increase the diversity of problem-solving opportunities
					Emphasize inquiry processes
					Use mentorship
					Create opportunities to use creativity; e.g., fluency, flexibility, originality, elaboration
					Create simulations
					Increase opportunities for application to real-world situations

189

190

Mathematics	Language Arts	Science	Social Studies	Process (continued)
✓	✓	✓	✓	✓	Process (continued)
					Use more inductive thinking; e.g., working from the specific to the general
					Use more deductive thinking; e.g., working from the general to the specific
					Increase the use of evidence of reasoning; e.g., supporting opinions, debates
					Create more opportunities for student choice; e.g., learning centres, tic-tac-toe menu, learning contracts
					Make activities more open-minded
					Create expanded opportunities for critical thinking, evaluating and decision making
					Create time for browsing and exploring
					Investigate possibilities for videoconferencing
					Organize partnerships through technological communications; e.g., e-mail, conference boards, e-mentor
					Create opportunities to teach others

Mathematics	Language Arts	Science	Social Studies		Product
✓	✓	✓	✓	✓	Product
					Provide for choice of product
					Incorporate service learning
					Apply to real-life problems and situations
					Challenge student to incorporate higher-order thinking skills; e.g., analysis, evaluation, synthesis
					Encourage different targets for assessment and evaluation; e.g., focus on learning logs and self-reflection rather than on completed project
					Create opportunities to reflect and record process

191

192

Mathematics	Language Arts	Science	Social Studies		
✓	✓	✓	✓	✓	**Physical Environment**
					Create interest centres that are available throughout the school day
					Increase access to computers and other technology
					Increase access to library
					Increase access to diverse materials and resources
					Share examples of excellence and exceptional achievement
					Increase access to community resources; e.g., colleges, universities, laboratory
					Social and Psychological Environment
					Use flexible grouping
					Create opportunities for partner and small group work
					Create opportunities for ability grouping for some tasks
					Create opportunities for interest grouping for some tasks
					Create opportunities for independent work
					Create opportunities for exchange of ideas
					Encourage intellectual risk taking
					Design self-pacing learning opportunities
					Create opportunities for self-reflection
					Offer choice
					Encourage risk taking and experimentation
					Organize self-directed learning that incorporates pursuit of interests

Mathematics	Language Arts	Science	Social Studies		Assessment, Evaluation and Reporting
✓	✓	✓	✓	✓	
					Create opportunities for demonstrating mastery early
					Incorporate student self-assessment including reflection on progress, achievements and challenges
					Create performance-based assessments
					Schedule regular student–teacher conferencing
					Incorporate student-developed criteria and standards
					Develop assessment based on application of skills to real problems
					Incorporate creativity as important criteria component
					Develop criteria for assessing critical thinking, evaluating and decision making
					Develop criteria for assessing decision-making skills
					Arrange for a real audience for student work
					Arrange for expert review of student work

193

English Language Arts

Contents of this chapter

11

195

"The classroom must be a place where literacy becomes inescapable because it is not only the password to connecting and making sense of the world, it is ultimately key to making the world a better place."
– Hill, 2006. p. 392.

Language arts instruction offers numerous opportunities to differentiate instruction. This chapter highlights research-supported best practices that foster student success in reading, writing and other language arts, and explores how these practices can support or be enhanced by differentiation. The chapter focuses on the context of the language arts program but many of the approaches discussed also apply to language tasks in other subject areas. This chapter also looks at best practice for assessment in language arts, and explores how this type of assessment supports differentiation.

Differentiating instruction in reading

Teachers can naturally differentiate reading instruction within the following best practices:

- promote frequent and varied reading
- teach skills for reading
- teach strategies for reading
- emphasize textual details
- offer varied options to extend text.

While these practices emphasize reading outcomes, many of the strategies relate to other language arts as well, as students typically participate in writing, speaking, listening, viewing and representing activities to develop reading skills related to comprehension.

Promote frequent and varied reading
Research tells us that students need to read frequently to become skillful readers. The following chart illustrates how instructional practices that encourage frequent reading can be excellent opportunities to differentiate instruction.

196

Instructional Practice	Opportunities to Differentiate
"Read-alouds" • Read aloud to students frequently. • Model and discuss how reading provides insight and enjoyment.	• Choose reading material to appeal to a wide range of student personal and cultural experiences. • Include informational and practical text in read-alouds. Some students, often boys, prefer practical, "how-to" texts to literary texts. • Invite students to respond to read-alouds in a variety of ways.
Independent reading • Create class time for independent reading. • Challenge students to read at home for information and enjoyment.	• Ensure that the classroom and library book collection includes both literary and informational texts at varying levels of difficulty. • Include audio books as part of the collection, especially for students reading below grade level. By following print as they listen, students learn to identify words and to comprehend.
"Read-alongs" or "shared reading" • Encourage students to follow and join in the reading of a text by a competent reader. • Have a large or small group read a text together.	• Create a risk-free environment so students of varied abilities feel comfortable to join in. • Follow up with differentiated assignments. For example, one group of students might work on identifying word families in the text while another group composes a story related to the text.

197

Consider ways to scaffold instruction for students by using a mix of these instructional practices in combination with varied-level texts. The following diagram illustrates ways of scaffolding reading.

Ways of Scaffolding Readers[1]

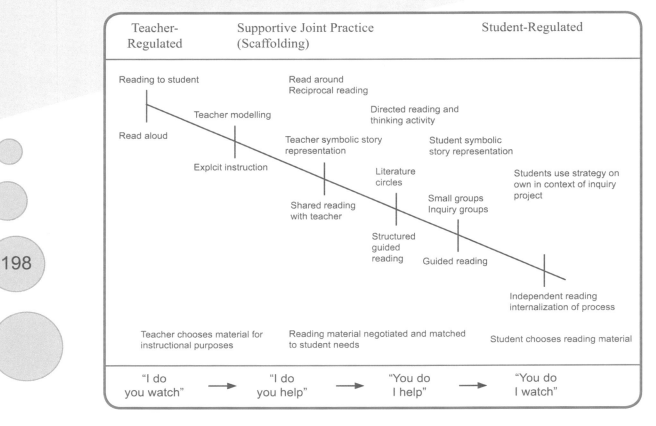

Teach skills for reading

Skills refer to what students must be able to demonstrate, such as identifying the author's purpose, a protagonist's motive or a character's dominant trait. Strategies refer to the know-how used to complete tasks. Most outcomes in the language arts program of studies are skills; however, the program also highlights strategies, with an emphasis on students discovering different strategies that work best for them. The next section of this chapter will consider strategies as critical components to differentiating instruction to meet a wider range of student needs.

---

1. Graphic reprinted with permission from *Strategic Reading: Guiding Students to Lifelong Literacy, 6–12* (p. 45) by Tanya N. Baker, Julie Dube Hackett, and Jeffrey D. Wilhelm. Copyright © 2001 by Tanya N. Baker, Julie Dube Hackett, and Jeffrey D. Wilhelm. Published by Boynton/Cook Portsmouth, NH. All rights reserved.

Instructional Practices	Opportunities to Differentiate
• Plan reading assignments to focus on specific learning outcomes. Students should know and be able to explain what skills they are expected to learn or demonstrate for each reading assignment.	• Have individual students or groups of students work on different skills within a selected text. Use ongoing assessment. • Have the class work on a selected skill (e.g., inference of main ideas) within different texts of varying difficulty and interest levels. Many reading materials are coded according to grade-level difficulty and interest.
• Use writing, speaking, listening, viewing and representing tasks to develop skills related to reading. For example, to work on identifying and assessing a response to a conflict, students could dramatize a story's conflict, visually illustrate the conflict, write a monologue to indicate the character's response to the conflict, and debate whether the character's choices to resolve the conflict were justified.	• Suggest and assign varied activities related to student learning preferences. For example, students who learn visually might illustrate the conflict, learners who are more kinesthetically strong might present a dramatization, and others who are strong auditory learners might share their written monologue in a small group and discuss different interpretations of the character's response to the conflict.

Teach strategies for reading

Students need to understand that strategies and skills are intertwined. Students who can identify the strategies they use to complete a learning task complete the task more skillfully. The following chart presents effective instructional approaches for teaching students reading strategies, along with related approaches for differentiation.

199

Instructional Practices	Opportunities to Differentiate

• Model strategies and create opportunities for students to identify strategies they might use before, during and after reading a selected text. For example, pre-reading strategies include:
  – build/recall prior knowledge
  – review purposes for reading
  – predict content
  – list questions to be answered by the text.
• Emphasize that individual readers use different strategies. Students should discover and use strategies that work best for them.
	• Use a "think-aloud" approach to explore strategies and response options students might use. Challenge students to identify their own preferred strategies and response options for selected texts.
	• Emphasize the value of strategies that appeal to a variety of learning styles and intelligences. For example, during reading strategies encourage students to:
	  – predict what might follow or ask questions as you read
	  – chunk the text by looking for periods, question marks, exclamation points, as well as paragraphs or stanza breaks in poems
	  – visualize as they read—make a movie in their minds
	  – link the text to personal experience; for example, if you are reading about friendship, consider familiar experiences about friendship that connect to the text
	  – check when something doesn't make sense
	  – paraphrase or summarize the text.
	• Discuss the options available within selected strategies such as:
	  – discussing ideas and responses with others
	  – preparing a chart or a sketch
	  – writing a journal entry or list of questions
	  – using graphic organizers
	  – role-playing or dramatizing.

200

Instructional Practices	Opportunities to Differentiate
The "Unfolding Method" 1. Ask students to cover a selected text with a piece of paper. Direct them to uncover only the title and illustrations and to listen carefully to your instructions for uncovering the remaining text. 2. Ask students to note background knowledge, to make predictions and to ask questions related to the title and illustrations. 3. Direct students to uncover the first chunk of text, often a complete sentence or a paragraph. Challenge students to use during-reading strategies. 4. Continue to lead the students through unfolding chunks of text. As you work through the unfolding, ask students why you unfolded the part that you did. Emphasize the importance of looking for meaningful chunks as you read. 5. Before unfolding the final chunk, students make a final prediction about what the text will include. Discuss how the final chunk often emphasizes a key point, presents a surprising twist or presents a character's or writer's reaction.	• During each phase of reading, describe a variety of strategies that could be used and discuss the value of these strategies. • As students work through each chunk of text, focus them on visualizing by asking them to note, diagram or chart what they saw. Students also can talk about, write about, chart or diagram predictions, summaries and questions. Use this opportunity to discuss the power of the strategies and response options in figuring out the meaning of an unfamiliar text. • Encourage students to select response modes that work best for them. • Challenge students to try at least one new response mode to build their strength in all learning styles and intelligences.

Emphasize textual details

Many students will benefit from prompts to attend to the detail in texts that they read. This attention to detail is critical to successful reading. Consider the following strategies to differentiate instruction while encouraging attentive reading.

- *"Split page"*

  Students draw a vertical line down the centre of their page to create a split page. In the first column, students write their first answer or interpretation. In the second column, students write their revised interpretation or answer. The following example represents a high school student's initial answer and the reconsidered answer that followed after re-reading a poem.

Title: "Freedom" by Louis Dude
Question: What does the poem suggest about freedom?

First answer	Revised answer
We like freedom.	We resent being told what to do even if we would choose to do what we're told.

This approach can be differentiated by exploring with students options that help them refine their interpretations beyond checking the text, such as:

- discussing answers with a partner or small group
- preparing an oral interpretation or dramatization of the text before revising the answer
- preparing a sketch or visual interpretation of the text before revising/refining the response.

202

- ***Graphic organizers***

  Many learners benefit when they use graphic organizers to organize information and explore meaning in a text. The following two examples illustrate possibilities.

"Sequence charts"

Title of Text: "Seven Years War in North America"

French Advantage

1. French defeat British at Fort Oswego **1756**	2. French defeat British at Fort Henry **1757**	3. French defeat British at Ticonderoga **1758**

British Advantage

4. British defeat French at Louisburg and Fort Frontenac **1759**	5. Wolfe defeats Montcalm on Plains of Abraham **1759**

"Thought webs"

The graphic on the following page illustrates a visual technique that encourages attention to details of text as students completed research about identity theft. As students use print, human and media resources to complete their research, they seek information related to four specific questions:

1. What is identity theft?

2. How are identities stolen?

3. What are the costs of identity theft?

4. How can you protect yourself from identity theft?

To differentiate, teachers can offer students the option of either creating an outline or identifying another strategy they can use to gather, organize and present information.

203

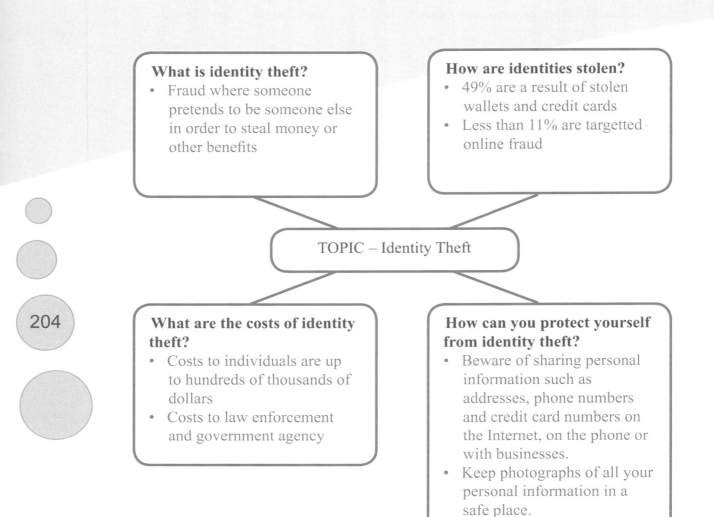

What is identity theft?
- Fraud where someone pretends to be someone else in order to steal money or other benefits

How are identities stolen?
- 49% are a result of stolen wallets and credit cards
- Less than 11% are targetted online fraud

TOPIC – Identity Theft

What are the costs of identity theft?
- Costs to individuals are up to hundreds of thousands of dollars
- Costs to law enforcement and government agency

How can you protect yourself from identity theft?
- Beware of sharing personal information such as addresses, phone numbers and credit card numbers on the Internet, on the phone or with businesses.
- Keep photographs of all your personal information in a safe place.

204

Offer varied options to extend text

One of the most powerful ways to develop and refine comprehension of a text is to do something with it—perform it, transform it or write about it. Extension activities can be differentiated by creating a range of options to meet the diverse needs, strengths and interests of students. The following examples illustrate possibilities.

Oral interpretation of text

Individually or in a group, students prepare an oral interpretation of a selected text.

- Students make a thoughtful determination about the most climatic point in the text for emphasis in the oral interpretation.
- Students decide about variations in the speed and the volume of their reading of the text.
- Students respect punctuation cues; e.g., pausing at commas, stopping at periods, showing appropriate tone for question marks and exclamation points.

Written extension of text

Students use the content of a text to inspire their own writing. Options could include:
- interview scripts with a character
- diary entries
- editorials
- descriptions of settings
- recollections of people inspired by the text
- a letter to express their response to the text
- sequel chapters
- original stories or poems on the theme explored in the text.

Visual extension of text

Students create visual representations. Possibilities could include:
- slide shows
- sketches
- cartoon versions
- book jackets
- games
- time lines
- maps
- collections of objects important in the text.

Artistic extension of text

Students use the arts to explore and reinterpret the text. Possibilities could include:
- dramatic performances
- songs or raps
- dances
- multimedia presentations.

In all of these extension activities, teachers challenge students to explain how their written, oral or visual interpretation connects to specific detail in the texts that inspired the extension. In relating speaking, listening, viewing, representing and writing extensions to specific textual details, students refine their comprehension of the text.

Differentiating instruction in writing

As teachers engage students in writing tasks, they can differentiate instruction by:

- promoting writing to learn and communicate
- engaging students with a range of writing genres and tasks, and related planning strategies
- creating opportunities for students to learn and use a range of drafting and revision strategies.

Promote writing to learn and communicate

Since students need practice to become more skillful, frequent writing is critical to becoming a skillful writer. One way to encourage frequent writing is to explore the question about why we write. Most students understand that people write to communicate. But they need to know that we also write to learn, to explore and to develop understanding. To encourage writing to learn, teachers across subject areas often include forms of journal writing or exploratory writing. Such writing focuses on risk taking and working through ideas rather than on correctness and conventional forms. Exploratory writing naturally incorporates opportunities for differentiation.

The following forms of exploratory writing provide opportunities for differentiation.

Learning logs

Students write to deepen their learning of a specific topic or experience. Teachers prompt students to write about their current understandings, their own uncertainties and their questions. By inviting students to discuss current understandings with partners and groups, to dramatize their concepts before they write and to incorporate visual illustrations in their writing, teachers differentiate instruction.

Personal responses to literature

Personal responses to literature focus on connections between one's life and a literary text as well as one's personal experience of a text. Students comment on likes, dislikes, current understandings, uncertainties, questions, predictions and judgements. To differentiate, teachers provide varied opportunities for students to discuss the text and to create oral interpretations (such as a song, poem or dramatic piece) or visual representations (such as a visual art piece or multimedia presentation) as a way of responding.

Journals

Journal writing creates choice about what students write. While learning logs and personal responses to literature are more connected to learning content, journal writing allows students to write about experiences of personal importance and significance. Teachers encourage students to consider the voice that is appropriate to their writing. A differentiated approach could include opportunities for discussion, role-playing and visualizing before writing, and for incorporating visual representations into the writing.

Engage students with writing variables and planning strategies

Writing variables provide a framework for writing to communicate. "R.A.F.T.S." is an acronym for writing variables—Role, Audience, Format, Topic and Strong Verb.

Explanation	Examples
R–ROLE From whose point of view am I writing?	• self • character in a story • parent • friend • historical or political figure • author
A–AUDIENCE To whom am I writing? What is my relationship to the audience?	• self • politician • friend • company • parent • editor • author
F–FORMAT What particular writing form is appropriate or assigned?	• letter • business letter • story • diary entry • song • eulogy • newspaper advertisement
T–TOPIC What am I writing about?	• friendship • job application • favourite activities • junk food • rights and responsibilities
S–STRONG VERB What is my purpose or what are my purposes? What do I wish to achieve in my writing?	• explain • complain • condemn • thank • describe • brag • argue • commend • deny

207

R.A.F.T.S. offers several advantages. It helps the writer to focus, to discover ideas and to capture appropriate voice. For example, students might be required to write a business letter (form) from the role of the president of the school council (audience) inviting her to speak at the graduation ceremony to offer advice to graduates (topic and purpose). R.A.F.T.S. offers natural opportunities for differentiation when teachers prompt individual students to choose different roles, audiences, formats, topics and purposes in their writing tasks.

Many students have a limited sense of possibilities beyond brainstorming and will need to learn a range of prewriting strategies that fit the R.A.F.T.S. variables and match their individual strengths, interests and learning preferences. Students will use a different prewriting strategy for story writing than they will use for description. The following table illustrates potential strategies for typical writing forms.

208

Format	Prewriting Strategy	Opportunities to Differentiate
Story/ Narrative	Students review critical story elements: • central character • setting • conflict • resolution of conflict • central character's final reaction.	• Students use discussion, role-playing, diagramming and note taking to review story elements represented by "somebody," "wanted," "but," "so," "then." 1. Identify your central character ("somebody"). 2. Think about where and when your story takes place, and your character's goal ("wanted"). 3. Identify the major problem or conflict your character must deal with ("but"). 4. Identify how the major conflict is resolved ("so"). 5. By presenting how your character reacted to the conflict and its resolution, you imply your story's theme ("then").

Format	Prewriting Strategy	Opportunities to Differentiate
Description	Students note the details that convey a dominant emotional response.	• Encourage students to use direct observation. For example, instead of students recalling a soccer game, ask them to observe a game with notepad in hand. Students might discuss observations or sketch observations as part of their written notations. • Students then note dominant emotional responses. Individual students will identify different emotional responses and will note different details. This will help them achieve an individual voice in their writing.
Explanations/ Exploratory Writing	Students organize relevant information under major subtopics related to their topic and purpose.	• Challenge students to identify approaches that work best for them in selecting topics and subtopics and in locating relevant information for subtopics. • Some students will prefer outlines while others will prefer thought webs to organize content.

Writing exemplars show rather than tell. Exemplars can help students learn about different formats, especially when the exemplars represent work of writers at a similar grade level or age. By examining exemplars of any selected writing form—eulogy, song lyric, editorial, position paper, business letter or other form— students may work on their own or in groups to create a graphic organizer or other planning strategy that works for the particular writing task.

Create opportunities for students to learn and use a range of drafting and revision strategies

In drafting, the writer's major focus is on keeping the flow going. The following suggestions apply when students are having a difficulty with a certain aspect of the writing process.

- Students may need to revisit their prewriting work to change plans or to gather further information.

- Writers often benefit from talking to someone about what they are trying to write.

- Students should place a check mark above sentences that seem unclear and an "S" above spelling uncertainties. They should keep drafting and leave these concerns until later when they are ready to move on to revising.

- Writers sometimes benefit from reading through everything that they have drafted to consider "what next" options.

- With some texts, especially explanations, it often is easier to begin with the second paragraph and to write the introductory paragraph last.

- Write on every second line or double space to make revisions easier. If students are using word processing, they need to save drafts.

Engage student writers in discussions and conferences about the drafting strategies that work best for them. Different students will have different preferences. Actively using criteria or questions to judge texts of their own or others will help students write more effectively.

Before reading and assessing student writing, teachers can guide students to review for criteria using prompts such as the following.

- I changed this sentence for clarity …

- I added the following detail to strengthen my writing …

- My introduction created interest by …

- I used the following transition techniques …

- Three precise and colourful words that I used are …

- An effective short sentence is …

- A sentence which begins with something other than the subject is …

- I checked on the following matters of grammar/usage …

While students may use checklists of selected criteria to report on their revisions, some students prefer to use highlighter pens or sticky notes. With the highlighter approach, students note key criteria on a piece of paper and establish colour-coding for each criterion. Students use the highlighter pen to mark parts of the composition that illustrate success with the criterion. With the sticky note approach, students write one revision criterion on each sticky note. They place the sticky notes in the margin of the composition and draw a line in pencil from the sticky note to the part of the composition that illustrates success with each criterion.

210

Language arts assessment

Best language arts assessment practice recognizes that assessment has purposes that extend beyond accountability. While teachers need to assess student achievement of outcomes, they also assess to instruct students and to help plan instruction. Teachers also use assessment to affirm students with positive comments and feedback, to celebrate success and to help students set personal goals. Best assessment practice involves students in self-assessment and in providing peer feedback. When students engage in assessment, they learn about what and how they are learning.

A balanced approach to language arts assessment includes:
- **observation**—informal, often rotationally planned
- **performance assessment**—learning task with specific criteria, often in the form of rubrics.

Using a variety of assessment approaches implies differentiated instruction. Teachers whose assessment guides planning are differentiating instruction. Grouping for instruction based on needs and interests of individual students flow from assessment. Teachers differentiate by highlighting varied assessment criteria for different students and by encouraging students to set individual learning goals. Informed by ongoing informal, observational assessment, teachers can provide ongoing differentiated instruction each day.

Rubrics are critically important in performance assessment. Teachers differentiate by highlighting varied criteria for students on selected rubrics. Students also can be involved in the creation of rubrics following study of an exemplar. Another possibility involves challenging students to examine a rubric developed by someone else, to paraphrase what each criterion means and to suggest additions, deletions or modifications to the rubric.

Exemplars are examples or illustrations of performances of various levels of quality. Exemplars can be:
- print samples
- artistic representations
- audiotape performances
- multimedia performances or presentations
- writing samples.

Exemplars help establish and communicate performance standards for a task, and communicate these expectations to students and parents. Exemplars complement rubrics by showing rather than telling. Students work more effectively with rubrics once they have first worked with corresponding exemplars.

211

From the perspective of differentiated instruction, exemplars allow teachers to show work that represents a reasonable goal for learners. Individual learners work with different exemplars with the focus on learning what will help the student achieve work of similar quality to the exemplar. Teachers who have worked with exemplars report steady improvement in student work. Students often seek to perform better than the work illustrated in the exemplar.

In collecting exemplars, respect jurisdictional and provincial privacy guidelines. Seek student and parental permission for use of exemplars. Use collected exemplars in subsequent years and present anonymously. Collect exemplars that represent grade-level expectations as well as exceptional performances for the grade level.

Mathematics

12

213

Contents of this chapter

"The use of manipulatives and a variety of pedagogical approaches can address the diversity of learning styles and developmental stages of students, and enhance the formation of sound, transferable, mathematical concepts."
– Western and Northern Canadian Protocol in *The Common Curriculum Framework for K–9 Mathematics*

The move toward differentiated instruction in the mathematics classroom represents a significant shift in the way teachers think about and teach mathematics. Today's classrooms are becoming more student-centred, focused less on direct instruction and more on experiential learning. Creating a differentiated mathematics classroom can begin with the following steps (Bender 2005).

- **Consider how students learn.** All of the instructional and assessment decisions you make should be based on the learning needs and preferences of your students.
- **Organize students into flexible groups.** In a differentiated classroom, students are subdivided into groups early and often. There also are multiple opportunities to work both with partners and independently.
- **Plan for a variety of activities.** Learners benefit when content is presented in multiple ways.
- **Connect to the students' world.** Connecting mathematics learning with reference points in the students' community is one way to increase engagement.
- **Create a safe and caring environment.** Create a learning environment in which students feel confident in taking risks and trying new things.
- **Begin differentiated instruction slowly.** Start with an area of mathematics you feel confident teaching. This increases the chances of success and will help create confidence to extend differentiated instruction into other areas.

Use flexible groupings

Effective flexible grouping depends on a thorough knowledge of the curriculum and of individual students in the classroom. Using this knowledge, you can plan a variety of group structures to help students learn mathematics and interact with others in useful ways.

Groups should be formed in a number of ways to give students a variety of learning experiences. For some activities, grouping based on readiness may be the most practical method. Groups also can be formed on the basis of students' general areas of mathematical strengths and challenges, learning preferences or interests. A variety of information, including ongoing assessment results, portfolios, grades and report card comments from previous years, and other achievement information, can be helpful in identifying groups of students who may need extra assistance and support throughout the year. Flexible grouping can increase students' engagement and success when they have learning opportunities that build on their strengths and needs.

Readiness grouping

Grouping students based on their readiness related to specific concepts or outcomes can allow you to effectively meet the needs of students at multiple levels. The "guess, assess and break away" strategy is one approach to readiness grouping. Using this strategy, you:
- *guess* which students have the concept
- *assess* those several students with one or two quick activities such as a journal prompt or a hands-on activity
- *break away* a small instructional group of those students who will benefit from a targetted instructional activity.

For example, teachers can identify and work with a small break-away group of students doing a follow-up instructional activity after each phase in a learning activity sequence. The break-away group could include students who require additional practice with the concept.

You can use break-away activities throughout a teaching plan. Structure learning activities so that different groups of students participate in the same activity at different times. Individual students might benefit from participating in the same activity with different groups of peers. The different groupings will provide increased opportunities for practice and improved opportunities for engagement. In addition, consider providing break-away activities that incorporate various multiple intelligences.

Use an assessment task prior to beginning a unit. Forming two short-term groups based on the information gathered is a good starting point for differentiating instruction. Similarly, a "do now" or warm-up activity at the start of a learning activity can be used to identify students who need to review a concept before moving on and those who are ready to move forward.

In addition to identifying student readiness levels, assessment tasks can be used to help determine student understanding on the continuum of concrete to abstract. This type of information provides insight into the way some students may need to begin processing the content.

Effective assessment in mathematics requires teachers to plan regular and specific ways to find out *what* students understand and *why* they may be making errors. The knowledge gained through this type of assessment lets teachers differentiate instruction to both assist and challenge students appropriately.

215

When working with diagrams and manipulatives, mixed-ability grouping may make sense; e.g., the student who works best with manipulatives is working alongside another student who prefers to work symbolically. The goal is that all students will eventually move to the symbolic.

Learning preference grouping

Learning preferences can be the basis of grouping for exploring and applying new mathematical concepts. Consider the following Grade 7 learner outcome related to patterns: Create a table of values from a linear relation, graph the table of values, and analyze the graph to draw conclusions and solve problems.

While learners with auditory strengths may be able to describe relationships demonstrated, learners who prefer visual opportunities will benefit from creating graphs, either with paper and pencil or with a software program.

Using tape to create a large graph on the floor will allow the kinesthetic learners in the class to actually become points on the graph.

In this learning activity, students are offered different ways to process the learning, yet the content is the same for every student. Students need opportunities to explore, practise and demonstrate their learning in a variety of ways.

Interest grouping

Students can be in groups based on their interests as well. In this example, all students reach the same goal, but through a choice of three different scenarios.

Consider the following Grade 2 learner outcome:
Formulate the questions and categories for data collection, and actively collect first-hand information.
In this activity:
- Group 1 is going to investigate something about student eating habits
- Group 2 is going to investigate something about student hobbies.
- Group 3 is going to investigate something about student families.

All groups consider the following same questions before constructing their graph.
- Will your group gather information by counting, measuring or surveying?
- How do you plan to keep a record of the information gathered?
- Will you make a bar graph or a pictograph?
- How will you sort and graph your data?

The simple act of including choice will increase student engagement, particularly if the scenarios for choice are developed based on information about student interests.

Cooperative grouping[1]

Students will benefit from opportunities to participate collaboratively in pairs or in small groups. This approach:

- involves students in working collaboratively to solve a problem or investigate a mathematical idea
- provides opportunities for students to learn from one another
- encourages discussion and sharing of ideas.

Students learn from one another with guidance from the teacher. Shared mathematics promotes the development of problem solving, reasoning and communication skills.

Independent mathematics[2]

Students also need opportunities to work independently to focus on and consolidate their own understanding. Independent mathematics provides opportunities for students to:

- develop, consolidate or apply strategies or skills on their own
- make choices independently
- work at their own pace and develop independence, perseverance and self-confidence
- demonstrate what they know and can do.

Although students are working independently, allow them to ask their peers or you for clarification or feedback. During this time, take the opportunity to observe, ask questions and record information about student understanding, strategies, procedures, skills and knowledge.

Plan differentiatiated learning experiences

Successful planning for differentiation in the mathematics classroom requires teachers to:

- consider the various dimensions of mathematical learning; e.g., computation, explanation, application and problem solving throughout instruction planning
- help students identify their own learning preferences, strengths and challenges, and where they need to grow
- use a variety of teaching strategies to explore a mathematical topic.

---

1. This section adapted from Expert Panel on Literacy and Numeracy Instruction for Students with Special Education Needs, *Education for All: The Report of the Expert Panel on Literacy and Numeracy Instruction for Students with Special Education Needs, Kindergarten to Grade 6* (Toronto, ON: Ontario Ministry of Education, 2005), p. 81. © Queen's Printer for Ontario, 2005. Adapted with permission.
2. Ibid., p. 84.

217

Plan for a variety of activities

Most students benefit from explicit and focused instruction in targeted chunks of five to 15 minutes. In addition, learners benefit most when content is presented in multiple ways. Present new mathematical concepts at three levels:
- concrete; e.g., using manipulatives such as blocks or other objects
- representational; e.g., pictures
- symbolic.

When planning a learning activity, build in different ways to explore and apply the specific skill or concept, as a whole class or in various grouping configurations. Manipulatives can be used across the grade levels to teach and explore mathematical concepts. Some students find it helpful to explore and visualize problems using manipulatives, and then explain the result to each other. Other students benefit from developing a representation of the problem, while other students learn best by considering it abstractly. The goal should be that students can each demonstrate learning in a variety of ways.

Many teaching resources offer additional activities under the heading of "enrichment" or "alternative teaching" ideas. These activities can serve as a starting point for differentiating instruction.

Limit number of tasks

Generally, students with difficulties in mathematics will achieve greater mastery by focusing on quality (versus quantity) and working with key concepts for longer periods of time.

Search for and emphasize patterns

The brain searches for patterns in order to reduce the information load on the system; therefore, teach using patterns. Present different types of strategies that use patterns (for example, using the patterns of counting by 3s or 5s to help with multiplication) and post these on walls as sample strategies. Use patterns as classroom games or quick and fun activities at various points throughout the school day.

Connect to the students' world

Make connections between students' prior knowledge and new concepts by using real-world examples. Connecting mathematical learning with reference points in the community is one way to increase engagement. Start with the classroom community and move out to include the school, and then the local community. Using local examples can make learning more authentic for students. For example, when learning about mass, students can write word problems with a local flavour; e.g., comparing the mass of various animals at home and then at the local zoo or nearby farm.

218

Scaffolding instruction

In scaffolded instruction, teachers use individual prompting and guidance tailored to the specific needs of individual students. This provides just enough support for the student to do a new task. Scaffolding can include an array of learning supports, including charts, graphics and cue cards.

For effective scaffolding in the mathematics classroom consider the following.

Identify what students know.
The level of support must be tailored to the students' ever-changing understanding of mathematical concepts. To do this, you need to know what students already know (background or prior knowledge), what misconceptions they have and their developmental level (i.e., which competencies are developing and which are beyond students' current level of functioning). For example, a teacher who knew that her students "think in terms of money," used the familiar concept of money to teach rounding.

Help students achieve successes quickly. If copying numbers is laborious for some students, consider pairing students who have difficulty with written production with a peer buddy who records the answers. This allows the other student to generate ideas on solving problems without having to worry about how to convey these ideas in writing.

Help students learn from each other. Create opportunities for students to teach each other, to summarize main points, and to tutor each other in new concepts in short (e.g., five-minute) tutoring sessions. These types of collaborative activities can enhance student motivation to learn mathematics as well as create opportunities to learn about working with others.

Help students be independent. Effective scaffolding involves listening and watching for clues from students as to when teacher assistance is or is not needed. Achieving independence is different for individual students. Some students may be at identical skill levels, but emotionally they may be at different levels regarding the amount of frustration they can tolerate. Some students will need more teacher support while learning to perform a task; others will demonstrate task mastery more quickly.

Consider the following examples of scaffolding that create choice and provide structured opportunities to reflect on mathematical learning.

Open-ended problem solving
Learning through problem solving needs to be the focus of mathematics at all grade levels. In a problem-solving classroom, problems are used as a vehicle to learn new mathematics.

One way to create this is to use open-ended tasks that provide multiple entry points for students at varying readiness levels. For example,

> The answer is 12, what is the question?

Broken calculator activities are also open-ended. For example,

> Suppose the only working keys are [3] [8] [x] [–] [=].
>
> - Show how you can still get all the answers from 1 to 10.
> - What is the least number of key strokes (button presses) it takes to get each one?

Multiple entry points

John Van de Walle (2001) introduced an interesting model for creating differentiated tasks. By providing multiple sets of data within one problem, students have multiple entry points.

> Maria has {12, 60, 121} pine cones. She gave Evan {5, 15, 46} pine cones. How many pine cones does Maria have now?

Students can complete the task with numbers that are within their reach. For example, a student who finds subtraction challenging can choose $12 - 5$, while a student ready for a challenge can choose $121 - 46$.

> How many people can you serve with $\{4, 4\frac{1}{2}, 2\frac{1}{4}\}$ pizzas, if each person eats $\{\frac{1}{2}, \frac{3}{4}, \frac{2}{3}\}$ of a pizza?

Give students a choice of which pair of numbers to work with first, and then encourage them to continue with a more challenging pair of numbers. This type of task differentiates by readiness, yet engages all students in solving word problems involving division of fractions.

220

Think-alouds

Modelling how to use "think-alouds" is particularly valuable for students who have difficulty knowing how to select and use appropriate strategies. As the teacher thinks aloud while working through a problem, students hear the thought process involved and see a model of problem-solving behaviour. Think-alouds can be used with the whole class and/or with individual students who need scaffolding support for applying problem-solving strategies.

Journals

Mathematics journals are an opportunity for students to demonstrate and reflect on their understanding of new mathematical concepts. They also provide an opportunity for teachers to learn more about student attitudes toward mathematics. Information from journal entries can be a starting point for grouping students based on:

- levels of understanding
- plans for gaining understanding
- real-world connections and personal interests.

Consider the following types of journal prompts.

- Explain how to solve this problem.
- Identify the error in this solution and explain how you know.
- Compare integers and fractions. How are they the same? How are they different?
- In yesterday's class we learned _____. This concept is important because _____.
- Write down everything you know about triangles.
- Reflect on how you did on the unit test. How did you prepare? How can you improve for next time?

Supporting success for all students

A variety of strategies support a diversity of learning needs in the differentiated mathematics classroom. Many of these strategies also can be used in other subject areas, depending on the content being learned and the level of support required by individual students.

In addition to the strategies taught by the teacher, students may have developed their own personal strategies, or may have learned strategies in other subject areas that are successful for them. Make opportunities during mathematics class to share strategies and encourage students to use their personal strategies in a variety of learning tasks.

Teach how to use textbooks effectively

- Teach text features and how to use them; e.g., bold to identify important ideas or vocabulary, special boxes to set information apart from the rest of the text.
- Teach students to highlight important information found in directions and word problems. Assign different colours for highlighting different parts of the problem (e.g., the question being asked) and have these remain consistent.

Promote comprehension

- Create opportunities for students to use visual images or concrete objects and manipulatives to represent what they have learned. For example, students can visually demonstrate an understanding of equality using a balance scale and 3-dimensional objects.
- Work collaboratively with students to create concept maps to visually represent and demonstrate specific mathematical concepts and/or personal strategies.
- Use word walls and other opportunities to reinforce and create a deeper understanding of new mathematical terms.
- Provide clear directions both verbally and visually.
- Present information in a variety of ways to help students see the information in more than one way. This will help them move the new information into their long-term memory.
- Provide variety and multiple opportunities for participation during learning activities.
- Provide immediate specific feedback for correct and incorrect responses.
- Make learning personally relevant by connecting it to student lives.
- Encourage students to talk aloud while working through a problem or calculation. This can help them organize their thoughts and remember the steps.
- Provide information in small chunks.
- Make connections between each new learning and students' prior knowledge and personal experience.
- Provide multiple opportunities for practise to ensure new learning is embedded in long-term memory.
- Use games for reinforcement and practice. Having fun makes learning more memorable.
- Provide a model of a completed problem and display it so students can refer to it as needed.
- Provide clear and consistent transitions between topics.

Provide supports to reduce frustration and increase success

- Reduce the number of questions on the page. In some cases consider presenting individual problems on single sheets of paper in order to reduce the visual load on students and allow them to focus on one question at a time.
- Provide assistive technology (such as word processors) for students with motor difficulties so they can legibly record their answers.
- Reduce the amount of copying required by providing copies of notes. Students can then highlight the key points on the copies as a way of engaging with the information.
- Reduce the number of assigned mathematical tasks by allowing students a choice; e.g., do any 10.
- Provide extra time to work on assessments tasks, on an as-needed basis.
- Encourage students to use a cue card or post-it note to keep their spot on the page or in the textbook.
- Encourage students to talk aloud while working through a problem or calculation to assist in their organization process and to provide insight into the approach being used.
- Establish a cue (e.g., a phrase or a distinct sound such as a chime) that alerts students that directions are about to be given or instruction is about to begin.

223

Use mathematics to develop oral, written and reading comprehension skills[3]

- Provide tasks that are worth talking and writing about.
- Model think-aloud techniques and encourage students to do the same; e.g., "I have 25 and need to subtract 7 but don't have enough ones so I need to regroup."
- Model the use of mathematical language.
- Ask good questions and encourage students to reflect on their thinking and ask their own questions.
- Ask, "How do you know?" and create opportunities for students to reflect on their own learning.

The following charts are sample strategies that promote different types of communication including:

- oral communication
- written communication
- reading comprehension.

---

3. This section and following charts on pages 224–229 adapted from Expert Panel on Literacy and Numeracy Instruction for Students with Special Education Needs, *Education for All: The Report of the Expert Panel on Literacy and Numeracy Instruction for Students With Special Education Needs, Kindergarten to Grade 6* (Toronto, ON: Ontario Ministry of Education, 2005), pp. 85–90. © Queen's Printer for Ontario, 2005. Adapted with permission.

Oral communication strategies

Oral communication strategies	Student areas of need that may have an impact on the effectiveness of the strategy	Considerations for implementation
"*Think-pair-share*"		

Students independently consider a task, strategy, and so on, then pair with another student and share ideas. Two pairs then join each other to discuss further.	• Language abilities—the ability to process information, make connections, and express ideas and solutions.
	• Prior knowledge and experience—level of content knowledge required to complete the task.
		• Consider pairings that support different levels of language ability. Pairings should:
		  – model good language
		  – challenge thinking.
		• Provide visual prompts or sentence starters to keep pairs on task.
		• Consider tasks that support different levels of understanding:
		  – pair a capable student with a less capable student to scaffold learning
		  – pair students of similar abilities to consolidate or extend learning.

"*Show-and-Tell*"		
Students explain the task to one another, build a representation of the solution and then share their work through pictures, words or diagrams.	• Cognitive abilities—being able to represent thinking in concrete ways. • Metacognitive abilities—identifying and selecting appropriate strategies and organizing information • Language abilities—the ability to process information, make connections and express ideas and solutions.	• Provide models of how to describe and show thinking concretely: "I found the total number of buttons by putting them into groups of 10. And then I counted 10, 20, 30, 31, 32, 33." • Provide a checklist that describes the steps in the process. • Provide a template to help organize work. • Provide a framework for showing and telling that might include prompts or sentence starters.

224

Oral communication strategies	Student areas of need that may have an impact on the effectiveness of the strategy	Considerations for implementation
"Mathematician's chair"		
Students prepare a problem, then share it with the class or small group.	• Language abilities—the ability to process information, make connections and express ideas and solutions. • Self-regulatory abilities—the ability to plan, organize information, to create and solve a problem, and then to share the solution.	• Model what and how to share using think-aloud. • Use a graphic organizer to model the steps needed to solve a problem.

225

Written communication strategies

Written communication strategies	Student areas of need that may have an impact on the effectiveness of the strategy	Considerations for implementation
"Mind mapping"		
The teacher records ideas about a concept using key words. He or she draws a mind map showing how the ideas are connected.	• This is a good strategy for all students.	• Provide blank or partial templates to help students organize their thinking.
"Think-talk-write"		

The teacher gives students a problem/question/prompt to think about.
 	
Students take turns in small groups to talk about their ideas. Students then write a response.
	• Language abilities—the ability to process information, make connections and express ideas and solutions orally, then in writing.
	• Prior knowledge and experience—level of content knowledge required to complete the task.
		• Consider pairings that support different levels of language ability.
		• Model mathematical language.
		• Challenge thinking by asking "How do you know?"
		• Utilize visual prompts to keep pairs on task.
		• Provide written prompts or sentence starters for sharing.
		• Consider pairings that support different levels of understanding:
		  – pair a capable student with a less capable student to scaffold learning
		  – pair students of similar abilities to consolidate or extend learning.

226

Written communication strategies	Student areas of need that may have an impact on the effectiveness of the strategy	Considerations for implementation
"Place mat"		

Students work in groups of four. Each student records responses in one quadrant of a large sheet of paper. A summary of all responses is written in the centre of the paper.	• Prior knowledge and experience—level of content knowledge required to participate in the task.	• Consider groupings that support different levels of understanding:
		  – group capable students with less capable students to scaffold learning
		  – group students of similar abilities to consolidate or extend learning.

"Graphic organizers"		
Students use Venn diagrams, flowcharts, and T-charts to arrange information visually.	• Self-regulation—the ability to know when to use an organizer, how to use it and how to evaluate its effectiveness.	• Model the appropriate use of different types of organizers. • Provide examples of different forms.
"Mathematics word wall" and *"Mathematics strategy wall"*		
Students refer to mathematics vocabulary and sample problem-solving strategies posted in the classroom while making oral and written responses.	• Working memory—the ability to keep in mind the words and strategies needed while completing a writing task.	• Review vocabulary and strategies often. • Provide examples of how the words and strategies are used. • Colour-code, classify or group words and strategies for easier reference.
"Journals" and *"Learning Logs"*		
Students represent their understanding of mathematical concepts by contributing responses, explanations and reflections, using pictures, numbers and/or words.	• Self-regulation—the ability to organize what has just been experienced and then provide a recording of it. • Working memory—the ability to hold in mind what to write, the grammar needed to write and the style to use.	• Provide sentence starters, outlines and models. • Model the use of pictures and diagrams. • Teach the writing form using different examples and contexts. • Provide a checklist of the content to be included in the journal/learning log.

227

Written communication strategies	Student areas of need that may have an impact on the effectiveness of the strategy	Considerations for implementation
"Mathematics picture books"		
Students write and illustrate a picture book individually, in pairs or as a whole class to explain a concept.	• Self-regulation—the ability to plan and organize an entire story.	• Provide a model using published picture books. • Provide think sheets for planning.
"Poster projects"		
Concepts are represented in poster form using pictures, diagrams and written explanations.	• Self-regulation—the ability to plan and organize a poster.	• Provide examples; use picture supports.
"Students' problem posing"		
Students write their own problems and share them with the class.	• Language abilities—the ability to process information, make connections and express ideas and solutions in writing, then orally.	• Provide a checklist for students to use to write their own problems. • Model what and how to share, using think-aloud.

228

Reading comprehension strategies

Reading comprehension strategies	Student areas of need that may have an impact on the effectiveness of the strategy	Considerations for implementation
"Retell, Reflect, Relate"		
Students answer questions before, during and after the reading of the problem or task.	• Language abilities—the ability to make connections, use vocabulary and express thinking. • Working memory—the ability to hold in mind important information from the text.	• Use alternative forms of presentation (oral: discuss the problem; visual: present the problem in a picture). • Discuss new vocabulary (add to mathematics wall). • Provide students with a graphic organizer to work through the problem.
"Mental Imagery"		
Students try to represent the problem through the use of images.	• Working memory—the ability to hold in mind important information from the text. • Prior knowledge and experience (vocabulary).	• Generate an image/drawing. • Act out the problem. • Present the problem to students using different media (e.g., audio, picture) to respond to varying learning styles.

229

Create a safe and caring environment

Create a learning environment in which students feel confident in taking risks and trying new things. Ways to do this include asking questions with no wrong answers and explicitly teaching students how to listen to and support one another.

In the differentiated mathematics classroom, as in any classroom, fostering a positive attitude toward learning is important. Create an environment that encourages success in mathematics. Stress the importance of mathematics as a life skill through the use of real-life situations, and incorporate a problem-solving approach to build on student ability to think analytically and creatively.

Reward and highlight student achievements and/or strengths. Set attainable goals with students and monitor progress on a predetermined schedule. Celebrate successes along the way, and encourage students to reinforce themselves for setting and achieving goals. Emphasize the effort that went into achieving the goals. Help them understand that mistakes help us learn and that mistakes point the way to success. Finally, create an atmosphere of cooperation in which all students are active learners who support each other throughout the learning process.

Science

Contents of this chapter

13

231

"The [scientific] inquiry process is active, engaging and transferable. Studies have found that not only are students learning more science content through inquiry, but they are also developing the ability to 'study the natural world and propose explanations based on the evidence derived from their work'[1] through inquiry."
— The Access Center and American Institutes for Research in "Science Inquiry: The Link to Accessing the General Education Curriculum"

Inquiry is an important component of science education and an ideal place to begin differentiating instruction. Inquiry-based learning is a process where students formulate questions, investigate widely and then build new understandings, meanings and knowledge. This knowledge may be used to answer a question, to develop a solution or to support a position or point of view. The knowledge is usually presented to others and may result in some sort of action. Although inquiry-based learning takes time and commitment to implement, the benefits are obvious—students learn to question, explore, research, test, analyze, compare and pose ideas. "Opportunities to think and behave as scientists provide relevance and credibility to student understanding of science. They learn that it is appropriate to ask questions and seek answers. In addition, students learn the challenges and pitfalls of investigations" (The Access Center and American Institutes for Research, p. 7).

Effective inquiry-based instruction naturally builds in elements of differentiation. You can further emphasize differentiated instruction by purposefully planning ways to:

- offer learning experiences that vary in complexity, open-endedness and structure
- deal with authentic, real-life problems within the context of the curriculum and community
- incorporate more student choice, including opportunities for students to generate and pursue their own science-related questions
- support students in multiple ways and scaffold instruction as they build understandings of science
- model behaviours, language and multiple processes for gathering and presenting information
- encourage meaningful personal connections and applications of scientific concepts
- make student understandings of scientific concepts visible at each phase of the inquiry process
- provide constructive and instructive feedback to students at each phase of the inquiry process.

---

1. Reprinted with permission from *National Science Education Standards* (p. 23), 1996, by the National Academy of Sciences, courtesy of the National Academies Press, Washington, DC.

This chapter provides suggestions for differentiating instruction in science within a scientific inquiry model. There are many types of inquiry and the sample process discussed in this chapter will focus on a research inquiry. For more information and strategies related to inquiry, see *Focus on Inquiry* (Alberta Learning 2004). available at http://education.alberta.ca/media/313361/focusoniquiry.pdf.

Plan for differentiated inquiry

Planning for inquiry-based science instruction begins with an understanding of relevant outcomes and the stages of inquiry. Most inquiry models include the following stages.
>   1. Planning.
>   2. Retrieving.
>   3. Creating and Sharing.
>   4. Evaluating.

These stages need not be followed in a lock-step sequence. Some students may need opportunities to approach inquiry from the middle or even end points within the process. Students also should be taught to go backwards or forwards in the process and to revisit some phases more than once.

An inquiry model outlines the skills and strategies that need to be taught explicitly in each phase of the process. Referring to the model frequently and consistently during the planning of inquiry-based learning activities keeps instructional concerns in the forefront as you plan learning activities and create instructional materials. Consider the following strategies to help you plan effective, differentiated inquiry activities.

Know your students
Use learner profiles, pre-assessments, observation, discussion and other strategies to learn about students' individual strengths, interests, experiences and background knowledge. This information is vital to choosing relevant topics and to making effective decisions about instruction and assessment. For more information about learner profiles, see *Chapter 3: Developing Learner Profiles*.

Identify topics
It is important to select a topic or theme that is worthy of the time and effort involved and that will be interesting to students for more than a short-term period. Early selection of a theme and inquiry activity will give you the time to build student background knowledge, to develop the inquiry skills and strategies that students will need, and to gather the required resources. The most successful curriculum inquiry projects emerge from topics that are of personal interest to the students (Wiggins and McTighe 1998). In a teacher-directed inquiry project, students need to have a choice of topics about which they truly wonder and care, and there needs to be an identifiable time when students work on their inquiries.

233

In student-directed inquiry projects, you may provide curriculum-related themes and allow students to generate their own topic questions. It is important to ensure that appropriate resources are available for the topics students will be investigating.

Separate content from process

Separating *what* students are learning from *how* they are learning can provide more opportunities to meet a greater range of differing student needs. Using this approach, you could have all students working with common content that is described in the program of studies. However, students will have different levels of engagement with that content, as well as different process skills. Learners will, therefore, differ in the depth, scope, detail and sophistication of the processes and products that stem from a given inquiry. By being mindful of the possibilities for separating content and process, there is a greater dimension of flexibility for differentiation.

Consider grouping options

There are many possible groupings for inquiry activities. Will students work individually, in pairs, small groups or as a whole class? If working in pairs or in small groups, how might student strengths and needs be balanced by the composition of the groupings? In upper elementary grades, consider how reading ability can affect this decision. Students who require more assistance could be partnered with students who require less support. Individual learner profiles and class profiles can be helpful in planning appropriate groupings to provide optimal levels of support.

Identify scaffolding opportunities

All learners of science need opportunities for appropriate challenge, growth and success. Some students will require concrete and tangible examples that provide clear, guided support. Others can develop and apply skills in increasingly independent, abstract and complex contexts. It may be helpful to consider student needs along a continuum of support through to independence. That is, students will vary in the degree of teacher support that will be required in order for them to successfully engage in scientific inquiry. Aim to provide students with multiple contexts, ranging from independent experiences to guided inquiries to group or partner-supported inquiry. Individual students also may require differing levels of assistance at the various stages of the inquiry process.

Direct modelling by the teacher; direct intervention and assistance is required and offered	Significant level of teacher assistance required	Moderate level of teacher assistance required	Student engages in inquiry independently

234

Assess student learning

An important way to differentiate instruction is to consider student needs and talents as learners of science before beginning the first phase of an inquiry-based project. Asking students to complete a simple inventory can help identify where and how to support them as they engage in scientific inquiry. Such pre-assessments also can be a valuable addition to learner profiles, and aid in planning other aspects of differentiation, such as activities differentiated by student interests or learning preferences. A sample inventory is included as *Tool 1: What Kind of Science Learner am I?* at the end of this chapter.

As you progress through the inquiry, contine to assess learning on an ongoing basis to help you effectively adjust teaching strategies and levels of support for individual students and student groupings. Assessment *for* learning may be accomplished individually, in pairs or small groups, by peers or as a whole class activity. It is important to use assessment tasks to make student understanding explicit and to provide feedback about both the inquiry itself and related skills such as teamwork. This feedback should describe and support progress and not necessarily be recorded as part of students' final evaluations.

Concept attainment

One useful assessment *for* learning strategy is concept attainment. This strategy is particularly helpful toward the end of the retrieving and processing phase to identify any misconceptions regarding a particular science concept under investigation. Concept attainment may be done with individual students, small groups or with the whole class, depending on learning needs. The basic steps involved are listed below and can be adjusted based on student developmental levels.

1. Set up a section of the board or a piece of paper with two columns: one labelled "Yes" and the other labelled "No."

2. Use individual strips of paper to record (a) the attributes of the science concept, (b) exemplars that illustrate the science concept, and (c) non-exemplars that help to illustrate what is *not* associated with the science concept. Note that student work on the inquiry to this point may be a source for non-exemplars if the student is misinterpreting information. However, this kind of feedback needs to be given with sensitivity; e.g., individually rather than in front of the group.

3. Without identifying the specific science concept to students, share the strips of paper with students, one strip at a time. Ask students to decide if the given strip belongs on the "Yes" side or the "No" side of the chart. Students should recognize the science concept as the activity unfolds; if not, this is an indicator that additional instruction may be required.

4. Lead and encourage discussion throughout the activity about why students are making certain choices. The goal is that, toward the end of the activity, students will be able to identify the science concept and to more solidly delineate the critical attributes of that concept.

Assessment and evaluation *of* learning is not required at every phase of an inquiry, nor even for every inquiry. Students need supportive opportunities throughout an inquiry to work toward independence without the pressure of evaluative scoring. When final evaluations are appropriate, watch for opportunities to differentiate the assessment process; e.g., How will students demonstrate and share their learning? What are the different possibilities for students to best demonstrate their learning while still allowing you to assess the same curricular outcomes for the class as a whole? Science assessment often relies on writing, which can create challenges for some students. Providing opportunities for students to communicate learning in a variety of ways, including using drawing and presentations, ensures that all students can accurately demonstrate their learning.

For more information, see *Chapter 4: Differentiated Assessment.*

Inquiry and differentiated learning experiences

Inquiries can be differentiated through pacing, complexity and degree of support; through providing a variety and choice of activities; and through actively engaging students at all phases of the inquiry. Ongoing reflection and dialogue with students are critical aspects of the entire inquiry process, as plans and questions should be revisited and, if necessary, revised as the process unfolds. Student understanding of inquiry is enhanced when you explicitly teach and frequently refer to the inquiry model you are using. Post the model in your classroom and the school library so students may reference it at any time.

The following list provides an overview of sample approaches and strategies for differentiated inquiry-based learning experiences. Although the strategies are organized by phases of the inquiry process, many of these strategies can be adapted and used at multiple phases. For more information on differentiating learning experiences through scaffolding, flexible grouping, student choice and other strategies, see *Chapter 5: Differentiated Learning Experiences.*

Planning phase
In this phase, students:
- identify a topic for inquiry
- identify possible information sources
- identify audience and presentation format
- establish evaluation criteria
- outline a plan for inquiry.

Consider the following sample strategies and approaches to differentiate instruction during the planning phase of inquiry.

Make connections

- Use visual, audio, narrative and musical examples to introduce a topic, inquiry question or investigation, draw out affective responses, and encourage students to make comparisons and draw inferences based on their prior knowledge and understandings.
- Connect personal life experiences to abstract ideas and concepts. Model using personal examples and insights related to a scientific inquiry or investigation.
- Encourage students to make predictions and hypotheses as they begin their inquiry. Ask them to reflect explicitly on prior knowledge and make their own connections to new science concepts and topics.
- Teach students how to use graphic organizers to describe their prior knowledge and organize their thinking and learning. For example, use a "K-W-L chart" to encourage students to track and reflect on their learning from the beginning of a topic of study to its completion. The "K-W-L chart" can help to establish direction for the inquiry and promote reflection at the end of the inquiry.

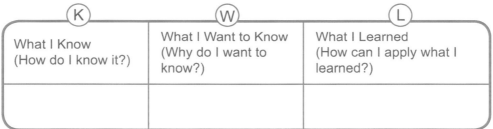

K — What I Know (How do I know it?)	W — What I Want to Know (Why do I want to know?)	L — What I Learned (How can I apply what I learned?)

Use flexible groupings

- Have students structure their plan for inquiry individually, in partners, in small groups or as a whole class.
- Have students find a partner who is interested in the same question or in using the same source of information.
- Invite students to "think-pair-share", by reflecting on the question, sharing their response with a partner and then contributing their ideas to a class discussion.
- Invite students to generate their own questions that will guide further research and exploration. Compare questions and use as the basis for forming research groups.

Use scaffolding strategies

- Use demonstrations and modelling with "think-alouds" to walk through steps in applying a skill.
- Provide multiple opportunities to practise skills and apply processes with support. Include guided practice in which you work through examples with students.

- Use inductive problem-solving activities to introduce and model the inquiry process. Provide students with a problem or issue and invite them to ask questions that can be answered with only "yes-no" responses to obtain more information. Emphasize skills of applying logic to information, processing responses and using information gained to lead to new questions. Once students believe they have enough information, they can present a hypothesis.

Provide opportunities for student choice
- Develop a list of inquiry questions or topics related to a concept from which students can select one that most interests them.
- Ensure that students have the opportunity, at one or more points in the year, to generate their own questions for inquiry. Some students may require assistance in the formation and refining of questions, but it is important that they are able to pursue topics that are of interest and are meaningful to them.

2 ▶ Retrieving and processing phase

In this phase, students:
- develop an information retrieval plan
- locate, collect and evaluate information resources
- establish a focus for inquiry
- evaluate, choose and record pertinent information
- make connections and inferences
- review and revise the plan for inquiry one or more times as they work through these steps.

Retrieving and processing can be bundled together, as the process of scientific inquiry often requires an interplay between them. Movement between them also will depend on personal preferences, student needs and teaching styles.

Consider the following sample strategies and approaches to differentiate instruction during the retrieving and processing phase of inquiry.

Vary the context, tasks and sources
- Have students complete the same task with different information sources.
- Have students use the same information source to complete different tasks or apply different processes.
- Have students use the same information source and process to complete different projects or products.

Use flexible groupings
- Provide different contexts in which students respond to questions or explore information, including whole class, small group and partner discussions, and individual student reflection.

- Have individual students pool research and information from different sources to share with the class. For example, provide each student with recipe cards, post-it notes or strips of paper. Have students record one fact per card. Post the recorded facts on a bulletin board or other common space so that other students can access their peers' research. Monitor the postings for accuracy, and discuss any misconceptions or inaccuracies with students so that they can be corrected together.
- Have students explore sources of information using "carousel" or "gallery walk" strategies. Organize different sources in stations or displays around the classroom and invite students to visit different stations to select, summarize, organize and analyze content.
- Establish learning centres using classroom areas, pizza box or other containers to hold different types of sources of information.
- Provide opportunities for students to chunk content, share understandings and apply knowledge and understandings by teaching others. For example, use a "cooperative learning jigsaw strategy" to divide responsibilities among groups of students and provide them with the opportunity to teach others what they have learned. Expert groups can be based on differing predictions or hypotheses, sources of information or experiments.
- Vary questioning strategies to provide opportunities for students to contribute meaningfully to discussions.

Provide information in multiple formats
- Provide multiple examples related to the topic and concepts.
- Present concepts through hands-on or concrete materials, experimentation, models and demonstrations.
- Provide visual supports, including videos, images, highlighted text and photocopies of key words and notes, to enhance understanding of the concepts under investigation and the inquiry process itself.
- Whenever possible, provide a variety of parallel texts on the same topic with a range of reading levels.
- Ask students to think of and share different ways they can represent information, terms and concepts. Encourage students to develop mental, symbolic and nonlinguistic representations of textual information.
- Read textual information out loud as students listen with their eyes closed, encouraging students to ask questions as they listen. Have students create a mental picture of what they 'see in their minds' and then share, categorize and prioritize their insights by using a graphic organizer.

Encourage active engagement and critical thinking
- Encourage students to use multiple sources of information to answer questions. Teach students to consider and evaluate multiple perspectives, and to explore consistencies and inconsistencies between sources.

239

- Encourage students to compare and contrast different data sets or information from different sources. Have students use an "interactive notebook format" or "split page organizer" to record information and reflect on similarities and differences. An interactive notebook or split page organizer divides a notebook page into two columns, and asks students to record facts and information on the right column and personal insights, questions and reflections on the left side.
- Provide a research retrieval chart that requires students to identify consistent and inconsistent information between different sources and compare with experimental data or personal hypotheses or predictions.

Help students organize, analyze and manage information

- Provide key information or use key questions as an advance organizer to help students organize and make sense of new content.
- Teach students to select the graphic organizer that best supports their learning needs and the specific task. Invite students to create their own graphic organizer, specific to an identified purpose.
- Chunk text and tasks into smaller, manageable sections.
- Colour-code handouts and text or use sticky notes to mark important sections of text.
- Pre-teach key vocabulary.
- Watch for students who are feeling frustrated or overwhelmed by finding too many or too few information sources. Teach students that these feelings are ones that many inquirers experience, and provide skills and strategies for selecting relevant information and for modifying inquiries when necessary.
- Teach students how to compare, contrast and synthesize data to choose pertinent information from resources.

3 ▶ Creating and sharing phase

In this phase, students

- organize information
- think about the audience
- create a product
- revise and edit
- present new understandings
- demonstrate appropriate audience behaviour.

Consider the following sample strategies and approaches to differentiate instruction during the creating and sharing phase of inquiry.

Encourage new interpretations

- Provide opportunities for students to organize and share their data in accordance with their own background knowledge, experiences and learning preferences.

- Use a "concept formation" strategy. Concept formation employs divergent thinking—every answer will be considered to be correct as long as students can articulate a logical and reasonable rationale. In this strategy, students do the following.
  1. Record facts on strips of paper. These facts must stem from a reliable source and should be monitored for accuracy.
  2. Spread out the information on a flat surface.
  3. Group the facts by physically moving the strips of paper into clusters and labelling each cluster. Students should be able to describe a rationale for each grouping, including only the critical attributes that define each category.

  When students are finished, review the labelled clusters, encouraging them to consider areas where additional research may be required. The process of organizing and expanding on the information base may go back and forth several times before a complete data set is created.

Provide variety and choice
- Provide choices for students to demonstrate skills with the same content.
- Invite students to demonstrate skills using different content, selected by interest, readability or differentiated topics.
- Offer students choice in product development and assessment; for example, provide the option to use choice boards, cubes or matrixes to create products that demonstrate knowledge and understandings.
- Provide options for students to communicate their learning through illustrated and/or textual storyboards, illustrated and/or text-based time lines, maps (bird's eye views), labelled diagrams, posters, tables, picture glossaries, diagrams to scale, analytic or cutaway diagrams, comparative diagrams, illustrated cross sections, flowcharts to flow diagrams (to illustrate change, growth or development, cause and effect, chain of sequence), tree diagrams, webs, concept maps, graphs (bar, column, line, pie), two- and three- dimensional models, and illustrated and/or textual tables.

Promote success
- Help students keep their creation to a manageable scope.
- Provide supports and scaffolds within the structure of a project to encourage students to demonstrate their learning on different levels.
- Provide agendas, menus or task lists to guide students through assignments or projects, especially when the task requires students to work with a learning preference that they are not the most proficient in.
- Set up learning centres with different projects as their focus. Work with groups of students to map their use and complete the tasks within all or some of the centres.
- Break long-term assignments or projects into smaller steps, with clear due dates and frequent feedback.

241

- Provide checklists to help students manage multi-step tasks or post daily assignment requirements.
- Provide instruction on when and how to use various formats (e.g., labelled diagrams, posters, tables, picture glossaries, diagrams to scale), and make samples or models available to students to encourage them to correctly use different modes for communicating their learning.
- Make sample completed projects available so students can plan projects and products with the end in mind.

Provide opportunities to share results

- Provide bulletin board or other display space to students on a regular basis.
- Have students share their inquiry work with others through a poster presentation, a format similar to that used at conferences where scientific research is shared with the larger professional science community.
- Set up a trade show where desks or tables are organized into a horseshoe shape and work is displayed.
- Invite other classes of students, parents or members of the community to the science classroom to view and hear about student research and inquiry products.
- Explicitly teach audience appreciation skills and strategies.

4 ▶ Evaluating phase

In this phase, students:
- evaluate the product
- evaluate the inquiry process and inquiry plan
- review and revise personal inquiry model
- transfer learning to new situations, including those beyond school
- identify new questions and applications for their learning.

Consider the following sample strategies and approaches to differentiate instruction during the evaluating phase of inquiry.

Create opportunities for self-assessment

- Include frequent opportunities for ongoing and formative assessment, such as rating scales and self-reflective writing assignments. In addition to more formal approaches, consider simple strategies such as asking students to hold up a number of fingers to self-assess understanding, or to use thumbs up or down to indicate agreement or disagreement.
- Provide regular opportunities for students to use and be involved in creating rating scales, criteria and rubrics.
- Use index cards as exit cards to have students self-assess and reflect on their application of a skill or process throughout the inquiry process by writing down an answer to a question or prompt such as "Name one thing you learned today about ...."
- Use the accumulated observations to assist in evaluating the process as a whole.

Encourage personal reflection

- Encourage students to reflect on and discuss questions such as:
  - What went well in each phase of this inquiry?
  - What might I change to make my work stronger and to increase my learning and skill level?
  - What have I learned in this inquiry?
  - What was the highlight of this assignment? Why?
  - What did I learn that I can transfer to other tasks in and out of school?
- Provide an opportunity for students to complete and reflect on their "K-W-L charts."
- Encourage students to read their personal journals and reflect on them.
- Have students write, draw, present or represent syntheses of their activities.

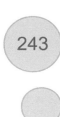

243

Tool 1: What Kind of Science Learner Am I?

1. On a scale of 1 to 10 (one being least and 10 being most), I enjoy learning about science.

   1   2   3   4   5   6   7   8   9   10

2. On a scale of 1 to 10 (one being least and 10 being most), I do well in science.

   1   2   3   4   5   6   7   8   9   10

3. When doing science, I like to work (check all that apply to you):
   ❑ alone
   ❑ with a partner
   ❑ in a small group
   ❑ as a whole class

4. In learning about science, I like to (check all that apply to you):
   ❑ read
   ❑ watch demonstrations of inquiries
   ❑ carry out inquiries that have been developed by others
   ❑ design and carry out my own inquiries
   ❑ other _____

5. I prefer to show my learning in science by (check all that apply to you):
   ❑ writing
   ❑ drawing
   ❑ charting
   ❑ sharing orally
   ❑ using models
   ❑ using a computer (e.g., PowerPoint presentations)
   ❑ other _____

6. Areas that I do well in science include: _____

   _____

7. Areas that I struggle with in science include: _____

   _____

   _____

8. An area that I would like to improve on in science is: _____

   _____

   _____

244

Social Studies

Contents of this chapter

14

245

"Social studies helps students develop their sense of self and community, encouraging them to affirm their place in an inclusive democratic society."
– Alberta Social Studies program of studies, p. 1.

Differentiated instruction is possible and valuable in all subject areas; in social studies it is a particularly natural fit. The emphasis on diversity in the social studies program parallels the reality of diversity in our classrooms. The messages that differentiation sends to students about choice, empowerment and respect for differences reinforce the core concepts of citizenship and identity that are embedded in the Alberta social studies program.

This chapter offers steps and strategies for considering key elements of the social studies program, including attitudes, knowledge, skills and assessment, in light of the individual students in your classroom.

Make connections

Establishing personal connections to the topics and concepts of the curriculum increases motivation, promotes active engagement with content, and recognizes the diversity of experiences that shape and influence understandings. Implementing strategies to facilitate personal connections sets a context that can allow multiple paths through the learning process.

Students need to connect new learning not only to their personal experiences and beliefs, but also to their existing knowledge. Strategies used to introduce a topic and activities used throughout a learning activity can be purposefully planned to connect new learning to what students already know, understand and can do. In doing so, these strategies and activities also can provide a context to pre-assess student levels of understanding and skill, as well as attitudes, learning preferences and interests. This information can help you identify additional learning activities, and provide an entry point for scaffolding and ongoing assessment decisions.

Planning units and individual learning activities around the big ideas or universal concepts in the program of studies can be an effective way to encourage connections. For more information on planning, see *Chapter 2: Purposeful Planning*.

The following approaches can be used to help students connect to social studies content in a variety of ways. Consider these sample strategies not only at the beginning of a unit of study, but throughout as new concepts are introduced.

Know your students

- Create learner profiles by using pre-assessments, observations, discussions and other strategies to learn about students' individual strengths, interests, experiences and background knowledge. This information is vital to making effective decisions about instruction and assessment. For more information about learner profiles, see *Chapter 3: Developing Learner Profiles*.

Elicit personal responses

- Introduce new topics with multiple examples that are meaningful to students with a variety of learning preferences, backgrounds and interests. Consider using visual, audio, narrative and musical examples.
- Use literature to evoke emotional responses and encourage students to make personal comparisons and connections.
- Connect abstract ideas and concepts to personal life experiences. For example, introduce an historical study by asking students to identify three aspects of their neighbourhood or community that have changed over time. How is it different? What are some of the reasons for the changes? Introduce a geographic study by asking students to write or talk about about a personal experience they had with a source of water, such as a lake, brook or ocean.
- Encourage students to compare and contrast historical events or time periods with current events and issues. For example, have students use an "interactive notebook format" or "split page organizer" to record information and reflect on similarities and differences. This organizer divides a notebook page into two columns, and asks students to record factual information on the right column and personal insights, questions and reflections on the left side.

Tap into background knowledge

- Teach students how to use graphic organizers to organize their thinking, and describe their prior knowledge, understandings and experiences. For example, use a "K-W-L chart" to encourage students to track and reflect on what they <u>k</u>now, what they <u>w</u>ant to know and what they <u>l</u>earned from the beginning of a topic of study to its completion.
- Give students a list of vocabulary and invite them to identify terms they know well, terms they are familiar with and terms they do not understand.

Integrate new learning

- Encourage students to make predictions, in order to elicit prior knowledge and make connections to new topics.
- Invite students to "think-pair-share" by reflecting on a new topic or question, sharing their response with a partner and then contributing their ideas to a class discussion.

247

- Invite students to explore and reflect on connections between two or more concepts or topics.
- Have students use an "interactive notebook" format to record their interactions with information and text. Students use the right page of the notebook to record notes during instruction, discussions, reading, viewing, group work and research activities. They use the left page to reflect, process, make connections, doodle ideas or pose questions in any way they would like.
- Invite students to generate their own questions that will guide further research and exploration. Compare questions and use as the basis for forming research groups or planning other activities.

Create multiple pathways to content

Deep understandings in social studies are developed when students have opportunities to:
- connect what they know to the big ideas and concepts in a topic of study or across multiple subject areas
- apply their learning to think critically, make inferences and solve problems
- recognize when new understandings challenge previous understandings
- transfer what they have learned across different contexts
- act on their new learning by contributing to the community.

Differentiated instruction assumes that all students, regardless of learning preferences, background, experiences and abilities, are capable of developing these understandings. It recognizes that in order for all students to be able to benefit from all outcomes, they will need multiple pathways to get there.

Bloom's taxonomy and Gardner's model of multiple intelligences can provide flexible pathways for organizing instruction. Providing content through different sources (e.g., artifacts, photographs, diaries, maps, sound or video tapes, music, literature) is one way to elicit different types of intelligences and provide an access point for more students to learn.

Creating multiple pathways also involves providing the resources and strategies that students need to think critically about the content you are teaching. Differentiated content sources and questioning strategies can provide opportunities for different levels of complexity in the development of critical thinking skills. Providing students with a variety of strategies for identifying, interpreting, organizing and analyzing information gives them the tools to select those strategies that work best for them.

The social studies program provides a multitude of possibilities for meeting diverse learning needs of students while encouraging them to develop deep understandings of content. Consider the following strategies.

Vary the context, tasks and sources

- Have students complete the same task with different information sources.
- Have students use the same information source to complete different tasks or apply different processes.
- Have students use the same information source and process to complete different projects or products.

Use and encourage a variety of formats

- Respect student limits regarding the length of teacher talk. Students respond best to short intervals of teacher talk; i.e., 5–7 minutes for primary grades; 7–12 minutes for intermediate; 12–15 minutes for secondary.
- Use a variety of visual supports to present topics and concepts, including videos, images, highlighted text, outlines, photocopies of key words and notes.
- Whenever possible, provide a variety of parallel texts on the same topic with a range of reading levels.
- Ask students to think of and share different ways they can represent information, terms and concepts. Encourage students to develop mental, symbolic and nonlinguistic representations of textual information.
- Read textual information out loud as students listen with their eyes closed, encouraging students to ask questions as they listen. Have students create a mental picture of what they 'see in their minds' and then share, categorize and prioritize their insights by using a graphic organizer.
- Provide students with opportunities to develop products such as comic books, picture books, songs and three dimensional models, and to use movement and drama to represent their learning of content.

Create flexible, active research options

- Encourage students to use multiple sources of information to answer questions. Teach students to consider and evaluate multiple perspectives, and to explore consistencies and inconsistencies between sources.
- Provide a research retrieval chart that requires students to use both fiction and non-fiction sources to investigate and explore information.
- Provide sources of information with varying degrees of difficulty and complexity. Offer these sources in different contexts that allow and encourage students to make choices about their research and learn at their own pace.
- Invite students to illustrate different perspectives represented in information and sources.

249

Help students organize and analyze information
- Provide key information or use key questions as an advance organizer to help students organize and make sense of new content.
- Provide students with graphic organizers that support the purpose of the learning experience.
- Teach students to select the graphic organizer that best supports their learning needs and the specific task. Invite students to create their own graphic organizer, specific to an identified purpose.
- Chunk text and tasks into smaller, manageable sections.
- Colour-code handouts and text or use sticky notes to mark important sections of text.

Use flexible groupings to support learning
- Use a variety of collaborative structures and contexts when grouping students. Structure groups according to common interests, learning preferences or readiness levels by using topics, levelled sources or tasks as the basis for groups. See *Chapter 5: Differentiated Learning Experiences* for more information on flexible grouping.
- Divide content responsibilities among groups of students and provide them with the opportunity to teach content to others.
- Organize different sources of information in stations or displays around the classroom and invite students to visit different stations to select, summarize, organize and analyze content.
- Establish learning centres using classroom areas, pizza boxes or other containers to hold different types of sources of information.
- Provide different contexts in which students respond to content or concept-based questions, including whole class discussions, small group and partner discussions, and individual student reflection.
- Work with students to develop strategies for selecting group members before allowing them to choose their own groups.

Offer diverse practice of skills and processes

In a social studies classroom, skills that are critical to student learning and growth include:
- reading for detail
- interpreting and analyzing primary sources
- organizing and categorizing information
- comparing and contrasting ideas and information
- recognizing multiple perspectives
- drawing conclusions.

250

Purposeful skill development should teach students to recognize, apply and extend their use of content beyond the comprehension level. Questions, discussions and activities should challenge all students to engage in problem solving, decision making, and critical and creative thinking. Activities should model and create opportunities for students to apply skills such as historical and geographic thinking.

At the same time, students need varying degrees of complexity, open-endedness and structure to develop these skills to their fullest potential. Some students require concrete and tangible examples that clearly and specifically provide guided support. Others can develop and apply skills very quickly in independent, abstract and complex contexts. Planning opportunities at all stages support students who are at different levels of learning readiness, and cognitive and affective development.

Differentiation of skills and processes allows students to apply their learning preferences and interests, while at the same time encouraging them to work in multiple learning contexts in order to strengthen areas of weakness. For example, flexible grouping strategies, including collaborative and cooperative learning contexts, emphasize participation in multiple group settings that provide students with different learning needs and opportunities to both succeed and grow.

It is easy for some students to get lost in large group discussions. But those quiet, shy students, who rarely participate in whole-class exchanges, often become more involved when they work with a partner. On the other hand, those students who tend to dominate class discussions must step back and take their lead from other students when they participate in a cooperative group activity. Students not only learn academic content and important skills from their peers in group settings, they learn how to be productive group members in a variety of situations (Dodge 2005, p. 104).

Consider the following sample strategies for promoting skill development in a differentiated social studies classroom.

Scaffold instruction

- Model skills and processes as part of ongoing instructional activities. Be particularly conscious of demonstrating discipline-based processes, including historical, geographic, archaeological and cultural.
- Introduce new processes with simple, step-by-step directions. Clarify and monitor student understanding throughout the process.
- Use a "think-aloud" approach to talk through steps in applying a skill.
- Provide multiple opportunities to practise skills and apply processes with support. Include guided practice in which you work through examples with students.

- Provide regular, meaningful feedback as students apply skills. Consider teacher-directed self-assessment checks; peer feedback in groups; peer feedback through project partners or learning buddies; and teacher feedback in individual or group conferencing.
- Provide students with tools, such as graphic organizers, that encourage them to apply skills and processes.
- Create opportunities for students to work as mentors or teachers to practise and refine skills.
- Check for understanding and application of skills and processes within authentic tasks.

Provide variety and choice
- Provide choices for students to demonstrate skills with the same content.
- Invite students to demonstrate skills using different content, selected by interest or reading level.
- Provide students with the option of applying skills and processes individually, with a partner or in a small group.

Encourage responsibility for learning
- Work with students to develop personalized learning goals and tasks.
- Invite students to develop and maintain weekly agendas that outline a set number of tasks that must be completed within a specified time period. Tasks may be related to research activities (such as citing sources or creating a bibliography), demonstrations of learning in specific skill areas (such as constructing a map or time line) or collaborative skills (such as conferencing with a partner to compare research or exchange feedback).
- Have students answer a question or complete a sentence at the end of an activity to self-assess and reflect on their application of a skill or process.
- Provide groups with file folders and invite them to use the folders to develop their group identity (front cover), organize tasks and responsibilities (back cover), and process group work and effectiveness (inside).

Emphasize research and inquiry skills
- Use "inductive problem-solving" activities to introduce and model the inquiry process. Provide students with a controversial topic or contemporary social issue or event and invite them to ask questions that can be answered with only "yes-no" responses to obtain more information. Emphasize skills of applying logic to information, processing responses and using information gained to lead to new questions. Once students believe they have enough information, they can present the hypothesis.
- Structure a variety of activities that require students to work with primary and secondary social studies sources.

- Have students use different strategies to analyze and interpret visual sources, such as historical photographs. For example, students could add "thought bubbles" to photographs to consider differing perspectives, or create captions to develop conclusions.
- Have students use learning logs to record information and research during a unit of study. Learning logs reinforce sequence and organizational skills and also can be used to track and assess student progress and learning.
- Develop a list of questions or topics related to a concept from which students can select an independent inquiry project. Inquiries can be further differentiated through pacing, complexity and degree of support.

Support literacy skills
- Scaffold writing skill development by using prompts and examples.
- Model writing by doing a collaborative piece of writing, with the teacher acting as scribe.
- Use graphic organizers to provide support in specific skills and processes; e.g., cause and effect charts to analyze and consider relationships, flowcharts and time lines to develop understandings of sequence, retrieval charts to gather and organize information.
- Directly teach skills for those students who need it.

253

Differentiate assessment tasks

Assessment strategies, used purposefully to determine student learning strengths and needs, provide an ongoing context for differentiation. Both formative and summative assessment strategies should be developed to allow flexibility, variety and choice. They also should clearly indicate expectations and criteria that students can use as a guideline for making decisions about how they are going to demonstrate what they have learned.

Differentiated assessment should be aligned with the same strategies used to differentiate instruction.

Differentiated products provide opportunities to support students who are at different levels of learning readiness, and cognitive and affective development. Providing students with variety and choices respects different learning preferences, empowers students and builds confidence in their ability to learn. Differentiated products in social studies also emphasize application of learning beyond the classroom by encouraging students to explore issues and take action.

According to Dodge (2005, p. 30) … students need an opportunity to personalize their learning by reorganizing the information and applying the new knowledge to new situations. Post-learning activities should include opportunities for forming opinions, determining importance, noting relationships, taking a position and providing evidence for that position, creating metaphors and analogies, comparing and contrasting concepts, participating in simulations, and using the new knowledge in different linguistic and nonlinguistic ways. By providing these reflective and summative closure opportunities, we help students to enhance the transfer of information into long-term memory.

For more information see *Chapter 4: Differentiated Assessment*.

When planning for differentiated assessment, the emphasis is not on the products and tasks themselves, but on the skills and understandings being demonstrated. Consider the following strategies.

Offer variety and choice

- Provide choices in assessment for learning tasks. Invite students to select from various tasks within tests or quizzes. Tasks can be structured around different learning preferences.
- Provide different formats for students to choose from to demonstrate their learning in assignments and projects.
- Use a product grid to create structured choices for culminating projects. A product grid can be created in different formats, including a "tic-tac-toe" grid, or a "choice board". For example, see *Chapter 5: Differentiated Learning Experiences*.
- Provide structured tasks for assignments and projects that can be completed around different topics or inquiry questions.
- Provide options that involve different learning preferences, including writing, speaking and representing. For example, a time line assignment could be created with text and visuals, in a three dimensional format, by videotaping vignettes or by creating poetry or a song.
- Provide choices about the types of sources students use to create a project. For example, students could investigate and compare places and ways of life by using maps, or tourism brochures and booklets, or the Internet.
- Provide options for completing assignments and projects that include independent or group structures.
- Include options that require students to work on areas in which they are challenged. When offered with the appropriate structure and support, such opportunities can push students to expand their learning abilities and broaden their interests.

254

Promote success

- Provide supports and scaffolds within the structure of a project to encourage students to demonstrate their learning on different levels.
- Provide agendas, menus or task lists to guide students through assignments or projects, especially when the task requires students to work with a learning preference that they are not the most proficient in.
- Set up learning centres with different projects as their focus. Work with groups of students to map their use and completion of the tasks within all or some of the centres.
- Break long-term assignments or projects into smaller steps, with clear due dates and frequent feedback.
- Provide checklists to help students manage multi-step tasks or post daily assignment requirements.
- Make sample completed projects available so students can plan projects and products with the end in mind.

Teach and require self-assessment

- Include frequent opportunities for ongoing formative assessment, such as rating scales and self-reflective writing assignments. In addition to more formal approaches, consider simple strategies such as asking students to hold up a number of fingers to self-assess understanding (e.g., one finger for "beginning to understand", five fingers for "really understand"), or use thumbs up or down to indicate agreement or disagreement.
- Share and discuss assessment strategies and the rationale for using them.
- Provide regular opportunities for students to be involved in creating rating scales, criteria and rubrics.

255

Bibliography

CHAPTER 1: Differentiated Instruction: An Introduction

Dodge, Judith. *Differentiation in Action*. New York, NY: Scholastic, 2005.

Gregory, Gayle H. *Differentiating Instruction with Style: Aligning Teaching and Learner Intelligences for Maximum Achievement*. Thousand Oaks, CA: Corwin Press, Inc., 2005.

Gregory, Gayle H. and Carolyn Chapman. *Differentiated Instructional Strategies: One Size Doesn't Fit All*. Thousand Oaks, CA: Corwin Press, Inc., 2002.

Heacox, Diane. *Differentiating Instruction in the Regular Classroom: How to Reach and Teach all Learners, Grades 3–12*. Minneapolis, MN: Free Spirit Publishing, 2002.

McQuarrie, Lynn, Philip McRae and Holly Stack-Cutler. *Differentiated Instruction: Provincial Research Review*. Edmonton, AB: Alberta Education, 2005.

Politano, Colleen and Joy Paquin. *Brain-Based Learning with Class*. Winnipeg, MB: Portage and Main Press, 2000.

Rose, David and A. Meyer A. *Teaching Every Student in the Digital Age Universal Design for Learning*. Alexandria, VA: ASCD Publications, 2002.

Tomlinson, Carol Ann. *The Differentiated Classroom: Responding to the needs of all Learners*. Alexandria, VA: Association for Supervision and Curriculum Development, 1999.

CHAPTER 2: Purposeful Planning

Bittel, Lester R. *The Nine Master Keys of Management*. New York, NY: McGraw-Hill, 1972.

Dodge, Judith. *Differentiation in Action*. New York, NY: Scholastic, 2005.

Erickson, H. Lynn. *Concept-based Curriculum and Instruction: Teaching Beyond the Facts*. Thousand Oaks, CA: Corwin Press, Inc., 2002.

Hall, Tracey. "Differentiated Instruction" (Wakefield, MA: National Center on Accessing the General Curriculum). *CAST: Universal Design for Learning*. 2002. http://www.cast.org/publications/ncac/ncac_diffinstruc.html (Accessed January 15, 2007).

Oaksford, Linda and Lynn Jones. *Differentiated Instruction Abstract*. Tallahassee, FL: Leon County Schools, 2001.

Ramsay, Douglas and Patricia Shields-Ramsay. *Purposeful Planning*. Edmonton, AB: InPraxis Learning Systems, 2006.

Tomlinson, Carol Ann and Jay McTighe. *Integrating Differentiated Instruction and Understanding by Design: Connecting Content and Kids*. Alexandria, VA: Association for Supervision and Curriculum Development, 2006.

CHAPTER 3: Developing Learner Profiles

Alberta Education. *Building on Success: Helping Students Make Transitions from Year to Year*. Edmonton, AB: Alberta Education, 2006.

Alberta Education. *Make School Work for You: A Resource for Junior and Senior High Students who want to be more Successful Learners*. Edmonton, AB: Alberta Education, 2001.

Armstrong, Thomas. *Multiple Intelligences in the Classroom*. Alexandria, VA: Association for Supervision and Curriculum Development, 1994.

Dodge, Judith. *Differentiation in Action*. New York, NY: Scholastic, 2005.

Dunn, Rita and Ken Dunn, 1987.

Edmonton Public Schools. "AISI Middle Literacy Project." Edmonton, AB: Edmonton Public Schools, 2001.

Gardner, Howard. *Multiple Intelligences: The Theory in Practice*. New York, NY: Basic Books, 1994.

Gregorc, Anthony F. *An Adult's Guide to Style*. Maynard, MA: Gabriel Systems, Inc., 1982.

Gregory, Gayle.H. *Differentiating Instruction with Style. Aligning Teacher and Learner Intelligences for Maximum Achievement*. Thousand Oaks, CA. Corwin Press Inc., 2005.

Hume, Karen. *Start where they are. Differentiating for Success with the Young Adolescent*. Toronto, ON: Pearson Education Canada, Inc., 2008.

Northey, Sheryn Spencer. *Handbook on Differentiated Instruction for Middle and High Schools*. Larchmont, NY: Eye on Education, 2005.

Ontario Ministry of Education. *Education for All: The Report of the Expert Panel on Literacy and Numeracy Instruction for Students with Special Education Needs, Kindergarten to Grade Six*. Toronto, ON: Ontario Ministry of Education, 2005.

Pavelka, Patricia. *Create Independent Learners: Teacher-tested Strategies for all Ability Levels*. Peterborough, NH: Crystal Springs Books, 1999.

Sternberg, Robert J. *Beyond IQ: A Triarchic Theory of Human Intelligence*. New York, NY: Cambridge University Press, 1985.

Turville, Joni. *Differentiating by Student Learning Preferences: Strategies and Lesson Plans*. Larchmont, NY: Eye on Education Inc., 2008.

Willingham, Daniel T. "Ask the Cognitive Scientist: Do Visual, Auditory, and Kinesthetic Learners Need Visual, Auditory, and Kinesthetic Instruction?" *American Educator* 29, 2 (Summer 2005), pp. 31–44.

CHAPTER 4: Differentiated Assessment

Black, Paul et al. "Working Inside the Black Box: Assessment for Learning in the Classroom." *Phi Delta Kappan* 86, 1 (2004), pp. 8–21.

Blaz, Deborah. *Differentiated Assessment for Middle and High School Classrooms*. Larchmont, NY: Eye on Education, Inc., 2008.

Chapman, Carolyn and Rita King. *Differentiated Assessment Strategies: One Tool Doesn't Fit All*. Thousand Oaks, CA: Corwin Press, 2005.

Dodge, Judith. *Differentiation in Action*. New York, NY: Scholastic, 2005.

Guskey, Thomas R. and Jane M. Bailey. *Developing Grading and Reporting Systems for Student Learning*. Thousand Oaks, CA: Corwin Press, 2001.

Marzano, Robert. *Transforming Classroom Grading*. Alexandria, VA: Association for Supervision and Curriculum Development, 2000.

Moll, Anne M. *Differentiated Instruction Guide for Inclusive Teaching*. Port Chester, NY: Dude Publishing, 2003.

Tomlinson, Carol Ann. "Grading and Differentiation: Paradox or Good Practice." *Theory Into Practice* 44, 3 (2005), pp. 262–269.

Wiggins, Grant P. and Jay McTighe. *Understanding by Design*. Expanded 2nd ed. Alexandria, VA: Association for Supervision and Curriculum Development, 2005.

Wormeli, Rick. *Fair isn't Always Equal: Assessing and Grading in the Differentiated Classroom*. Portland, ME: Stenhouse Publishers; Westerville, OH: National Middle School Association, 2006.

CHAPTER 5: Differentiated Learning Experiences

Bower, Bert, Jim Lobdell and Lee Swenson. *History Alive! Engaging all Learners in the Diverse Classroom.* 2nd ed. Palo Alto, CA: Teachers' Curriculum Institute, 1999.

Bowler, Leanne et al. "Children and Adults Working Together in the Zone of Proximal Development: A Theory for User-centered Design." *Conference Proceedings.* 2005. http://www.cais-acsi.ca/proceedings/2005/bowler_2005.pdf (Accessed February 7, 2007).

Coil, Carolyn. "Flexible Grouping: It's More than just moving Their Seats." *Carolyn Coil.* 2007. http://www.carolyncoil.com/ezine31.htm (Accessed June 28, 2007).

Corley, Mary Ann. "Differentiated Learners: Adjusting to the Needs of all Learners." *Focus on Basics: Connecting Research & Practice.* Volume 7, Issue C, March 2005. www.ncsall.net/?id=736 (Accessed June 29, 2007).

Dodge, Judith. *Differentiation in Action.* New York, NY: Scholastic Inc., 2005.

Ford, Michael P. *Differentiation through Flexible Grouping: Successfully Reaching all Readers.* Naperville, IL: Learning Point Associates, 2005. http://www.learningpt.org/pdfs/literacy/flexibleGrouping.pdf (Accessed June 27, 2007).

Gardner, Howard. *Multiple Intelligences: The Theory in Practice.* New York, NY: Basic Books, 1993.

Heacox, Diane. *Differentiating Instruction in the Regular Classroom: How to Reach and Teach all Learners, Grades 3–12.* Minneapolis, MN: Free Spirit Publishing, 2002.

Hickey, Daniel T. and Ann C. H. Kindfield. "Assessment of Oriented Scaffolding of Student and Teacher Performance in a Technology-supported Genetics Environment." Presentation to the Annual Meeting of the American Educational Research Asssociation, Montreal, April 1999. http://genscope.concord.org/research/pdf/hic99all.pdf (Accessed February 9, 2007).

Holbrook, Jennifer and Janet L. Kolodner. "Scaffolding the Development of an Inquiry based (Science) Classroom." In Barry J. Fishman and Samuel F. O'Connor-Divelbiss (eds.), *Proceedings of International Conference of the Learning Sciences 2000* (Mahwah, NJ: Lawrence Erlbaum Associates, Inc., 2000), pp. 221–227.

Kagan, Spencer. *Cooperative Learning.* San Clemente, CA: Kagan Cooperative Learning, 1992, 1994.

Kingore, Bertie. *Differentiating Instruction: Rethinking Traditional Practices.* Alexandria, VA: Association for Supervision and Curriculum Development, 2005.

Kolodner, Janet L. et al. "Problem-based Learning meets Case-based Reasoning in the Middle-School Science Classroom: Putting Learning by Design™ into Practice." *The Journal of the Learning Sciences* 12, 4 (2003), pp. 495–547.

McKenzie, Jamieson A. *Beyond Technology: Questioning, Research and the Information Literate School.* Bellingham, WA: FNO Press, 2000.

Newman, Denis, Peg Griffin and Michael Cole. *The Construction Zone: Working for Cognitive Change in School.* New York, NY: Cambridge University Press, 1989.

Ontario Ministry of Education. *Combined Grades: Strategies to Reach a Range of Learners in Kindergarten to Grade 6.* Toronto, ON: Ontario Ministry of Education, 2006.

Ontario Ministry of Education. *Guide to Effective Literacy Instruction, Grades 4 to 6: Volume One.* Toronto, ON: Ontario Ministry of Education, 2006.

Puntambekar, Sadhana and Roland Hübscher. "Tools for Scaffolding Students in a Complex Learning Environment: What have we Gained and What have we Missed?" *Educational Psychologist* 40, 1 (2005), pp. 1–12.

Reiser, B. J. "Why Scaffolding should Sometimes make Tasks more Difficult for Learners." In T. D. Koschmann, R. Hall and N. Miyake (eds.), *Carrying Forward the Conversation: Proceedings of the International Conference on Computer Support for Collaborative Learning* (Mahwah, NJ: Lawrence Erlbaum Associates, Inc., 2002), pp. 255–264.

Strickland, Cindy A "Differentiated Instruction: An Overview." *Educators Publishing Service.* 2004. http://www.epsbooks.com/flat/newsletter/vol05/vol05iss05/Differentiated_Instruction.pdf (Accessed January 29, 2007).

Strickland, Cindy A. *Professional Development for Differentiating Instruction.* Alexandria VA: ASCD Publications, 2009.

Theroux, Priscilla. "Strategies for Differentiating." *Enhance Learning with Technology.* June 20, 2004. http://members.shaw.ca/priscillatheroux/differentiatingstrategies.html (Accessed June 29, 2007).

Tomlinson, Carol Ann. *How to Differentiate Instruction in Mixed-ability Classrooms.* 2nd ed. Alexandria, VA: Association for Supervision and Curriculum Development, 2001.

Vygotsky, Lev S. *Thought and Language.* Revised ed. Cambridge, MA: MIT Press. 1986.

Wilhelm, Jeffrey D., Tanya N. Baker and Julie Dube. *Strategic Reading: Guiding Students to Lifelong Literacy.* Portsmouth, NH: Boynton/Cook Publishers, Inc., 2001.

261

CHAPTER 6: Leveraging Technology

Benjamin, Amy. *Differentiated Instruction using Technology: A Guide for Middle and High School*. 2005.

Pitler, Howard, E. Hubbell, M. Kuhn and K. Malenoski. *Using Technology with Classroom Instruction that Works*. Alexandria VA: ASCD Publications, 2005.

CHAPTER 7: A Schoolwide Approach

Alberta Teachers' Association. *Action Research Guide for Teachers*. Edmonton, AB: The Alberta Teachers' Association, 2000.

Carolan, Jennifer and Abigail Guinn. "Differentiation: Lessons from Master Teachers." *Educational Leadership* 64, 5 (February 2007), pp. 44–47.

Ciurysek, Sandra et. al. *Professional Learning Communities: A Literature Synopsis*. Lethbridge, AB: The University of Lethbridge, 2005.

DuFour, Richard. "Schools As Learning Communities." *Educational Leadership* 61, 8 (2004), pp. 6–11.

DuFour, Richard and R. Eaker. *Professional Learning Communities at Work – Best Practices for Enhancing Student Achievement*. Bloomington, IN: National Education Service, 1998.

Fullan, Michael et. al. *Breakthrough*. Thousand Oaks, CA: Corwin Press, 2006.

InPraxis Group Inc. "Effective Professional Development: What the Research Says." *Alberta Initiative for School Improvement*. 2006. http://education.alberta. ca/media/618572/effec_pd_research_says_2006.pdf (Accessed October 10, 2007).

Loucks-Horsley, Susan et. al. "Professional Development for Science Education: A Critical and Immediate Challenge." In Rodger W. Bybee (ed.), *National Standards and the Science Curriculum: Challenges, Opportunities, and Recommendations* (Dubuque, IA: Kendall Hunt, 1996), pp. 83–95.

Sirotnik, Kenneth A. "Evaluation in the Ecology of Schooling: The Process of School Renewal." In John I. Goodlad (ed.), *The Ecology of School Renewal: Eighty-sixth Yearbook of the National Society for the Study of Education, Part I* (Chicago, IL: The National Society for the Study of Education, 1987), pp. 41–62.

Tomlinson, Carol Ann. "Traveling the Road to Differentiation in Staff Development." *Journal of Staff Development* 26, 4 (Fall 2005), pp. 8–12.

University of Lethbridge. *Effective Professional Development*. Lethbridge, AB: The University of Lethbridge, 2005.

CHAPTER 8: Students with Disabilities

Alberta Education. *Supporting Positive Behaviour in Alberta Schools*. Edmonton, AB: Alberta Education, 2008.

Alberta Education. *Individualized Program Planning*. Edmonton, AB: Alberta Education, 2006.

Alberta Education. *Focusing on Success: Teaching Students with Attention Deficit/Hyperactivity Disorder*. Edmonton, AB: Alberta Education, 2006.

Bender, William. N. *Differentiated Instruction for Students with Learning Disabilities*. Thousand Oaks CA. Corwin Press, 2008.

Gaskins, Irene and Thorne T. Elliot. *Implementing Cognitive Strategy Instuction across the School: The Benchmark Manual for Teachers*. Cambridge, MA: Brookline Books, 1991.

Hitchcock, Chuck et al. "Providing New Access to the General Curriculum: Universal Design for Learning." *Teaching Exceptional Children* 35, 2 (2002), pp. 8–17.

Ontario Ministry of Education. *Education for All: The Report of the Expert Panel on Literacy and Numeracy Instruction for Students with Special Education Needs, Kindergarten to Grade 6*. Toronto, ON: Ontario Ministry of Education, 2005.

McQuarrie, Lynn, Philip McRae and Holly Stack-Cutler. *Differentiated Instruction: A Research Brief for Practitioners*. Edmonton, AB: Alberta Education, 2005.

Winebrenner, Susan. *Teaching Kids with Learning Disabilities in the Regular Classroom: Strategies and Techniques Every Teacher can use to Challenge and Motivate Struggling Students*. Minneapolis, MN: Free Spirit Publishing, 1996.

Woloshyn, Vera, A. Elliott and S. Kaucho. "So What Exactly is Explicit Strategy Instruction? A Review of Eight Critical Teaching Steps." *The Reading Professor* 24, 1 (2001), pp. 66–114.

CHAPTER 9: English Language Learners

Abate, Laura. "Differentiating Instruction for Limited English Proficient Students." *BETAC Interchange* 12, 2 (Spring/Summer 2004), pp. 1, 3.

Alberta Education. *English as a Second Language: Guide to Implementation, Kindergarten–Grade 9*. Edmonton, AB: Alberta Education, 2007.

Carlo, Maria et al. "Closing the Gap: Addressing the Vocabulary Needs of English Language Learners in Bilingual and Mainstream Classrooms." *Reading Research Quarterly* 39, 2 (2004), pp. 188–215.

Crandall, Joann et al. "Using Cognitive Strategies to Develop English Language and Literacy." ERIC Digest ED469970 (October 2002), pp. 1–7. http://www.eric.ed.gov/contentdelivery/servlet/ERICServlet?accno=ED469970 (Accessed May 11, 2007).

Cummins, Jim. "Teaching and Learning in Multilingual Ontario" (webcast). Curriculum Services Canada. December 7, 2005. http://www.curriculum.org/secretariat/december7.html (Accessed January 2008).

Earle-Carlin, Susan. "Providing Language Feedback." National Clearinghouse for English Language Acquisition. n.d. www.ncela.gwu.edu/oela/summit/Language_Feedback.pdf (Accessed January 2008).

Edmonton Public Schools. *Thinking Tools for Kids: Practical Organizers*. Edmonton, AB: Resource Development Services, Edmonton Public Schools, 1999.

Everything English Language. "Quick Tips: Short, Helpful Tips for the Educator in the hurry." everything ELS.net. 1998–2008. http://www.everythingEnglish language.net/quicktips/ (Accessed January 2008).

Heydon, Rachel. "Literature Circles as a Differentiated Instructional Strategy for including English Language Students in Mainstream Classrooms." *The Canadian Modern Language Review* 59, 3 (March 2003), pp. 463–475.

Hill, Jane D. and Kathleen M. Flynn. *Classroom Instruction that Works with English Language Learners*. Alexandria, VA: Association for Supervision and Curriculum Development, 2006.

Huerta-Macias, Ana. "Alternative Assessment: Responses to Commonly Asked Questions." *TESOL Journal* 5, 1 (1995), pp. 8–10.

Kagan, Spencer. "We Can Talk. Cooperative Learning in the Elementary English Language Classroom." ERIC Digest. 1995. http://www/ericdigests.org/1996-1/English language.html (Accessed November 21, 2006).

McLaughlin, Barry et al. "Vocabulary Improvement and Reading in English Langauge Learners: An Intervention Study." Paper presented at a research symposium of the Office of Bilingual Education and Minority Language Affairs, US Department of Education, Washington, DC, April 2000.

Tannenbaum, Jo-Ellen. "Practical Ideas on Alternative Assessment for English Language Students." ERIC Digest. 1996. http://www/ericdigests.org/1997-1/English language.html (Accessed November 21, 2006).

Villegas, Ana Maria and Tamara Lucas. "The Culturally Responsive Teacher." *Educational Leadership* 64, 6 (March 2007), pp. 28–33.

264

CHAPTER 10: Students who are Gifted

Alberta Learning. *The Journey: A Handbook for Parents of Children who are Gifted and Talente*d. Edmonton, AB: Alberta Learning, 2004.

Bloom, Benjamin S. (ed.). *Taxonomy of Educational Objectives: The Classification of Educational Goals*. New York, NY: David McKay, 1956.

British Columbia Minstry of Education. "Process." *Gifted Education – A Resource Guide for Teachers*. http://www.bced.gov.bc.ca/specialed/gifted/process. htm (Accessed January 2009).

Delisle, Jim and Judy Galbraith. *When Gifted Kids don't have all the Answers: How to Meet their Social and Emotional Needs*. Minneapolis, MN: Free Spirit Publishing Inc., 2002.

Department of Education, Employment and Training, State of Victoria. *Bright Futures Resource Book: Education of Gifted Students*. Melbourne, AU: Department of Education, State of Victoria, 1996.

Galbraith, Judy. *The Gifted Kids' Survival Guide: For Ages 10 and Under*. Revised and updated ed. Minneapolis, MN: Free Spirit Publishing Inc., 1999.

Galbraith, Judy and Jim Delisle. *The Gifted Kids' Survival Guide: A Teen Handbook*. Revised, expanded, and updated ed. Minneapolis, MN: Free Spirit Publishing Inc., 1996.

Harvey, David. *The Progressive Approach: A Model for Gifted Programming in Regular Classrooms*. Edmonton, AB: Open Mind Educational Resources, 2000.

University of Calgary. "Understanding Giftedness: Generalizations from the Research and Resources for Educators and Parents." *Alberta Initiative for School Improvement (AISI)*. 2005. http://education.alberta.ca/apps/aisi/literature/pdfs/ UofC_Literature_Synopsis.pdf (Accessed January 2009).

Winebrenner, Susan. *Teaching Gifted Kids in the Regular Classroom: Strategies and Techniques Every Teacher can use to meet the Academic Needs of the Gifted and Talented*. Revised, expanded, updated ed. Minneapolis, MN: Free Spirit Publishing Inc., 2001.

CHAPTER 11: English Language Arts

Chapman, Carolyn and Rita King. *Differentiated Instructional Strategies for Reading in the Content Area*. Thousand Oaks, CA: Corwin Press, 2003.

Chapman, Carolyn and Rita King. *Differentiated Instructional Strategies for Writing in the Content Areas*. Thousand Oaks, CA. Corwin Press, 2003.

Foster, Graham. *Language Arts Idea Bank*. Markham, ON: Pembroke Publishers, 2004.

265

Grant, Janet Millar, Barbara Heffler and Kadri Mereweather. *Student-led Conferences: Using Portfolios to Share with Parents*. Markham, ON: Pembroke Publishers, 1995.

Gregory, Gayle. H and L. Kuzmich *Differentiated Literacy Strategies for Student Growth ad Achievement in Grades K–6*. Thousand Oaks, CA. Corwin Press Inc., 2005.

Hill, S. "Our Visions of Possibility for Literacy: Keeping the Passion: What Really Matters." *Language Arts* 83, 5 (2006), pp. 392–393.

Hillocks, George Jr. *Research on Written Composition, New Directions for Teaching*. Urbana, IL: National Council of Teachers of English, 1986.

Hinson, Bess (ed.). *New Directions in Reading Instruction*. Newark, DE: International Reading Association, 2000.

Langer, Judith A. and Arthur N. Applebee. "Reading and Writing Instruction: Toward a Theory of Teaching and Learning." *Review of Research in Education* 13, 1 (1986), pp. 171–194.

Macoun, James M., Diane Bewell and Mary Ellen Vogt. *Responses to Literature, Grades K–8*. Newark, DE: International Reading Association, 1991.

Mariconda, Barbara. *The Most Wonderful Writing Lessons Ever*. New York, NY: Scholastic Publications, 1999.

Parsons, Les. *Response Journals Revisited*. Markham, ON: Pembroke Publishers, 2001.

Wilhelm, Jeffrey D., Tanya N. Baker and Julie Dube. *Strategic Reading: Guiding Students to Lifelong Literacy, 6–12*. Portsmouth, NH: Boynton/Cook Publishers, Inc., 2001.

CHAPTER 12: Mathematics

Bender, William N. *Differentiating Math Instruction: Strategies that Work for K–8 Classrooms!* Thousand Oaks, CA: Corwin Press, 2005.

Burns, Marilyn. "Looking at How Students Reason." *Educational Leadership* 63, 3 (November 2005), pp. 26–31.

Ontario Ministry of Education. *Education for All: The Report of the Expert Panel on Literacy and Numeracy Instruction for Students with Special Education Needs, Kindergarten to Grade 6*. Toronto, ON: Ontario Ministry of Education, 2005.

Silver, Harvey E. and Richard W. Strong. *Learning Style Inventory*. Ho-Ho-Kus, NJ: Thoughtful Education Press, 2003.

Sliva, Julie A. *Teaching Inclusive Mathematics to Special Learners, K–6.* Thousand Oaks, CA: Corwin Press, Inc., 2004.

Strong, Richard et al. "Creating a Differentiated Mathematics Classroom." *Educational Leadership* 61, 5 (February 2004), pp. 73–78.

Van de Walle, John. *Elementary and Middle School Mathematics: Teaching Developmentally* (4th edition). Boston, MA: Addison Wesley Longman, Inc., 2001.

Van de Walle, John A. and LouAnn H. Lovin. *Teaching Student-centered Mathematics, Grades K–3.* Boston, MA: Pearson Education, Inc., 2006.

Van de Walle, John A. and LouAnn H. Lovin. *Teaching Student-centered Mathematics, Grades 3–5.* Boston, MA: Pearson Education, Inc., 2006.

Van de Walle, John A. and LouAnn H. Lovin. *Teaching Student-centered Mathematics, Grades 5–8.* Boston, MA: Pearson Education, Inc., 2006.

Western and Northern Canadian Protocol. *The Common Curriculum Framework for K–9 Mathematics.* Edmonton, AB: Western and Northern Canadian Protocol, 2006.

267

CHAPTER 13: Science

The Access Center and American Institutes of Research. "Science Inquiry: The Link to Accessing the General Education Curriculum." *The Access Center: Improve Outcomes for All Students K–8.* http://www.k8accesscenter.org/training_resources/ScienceInquiry_accesscurriculum.asp (Accessed October 9, 2008).

Alberta Learning. *Focus on Inquiry: A Teacher's Guide to Implementing Inquiry-based Learning.* Edmonton, AB: Alberta Learning, 2004.

National Academy Press. *National Science Education Standards.* Washington, DC: National Academy Press, 1996.

Wiggins, Grant and Jay McTighe. *Understanding by Design.* Alexandria, VA: Association for Supervision and Curriculum Development, 1998.

CHAPTER 14: Social Studies

Dodge, Judith. *Differentiation in Action.* New York, NY: Scholastic Inc., 2005.

Tomlinson, Carol Ann. "Reconcilable Differences? Standards-based Teaching and Differentiation." *Educational Leadership* 58, 1 (September 2000), pp. 6–11.

Related Alberta Education Resources that Support Differentiation

AISI – Differentiated Instruction Provincial Research Review (2008)

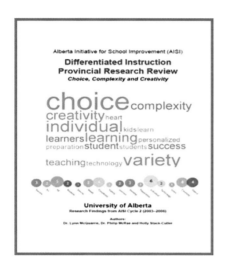

This 2008 research review, conducted by the University of Alberta, focuses on Cycle 2 of Alberta Initiative for School Improvement (AISI) projects on differentiated instruction. The review looks at approaches to planning and instruction that accommodates diverse student learning needs. The review identifies effective teaching strategies, assessment practices and professional development activities as well as the supportive behaviours of administrators, teachers, parents and district office staff.

To find a free PDF version of this resource, go to: http://education.alberta.ca/media/747920/differentiated_aisi99xx.pdf

The Heart of the Matter: Character and Citizenship Education in Alberta Schools (2006)

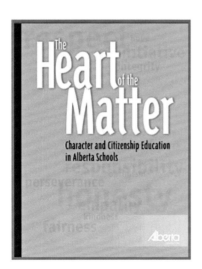

This resource provides an overview of what character and citizenship education is and offers a sample framework for building and sustaining a culture of character. The resource also provides information and sample strategies for choosing an approach; assessing outcomes; fostering a positive school culture; infusing character and citizenship education across subject areas; choosing resources; linking with extracurricular activities; and involving parents and community. (Grades K–12)
Order No. 616542*

To find a free PDF version of this resource, go to: http://education.alberta.ca/admin/resources/heart/print.aspx

Supporting Positive Behaviour in Alberta Schools (2008)

This three-part resource provides information, strategies, stories from schools and sample tools for systematically teaching, supporting and reinforcing positive behaviour. This integrated system of schoolwide, classroom management, and individual student support is designed to provide school staff with effective strategies to improve behavioural outcomes in their school. (Grades 1–12)

Part 1: *A schoolwide approach* describes a comprehensive schoolwide approach that involves *all* students, *all* staff and *all* school settings.

Part 2: *A classroom approach* provides information and strategies for systematically teaching, supporting and reinforcing positive behaviour in the classroom.

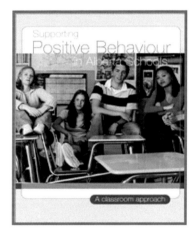

Part 3: *An intensive individualized approach* provides information and strategies for providing intensive, individualized support and instruction for the small percentage of students requiring this level of intervention.
Order No: 708951*

To find a free PDF version of this resource, go to: http://education.alberta.ca/admin/special/resources/behaviour.aspx

270

English as a Second Language (ESL) Guide to Implementation Kindergarten to Grade 9 (2007)

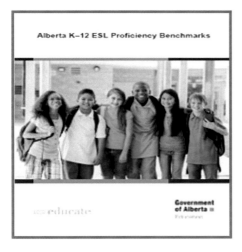

This resource provides an overview of English language learners and English as a second language (ESL) programming in Kindergarten to Grade 9, and includes information on second language acquisition, suggestions for the reception, placement and orientation of English language students, guidelines for ESL programming and connections to Alberta's programs of study and suggestions for assessment and evaluation of student learning and progress. (Grades K–9) **Order No: 708266***

To find a free PDF version of this resource, go to: http://education.alberta.ca/teachers/com/esl/resources.aspx

Alberta K–12 English as a Second Language (ESL) Proficiency Benchmarks (2009)

These benchmarks provide a description of the English language abilities that students typically demonstrate at each of the five proficiencies (at Kindergarten and each of the four grade-level divisions). These benchmarks can help teachers plan for language instruction within everyday classroom situations. (Grades K–12)

To find a free PDF version of this resource, go to:
http://education.alberta.ca/media/1111060/esl_benchmark1.pdf

Focusing on Success: Teaching Students with Attention Deficit/Hyperactivity Disorder (2006)

This research-based resource provides classroom teachers with information and practical strategies to better meet the needs of students with attention difficulties.
(Grades 1–12)
Order No: 673667*

To find a free PDF version of this resource, go to:
http://education.alberta.ca/admin/special/resources/adhd.aspx

272

Unlocking Potential: Key Components of Programming for Students with Learning Disabilties (2003)

This resource identifies nine key components of programming for students with learning disabilities and contains sample strategies and outcomes for each of the components.
(Grades 1–12)
Order No. 510851*

To find a free PDF version of this resource, go to:
http://education/alberta.ca/admin/special/resources/unlocking.aspx

Re: defining Success: A Team Approach to Supporting Students with FASD: A Strategy Guide for Mentors and Coaches Working in Schools (2009)

This guide offers ideas, actions and strategies for mentors, community support workers and coaches to use for supporting students with FASD in their school environment. (Grades 1–12)
Order No: 752858

To find a free PDF version of this resource, go to: http://education.alberta.ca/admin/special/resources/re-defining.aspx

273

Teaching Students with Fetal Alcohol Spectrum Disorder (FASD): Building Strengths, Creating Hope (2004)

This guide includes information on what FASD is, and strategies for creating positive classroom climates, organizing for instruction and responding to the needs of individual students. (Grades 1–12)
Order No: 538019*

To find a free PDF version of this resource, go to: http://education.alberta.ca/admin/special/resources/fasd.aspx

Our Words, Our Ways: Teaching First Nations, Métis and Inuit Learners (2005)

This resource offers information and sample strategies that classroom teachers can use to create opportunities for First Nations, Métis and Inuit (FNMI) students to be successful learners. The resource provides information on FNMI cultures and perspectives, and discusses the importance of family and community involvement. It includes shared wisdom from Elders and FNMI scholars, and related stories from teachers of FNMI students. The resource also includes information on learning disabilities and recognizing the gifts of individual students. (Grades K–12) **Order No: 619166***

To find a free PDF version of this resource, go to::
http://education.alberta.ca/teachers/resources/cross/ourwordsour ways.aspx

274

Building on Success: Helping Students Make Transitions from Year to Year (2006)

Provides practical strategies and sample tools for helping students make successful transitions from one school year to the next. The sample tools can be used to help students, parents and teachers collect, organize and share information about a student's individual strengths, abilities and learning needs.

Order No: 672594*

To find a free PDF version of this resource, go to::
http://education.alberta.ca/admin/special/resoruces.aspx

*All resources with order numbers are available for purchase from the Learning Resources Centre (LRC) at www.lrc.education.gov.ab.ca.

Index

277

281

282

283

285

287

289

291

293

questions
  essential questions, 17–19
  for gifted students, 183
  in assessment, 49, 55–56
  in scaffolding, 18, 77
  questioning strategies, 77
  unit questions, 19–20
questions, essential. *See* essential instructional components

RAFTS writing assignment (Role, Audience, Format, Topic and Strong verb)
  "choice board" strategy for, 83–84
  for differentiating writing, 207–209
"read around" strategy
  for unfamiliar vocabulary, 163
"read-alongs" strategy, 197
"read-aloud" strategy
  to model reading, 197
reading, 196–206. *See also* language arts, English
  about differentiation, 196–206
  assessment of, 210–212
  by English language learners, 151, 156, 158–166
  by students with disabilities, 124
  flexible groups for, 151
  graphic organizers, 203–204
  in class profiles, 29–31
  in learner profiles, 28
  in social studies, 253
  independent, 197
  language experience approach, 160
  literature circles, 159–160
  reading extensions, 204–206
  scaffolding, 198
  skill instruction, 198–204
  technology for, 90–91, 101–104, 122, 136–138
  Tool: 20 Questions About Me, 34–35
  Tool: A Reading Interview, 37
  Tool: Interest Inventory, 36
  Tool: Reading Attitudes Interview, 38
  Tool: Reading Strategies Survey, 39–40
  Tool: Sample Academic and Instructional Supports for Students with
    Disabilities, 141–142
  vocabulary development, 162–163
Reading Attitudes Interview (Tool), 38
Reading Interview (Tool), 37
Reading Strategies Survey (Tool), 39–40

294

295

297

299

301

302

303

305